D1558863

Under the Shadow of War

Fascism, Anti-Fascism, and Marxists, 1918–1939

Under the Shadow of War

*Fascism, Anti-Fascism, and Marxists,
1918–1939*

Larry Ceplair

Columbia University Press
NEW YORK   1987

Library of Congress Cataloging-in-Publication Data

Ceplair, Larry.
  Under the shadow of war.

  Bibliography: p.
    1. World Politics—1900–1945. 2. Anti-fascist
movements—Europe. 3. Anti-fascist movements—
United States. I. Title.
D727.C43 1987   940.5′1   86–32652
ISBN 0-231-06532-9

Columbia University Press
New York Guildford, Surrey
Copyright © 1987 Columbia University Press
All rights reserved

Printed in the United States of America

Book designed by Ken Venezio

To Tom Gatch, the most excellent of men

Contents

Acknowledgments

Three people deserve special mention for the assistance they gave me during the research and writing of this book. Dorothy Healey devoted many hours to discussing the people's front from its (and her) many perspectives. Jack Langguth provided moral and intellectual support and a careful reading of the manuscript. Kate Wittenberg never failed to be an ideal editor: enthusiastic, helpful, and critical.

Abbreviations

ADGB	General Federation of German Trade Unions
AFL	American Federation of Labor
ASP	American Socialist Party
BUF	British Union of Fascists
CGL	Italian Confederation of Labor
CGT	French Confederation of Labor
CIO	Congress of Industrial Organizations
Comintern	Communist (or Third) International
CPGB	British Communist Party
CPUSA	American Communist Party
ECCI	Executive Committee of the Communist International
EPIC	End Poverty in California
IFTU	International Federation of Trade Unions
ILP	Independent Labour Party (Great Britain)
KPD	German Communist Party
KPÖ	Austrian Communist Party
LP	Labour Party (Great Britain)
LSI	Labor and Socialist International
Narkomindel	Commissariat of Foreign Affairs (USSR)
NSDAP	National Socialist German Workers Party (Nazis)
PCd'I	Italian Communist Party
PCF	French Communist Party
PSI	Italian Socialist Party
RCP(B)	Russian Communist Party (Bolshevik)
RILU	Red International of Labor Unions
SFIO	French Socialist Party
Sopade	Executive of the German Social Democratic Party (Prague exiles)

SPD	German Socialist Party
SPÖ	Austrian Socialist Party
TUC	Trades Union Congress (Great Britain)
USPD	Independent German Socialist Party
VKPD	German People's Communist Party

Under the Shadow of War

Fascism, Anti-Fascism, and Marxists, 1918–1939

Introduction

Over sixty years ago, Benito Mussolini won political power in Italy by means of a movement labeled "Fascism," named after the organization Mussolini had built: the Fasci di Combattimento. That title was subsequently applied to dozens of groups that resembled Mussolini's in style or substance, to a type of state, and to an era. Nevertheless, during the time that has elapsed since November 1922, neither the movement's victims, rivals, or enemies, nor historians or political theorists, have developed a set of defining characteristics for Fascism that is generally accepted. Instead, the effort to arrive at a consensual understanding and definition of Fascism has created a major intellectual industry. As Pierre Ayçoberry has noted in the case of the German variant, Nazism, studies "have multiplied at such a rate that a single reader would be unable to glance through all of them even if he were to devote his life to the task."[1]

In addition, no two historians agree on which movements, parties, or organizations were "Fascist," "Fascistic," "Fascoid," or "Fascist-like." Although all Fascists tried to build mass movements of the radical Right, none succeeded, during the interwar period, in toppling a standing government or seizing power directly. Only two Fascist movements were invited to share power (Italy, 1922, and Germany, 1933), and though each quickly assumed a monopoly of government power, no other Fascist movement achieved a similar success, by itself, during the interwar era. Finally, Italian Fascism and German Nazism differed as movements, doctrines, and governing entities.

Any set of defining characteristics offered for the phenomenon known as Fascism cannot, therefore, be an exact label. "Fascism" should be used as a term of historical convenience, one that summons forth images of a political movement that features a demagogic and charismatic leader, a paramilitary organization devoted to violence and public demonstrations of force, and emphasis on "will" and "power," and a program or ideology that is flexible, pragmatic, inconsistent, and functionally designed to mobilize the largest possible number of dissatisfied people. The programmatic elements common to most are nationalism, usually of an irredentist nature, anti-Marxism, opposition to parliamentary-capitalist society, and devotion to the creation of a new order.

Arno Mayer has provided the most persuasive framework for understanding Fascism. He places it where it belongs, on the Right, and distinguishes it from two other political groupings that also inhabit that antirevolutionary domain: reactionaries, critics of the status quo who advocate a return to a mythical and romanticized past; and conservatives, who are basically satisfied with the status quo and are not opposed to pragmatic, gradual alterations of it. Fascists, according to Mayer's classification, are counterrevolutionaries, the "pre-emptive" type.[2]

As the term indicates, it is the specter of revolution, specifically working-class revolution, that catalyzes this modern counterrevolutionary phenomenon. The crisis that promotes a potential revolutionary enterprise also produces what Mayer terms "crisis strata," segments of the population deeply threatened by the prospect of a working-class revolution. Counterrevolutionary leaders arise and commence, *de novo*, rationally and methodically exploiting, inflaming, and manipulating the fears, resentment, and alienation of the "crisis strata," improvising and altering the standards of admission to the movement and its appeals as circumstances warrant. Since the strata the counterrevolutionaries are attempting to mobilize are so highly diversified, counterrevolution is essentially pragmatic, not theoretical; its ideology and program necessarily become inconsistent. It is not, however, a revolution of the Right. "In the last analysis, the counterrevolutionary project is far more militant in rhetoric, style, and conduct than in political, social, and economic substance," and counterrevolutionary propaganda places "greater stress on profound changes in attitude, spirit, and outlook than in economic and social structures." Skilled experts in modern forms of communication and specialists in street politics, counterrevolutionaries use propaganda, violence, and demonstrations as techniques to heighten the climate of insecurity and transform a potential prerevolutionary situation into a concrete precounterrevolutionary one.[3]

"Anti-Fascism," like "Fascism," is a term of historical convenience that must be placed within a larger framework to make it intelligible. Although there were conservatives and reactionaries who steadfastly opposed Fascist movements, anti-Fascism was a Left-wing phenomenon. Anti-Fascists, however, cannot be effectively categorized as a separate entity on the Left. It is true that a significant minority of anti-Fascists were political newcomers, brought into activity by events such as Nazi race policies, the Italian invasion of Ethiopia, and the Spanish Civil War, but by far the greater number of anti-Fascists were already engaged in Left-wing political activity, as liberals, trade unionists, Socialists, Communists, anarchists, or Trotskyists. Anti-Fascism was part and parcel of their reform or revolutionary effort; it was a defensive tactic designed to protect them from a movement or form of government that promised to destroy what they had achieved, obstruct what they hoped to achieve, and eliminate them altogether.

Since each group on the Left had a different agenda, anti-Fascism had a distinctive meaning for each. In addition, the international Fascist threat varied in intensity and immediacy during the interwar decade, as did the Left's perceptions, understanding, and appreciation of it. As a result, no anti-Fascist party per se emerged; instead, various types of temporary coalitions, alliances, and constellations of front groups constituted the anti-Fascist movement. Therefore, anti-Fascism became a monumental ambiguity, reflecting the profound differences of the political parties and trade unions that constituted it and the deep contradictions of the era that produced it. What at first seemed a catch basin large enough to contain both the Marxist Left and those dedicated to defending democratic values and civil liberties became a crowded vessel that broke and sank under the pressure of the hidden agendas of its inhabitants.

In addition to the ever-present problem of unity, anti-Fascists had difficulty in distinguishing Fascist regimes from the general range of authoritarian governments, and separating Fascists from reactionaries. Even though the agenda of the Left, from moderate to ultra-radical, faced a bleak future under any Right-wing dictatorship, it did matter whether that dictatorship was dominated by the military (Poland and Spain), the old-line aristocracy (Hungary), the monarchy (Yugoslavia), or a counter-revolutionary party (Italy and Germany). Not every authoritarian regime suppressed the Left; some allowed parties and trade unions to exist and remain active. In addition, authoritarian regimes were not necessarily militarist and expansionist.

The anti-Fascist cause of the interwar period allowed within its spacious domain more contradictions and condoned more blurrings and shadings than are healthy for an effective political movement. Left-wing challenges to radical Right movements and governments require more precise analyses, strategies, and tactics than interwar anti-Fascism produced. James Waterman Wise, the editor of *Opinion*, a liberal Jewish publication, warned against the danger of failing to make distinctions when he wrote in 1934: "Nazism, whatever its relation to other current political and social trends, must be considered sui generis if its meaning and implications are to be correctly appraised and its challenge met. . . . [T]o dismiss Nazism as a German variant of Fascism and nothing more is to confuse, not clarify the issue. Differences in degree, if they are great enough, become differences in kind."[4]

But Marxist party theoreticians, propagandists, and bureaucrats, particularly those from the Communist movement, tended to ignore the objective (material and historical) reality and to treat Fascism as a subjective form, elastic enough to fit any political situation. The indiscriminate application of it during the twenties and early thirties, therefore, trivialized the subject and the object, rendering it difficult for parties to comprehend and confront effectively the real thing, Nazism, when it became a significant factor in German then world politics.

Marxist anti-Fascists committed their most fatal error, however, when they refused to believe that Fascists could be anything but instruments of the capitalist bourgeoisie. In fact, Fascists were power seekers with plans of their own who made use of the bourgeoisie to gain power. Though Fascists in power left the bourgeoisie undisturbed and its economic power intact, the agenda followed by Mussolini or Hitler was his alone, determined by his movement's needs or his personal desires. The instrumentalist bias of anti-Fascism made its goals peripheral to the main political tasks of the Left-wing parties and trade unions that created it and supplied most of its followers. Anti-Fascism, therefore, tended to become another agenda item, front group, or programmatic thesis. In the final analysis, it meant that anti-Fascism did not develop a life of its own as a direct counter to Fascism.

Although many very intelligent Marxists spent a great deal of time observing, pondering, and analyzing the origins, modes, and activities of Fascist movements, theoretical analysis was literally an academic venture as far as the decision-making bodies of the Marxist internationals and their member parties were concerned. Party "lines" developed from organizational contingencies, not the persuasiveness or logic of theories.

Theorists whose views and interpretations of events differed from those of party leaders could be ignored, censored, or expelled. These procedures could not, however, be applied to the large number of people attracted into the ranks of anti-Fascism, or into parties trumpeting an anti-Fascist tactic. The rank and file were predominantly concerned with the victims of Fascist regimes, avoiding war, and the preservation of democracies such as Austria, Spain, and Czechoslovakia, whereas party bureaucrats and the executives of front groups focused on organizational matters. This latent divergence became manifest during the years of the Moscow purge trials, the Spanish Civil War, and Munich, producing great strain on anti-Fascist unity, and, with the German-Russian Nonaggression Pact of August 1939, finally shattering it.

Anti-Fascists fell well short of their goals basically because the essential political tasks of each significant group on the Left could not effectively accommodate anti-Fascism. It was a satellite, rotating around the center of Communist, Social Democratic, and Trotskyist endeavors. The Social Democrats, the largest group, focused on defending whatever democratic institutions existed, defending themselves against Communist attacks, protecting social and economic reforms, and maintaining a facade of unity for their disintegrating international. The Communists were concerned with complete domination of the working-class movement and full support of Soviet foreign policy. The Trotskyists wanted to construct a new Marxist revolutionary party. Trade unions, which were mostly of a Social Democratic or liberal stripe, needed to protect their workers from the harsh economic winds blowing through the thirties and, in some countries, from the even harsher political blasts. Anti-Fascism had to be fitted in and around these core principles, and tended either to become a rhetorical exercise with little in the way of concrete activity, as with many of the Social Democratic parties, or a concrete activity paving another path to traditional goals, as in the case of all Communist parties. As a result, the anti-Fascist offensive was compromised from the start, regularly bowed before more pressing matters of institutional concern, and weakly stood aside as Italian Fascism, German Nazism, and Fascist-supported Austrian reaction monopolized political power. Only in Spain was resistance offered.

The Spanish Civil War, however, did not originate as a contest between Fascists and anti-Fascists. It became an international cause, *the* symbolic, climactic Fascist versus anti-Fascist event of the decade, for reasons that had little to do with the identity of the contending sides, and much to do with the state of international relations. Among the rebels, the tiny Spanish Fascist Party, the Falange, neither planned, controlled, nor shaped the uprising or its postvictory consolidation of power. The Loyalists came to be dominated by a Soviet-inspired people's front mentality (and Soviet Russian "advisers") in the vacuum created by the refusal of the democratic countries to aid the beleaguered Spanish republic.

In fact, the traditional Right, with its vast resources, not the radical, Fascist variant, benefited most from the weaknesses of the interwar Left (divisions in its ranks, limits of its class appeal, and its inability to transform periodic bursts of worker militancy into enduring political effectiveness), and the public's impatience or lack of familiarity with democratic and republican institutions. Indeed, nine Right-wing authoritarian governments assumed power in Europe during the interwar decades.

Meanwhile, aside from Russia in November 1917, Communist revolutions suffered defeat after defeat, while Social Democratic parties outside the Scandinavian countries found themselves constantly on the defensive, even when, as in Germany, Austria, France, or Spain, they had won a significant plurality in a legislative election. Alone, neither Marxist party could withstand militant surges from the Right. Social Democrats, who had the larger membership, had played the parliamentary game too long, and its leaders had become ideologically and psychologically incapable of organizing, ordering, or approving armed resistance or preventive revolution. Communists, on the other hand, seemed ideologically prepared for forceful confrontation, but had not attempted it since the German fiasco of 1923, and lacked enrollment, the ability to rally non-Communists to their side, clear and sensible tactics, and Comintern approval for the use of mass violence or national uprisings. Thus during times of political crisis, when the Right was on the verge of destroying democratic rights, republican institutions, and civil liberties, Communist leaders exhibited the same uncertainty and paralysis of will as their Social Democratic counterparts. Only in Spain, where both parties were constituent elements of a government under direct attack, did Communists and Social Democrats launch an armed counteroffensive against the Right.

The ability of the Right, during unsettled times, to gain backing from the most powerful forces in a country (police, army, bureaucracy, church, and wealthy people) and the ability of its elements (conservatives, reactionaries, and counterrevolutionaries) to fuse effectively, if only temporarily, on behalf of protecting property and tradition made it too formidable a force for the divided Left to overcome between 1919 and 1939. Similarly, the respective reasons of state of the non-Fascist, democratic powers—France, Great Britain, and the United States—proved too strong for the disunited forces of the Left to transform. Until faced with the united aggression of the "Fascist" Axis between 1939 and 1941, the governments of those countries could not be persuaded to formulate an anti-Fascist foreign policy. Whereas the other major non-Fascist power, the Soviet Union, immune from the pressure of domestic public opinion that might have affected democratic leaders, but equally motivated by reasons of state, reversed itself several times on the issue.

The failure of anti-Fascists in the democratic countries to mobilize public opinion into a force powerful enough to persuade or intimidate government leaders to pursue a foreign policy that would effectively contain the ambitions of Mussolini and Hitler was not, however, solely the result of the Left's institutional blindness or disunity. It stemmed in large part from the double-bind position in which Fascism placed people during the post–World War I period. On the one hand, the rallying cry against Fascism was that it would unleash a war; on the other hand, it was obvious to any average informed citizen that only war could effectively stop the spread of Fascism. The citizens of France, Great Britain, and the United States and the leaders of the Soviet Union chose to postpone war as long as possible. Statesmen and diplomats of non-fascist countries, then, when faced with international episodes that did not appear immediately threatening to vital national interests, pursued a diplomacy of conciliation or appeasement (neutrality, nonintervention, nonaggression, various forms of wrist slapping, and territorial concessions).

The war that began in 1939, as most events of the two decades that led up to it, had a double edge, representing both a victory and a defeat for anti-Fascism. Fascism was virtually eliminated as a significant political force in the world, but the rest of the anti-Fascist program, and many anti-Fascists, became victims of Cold War politics.

The purpose of this book is to present an analytical description of the failures of Left-wing anti-Fascism. Of necessity, the narrative must include detailed considerations of intra-Left relations; Left-wing unity was the *sine qua non* of a successful popular anti-Fascism. Because the politics of Left-wing parties oscillated during the interwar period, political anti-Fascism also followed a sinuous course, often dropping from sight altogether.

The first five chapters will evaluate the nature of the Fascist problem, the Left-wing response in Italy and Germany, and the effort to construct an international front against further Fascist success. The last three chapters will examine the efforts of French, British, and American anti-Fascists to mobilize public opinion and alter the internal and external policies of their governments.

Chapter 1

Revolutions, Counterrevolutions, and the First Fascist State

There was no "Fascist era" between the two world wars of the twentieth century. No Fascist wave threatened to engulf Western civilization between 1919 and 1939. Instead, a powerful conservative-centrist tide washed across Europe and the United States. It restored, or preserved and strengthened, the grips of the traditional elites on power and provided them with the necessary means to limit or break workers' strikes, suppress Bolshevik or Communist activities, curtail Social Democratic political power, block social and economic reforms, and, usually, forestall the efforts of the radical Right. A war of unprecedented magnitude had unleashed those potentially shattering forces; it had mobilized and threatened with death and destruction unheard-of numbers of people, and then set into motion hordes of people, many previously passive, in large-scale, often spontaneous and leaderless activity. Governments, already reeling from the effects and costs of the war and the extraordinary transformations it had wrought (mutinies in the trenches, strikes behind the lines, two revolutions in Russia, and the fall of four dynasties), stood uncertainly before these social forces. Millions of returning veterans, many demanding and angry, would increase the instability. By the end of 1919, governments on both sides of the Atlantic Ocean, whether democratic or authoritarian, had resorted to force as the surest means to restore social peace and political order.

Fascism arose, unbidden, from the postwar maelstrom, to bolster the antirevolutionary forces. Although there had been, notably in *fin-de-siècle* France and Austria, precursors of what would later be considered prototypical Fascist traits, no radical Right group in the prewar or postwar era accomplished what Benito Mussolini and Adolf Hitler did in postwar

Italy and Germany respectively. The latter two combined extremist violence, nationalism, irredentism, and militarism into a mass movement, brought it to the threshold of political power, connived governing authority from legitimate hands, and then used that authority to create a totalitarian state.

The distinctive Fascist goal—simultaneously countering Left-wing revolution and transforming the political order by revolutionary means— required equally large doses of skill, luck, generalized popular anxiety, and government paralysis to succeed. Single-minded devotion to forging a cadre, repetition of simple promises, and regular demonstrations of elemental force and will enabled Mussolini and Hitler to build well-organized mass movements of dissatisfied veterans, frustrated nationalists, and the various strata of people angry with the unfulfilled promises of parliamentary parties and government, frightened by strikes and revolutionary rhetoric, and worried about their loss of social and economic status in unsettled economies increasingly dominated by massive, faceless corporate and bureaucratic entities.

Financed by wealthy industrialists and landlords, publicized by conservative newspapers, and protected from police and army suppression by moderate and conservative political leaders who feared revolution from the Left far more than violence from the Right, the Fasci di Combattimento and the National Socialist German Workers Party ultimately came to appear indispensable to the maintenance or restoration of order within Italy and Germany respectively. Mussolini and Hitler did not seize power; they used the violence and votes of skillfully built mass organizations as a means of consummating a deal to provide them with a share of power. Then, demonstrating they were nobody's instrument but their own, they undercut their political allies, jettisoned their more radical followers and promises, and built a dictatorial state by means of artful use of the instruments of executive power, a nucleus of trusted lieutenants, their party organizations, the opportunism of a large mass of citizens eager to profit from the new order, and the cooperation of the established elites of industry, agriculture, finance, the church, and the armed forces.

The strength of Fascism on the threshold of and in power resided in the ability of the party to manufacture among its followers a consensus, "to give the masses the impression that they are always mobilized, that they have a direct relationship with the leader. . . . They are led to believe not only that they can participate in and contribute to the restoration of a social order whose limits and historical inadequacy they have experienced, but that they can be prime movers in a revolution that will gradually lead to a new and better social order."[1]

Italian Fascism was not perceived as a threat to Europe, because, as Arno Mayer has noted, "pre-emptive" counterrevolutionaries seek exclusive control of the machinery of government, actual or potential checks on goverment power, and mass communications; they do not intend to uproot or transform social or economic structures. "In fact, as a trade-off for monopolistic control in the political realm [and, he should have added, cultural realm] and for parallel preserves for social and economic advancement, the established classes and status groups are left undisturbed."[2] The Fascist threat to Europe arose from, in Mayer's words, "the incongruities of this superstructural transformation and infrastructural permanence,"[3] which fueled the nationalist and militarist tendencies within Italian Fascism. Or, as De Felice describes it, the Fascist consensus has a tendency to dissolve in the face of indiscernible social progress and to create the need for "irrational substitutes aimed outside the national collectivity."[4] But it required the manifestation of these traits in Germany in 1933 and 1934 to produce a genuine Fascist threat to Europe, a threat that had more to do with German power than Fascist potential.

The threat to Western countries that dominated political and governmental thinking, at least until the mid-twenties, was Bolshevism. Internationally and nationally, from the peace conference at Versailles to the meeting of the Allied Reparations Committee in Paris (1924), from United States Attorney General A. Mitchell Palmer's office in Washington, D.C., to the Emperor's palace in Japan, the forces of order, frequently including Social Democrats, mobilized against working-class radicalism. Success was complete, most spectacularly in Poland, where the Poles defeated the Red Army, and Hungary, where a Soviet regime was overthrown with the assistance of the Romanian army. Elsewhere, the police, the courts, extralegal vigilante groups, and divisions within the Left ended, by the summer of 1920, the threat of Bolshevik revolution in Europe.

Authoritarian regimes were not necessary to solve the problem; authoritarian methods in the hands of democratic leaders served very effectively. In many countries, however, authoritarian regimes were needed to overcome the political paralysis and social instability that resulted from the war and postwar upheavals. With the exception of Italy, none of the Right-wing authoritarian successes of the 1920s was based on a mass or popular movement. Hungary's reactionary regency, controlled by Admiral Miklós Horthy, had a military base, as did the regimes of General Miguel Primo de Rivera in Spain, Marshal Józef Piłsudski in Poland, and General Manuel Gomes de Costa in Portugal. The successful coups in Greece, Albania, and Bulgaria all came from above. The attempted coups, of the Freikorps and Bavarian nationalists in Germany and the Heimwehr in Austria, had popular bases, but they were not sufficiently extensive, the government was not sufficiently paralyzed, and the Left was not sufficiently weakened for them to succeed.

Italy became the *locus primus* of Fascism in Europe because it contained the requisite amounts of the necessary building blocks: on the one hand, all the ingredients for a mass movement of the dissatisfied and dispossessed (a costly war effort with few rewards, uneven economic growth, ineffective parliamentary government, and class-based militancy in the form of huge worker strikes); on the other hand, a Left that had been, and still appeared to be, a threat to tradition and order, but which was, actually, exhausted, splintered, and hopelessly confused about what to do next. Mussolini was able to mobilize the former and take advantage of the latter to elevate his movement into the epicenter of Italian politics.

The traditional European Right proved to be more effectively anti-Fascist than the Italian Left. In other countries, Right wingers either stabilized the political and social situation by means of traditional legal or forceful methods, thoroughly suppressed the militant Left, eliminated the seeds of native Fascism, or devised some combination of those policies. None of the four Right-wing leagues that emerged in France during the 1920s—Jeunesses Patriotes, La Faisceau, Croix de Feu, or Défense Paysanne—provoked serious trouble or exhibited markedly Fascist characteristics. The nucleus of Romanian Fascism, the Legion of the Archangel Michael, had not yet formed its paramilitary force. The large network of secret societies, patriotic associations, and vigilante groups in Hungary were placated with minor bureaucratic posts and limited freedom to promote popular demonstrations, attack Left groups, and terrorize Jews, but their basic demands were not met and they were never allowed to present a remote threat to Horthy's control.[5] In fact, the only Right-wing group that caused severe problems for any regime in Europe during the twenties, the Austrian Heimwehr, only did so because it was a useful weapon for the Christian Social Party to use against its rival, the Social Democrats. It lacked unity and doctrine, and was "in effect a federation of provincial associations, each mirroring the characteristics and political conditions of its *Land*."[6] Not even the money, weapons, and advice of Mussolini and Hungarian Prime Minister István Bethlen could engender a successful Heimwehr uprising in 1928.[7]

Counterrevolution from Above: Governments Against Bolshevism

Part of the reason that Marxists had difficulty identifying Fascism as a new form of counterrevolution, requiring new forms of battle, was that it seemed to emerge, in Italy, as an adjunct to traditional counterrevolution and white terror. The various episodes of revolution and mass workers' strikes that broke out in Europe and the United States during the last years of the war and first year of the postwar era were met with a variety of antirevolutionary forces. In the storm of civil war and outside intervention that followed, it was not easy to distinguish between categories of hostile elements.

All revolutionary efforts between 1917 and 1920 involving Communists or soon-to-be Communists met fierce resistance. The several attempts by German and Austrian Communists to extend the Social Democratic–controlled revolutions in those countries were brutally defeated by, respectively, government-authorized vigilante groups (the Freikorps) and a government-created army (the Volkswehr). The Hungarian Soviet regime headed by the Communist Béla Kun was eliminated by the Romanian army. Only the Russian Revolution survived.

The events and perceptions of those years laid the fault-ridden foundation of Marxist anti-Fascism. The Bolsheviks' revolutionary *idée fixe* percolated strongly behind the acknowledgment by the Russians that this particular revolutionary phase had ended. For most of the twenties, therefore, they remained preoccupied with constructing the means for the next revolutionary phase, not with responding to Fascism, which was, in their eyes, a counterrevolutionary variant. Since Social Democrats had generally failed to support revolution and, in particular, had actively limited those in Germany, Austria, and Hungary, Communist propaganda labeled them enemies of the working class.

The failure of revolution in Europe heightened both the Russian Bolsheviks' sense of isolation and vulnerability and their feeling of revolutionary superiority. The ensuing "Bolshevization" of their supporters by means of Moscow-orchestrated schisms, purges, and party rebuilding further splintered the Left and widened the gap between Social Democrats and Communists. Finally, the Bolshevik perception that it was the duty of the workers of Europe to defend the Russian Revolution and the Russian workers' state made uncritical defense of the Soviet Union the irreducible base of any coalition with Communists.

The counterrevolution began in Russia. Between March 1918 and January 1919, 15,000 Allied soldiers were sent to northern Russia, and several Japanese, British, French, Italian, and American units landed in the east. Major cities in all parts of the country were occupied, coasts and borders blockaded, and Allied ambassadors called home. The Allies wanted to deprive Germany of a secure front, raw materials, and military supplies; France wanted to protect her huge prerevolutionary investments; and Japan wanted territory.[8] None wanted to see the largest country in Europe ruled by Communist revolutionaries.

The combination of an antagonistic Allied presence and the revolt of the Russian army's Czech and Slovak brigade stimulated the processes of internal revolt, and a full-scale counterrevolution emerged by July. On July 29, the Central Executive Committee of the Soviets declared "the socialist fatherland in danger," and sent out an appeal "To the Toiling Masses of France, England, America, Italy, and Japan" to bring pressure on their governments to halt the intervention.[9] Instead, however, the Allied victors took advantage of Germany's surrender to send more troops, material and technical aid, and moral support. The Social Democratic governments of Germany and Austria did not dare to open diplomatic relations with Russia or offer moral or material support, for fear the Allies would either invade their countries, refuse to deliver food, or impose a crushing peace treaty.[10] Only when it became clear, in January 1920, that the counterrevolutionary forces could not defeat the Red Army was the blockade called off and most of the foreign presence ended. France, alone, continued to support General Wrangel until November.[11]

Meanwhile, the Polish army, led by Marshal Pilsudski, a nominal Social Democrat, took advantage of the civil war in Russia to occupy disputed territory, forge an alliance with the Ukrainian army of Semeon Petliura, and advance to Kiev. The Red Army launched a successful counterattack in May, but when it reached the so-called "Curzon Line," a debate broke out in the Politburo over the next step. Leon Trotsky urged the Bolsheviks to accept the British offer of mediation and try to arrange an armistice that would lead to peace with the Entente. Vladimir Lenin, unaware of the battered state of Polish Communism, the isolated minority status of

German Communists, and the general waning of revolutionary aspirations in Europe as a whole, argued that the appearance of the Red Army in Europe would stimulate revolution there. He was wrong. The French sent military aid to Pilsudski, the Russians poorly coordinated their invasion, and the Polish counteroffensive drove the Red Army out of Poland in August.[12]

Though the Russian Revolution remained intact, its leaders alive, its party in full control of the great majority of prerevolutionary territory, the revolutionary project had failed in the West. The major strikes of 1919 and 1920 neither attained their goals nor developed into revolutionary movements, and Communist revolutions in Central Europe notably in Germany, the focus of Russian Bolshevik hopes, were smashed.

The German Communist Party (KPD) was a small unit in a severely fragmented working-class Left. Division had begun in April 1917, when a group calling themselves the Independent Social Democrats (USPD) split from the Social Democrats (SPD) over the issue of war credits. The ranks of the USPD contained the Spartacus Union, led by Rosa Luxemburg and Karl Liebknecht, which would become the KPD in January 1919. The revolution that broke out in Germany in November 1918 was organized and led by none of these organizations; it was a spontaneous affair of soldiers, sailors, and workers, who formed revolutionary Workers' and Soldiers' Councils. The provisional government, led by Prince Max of Baden, resigned in the face of a Berlin general strike of November 9, and handed power over to Friedrich Ebert, chairman of the SPD. Negotiations between the SPD and USPD led to the creation of a Council of People's Commissars, composed of three representatives from each party, to govern until a constituent assembly could be convened. The Berlin Workers' and Soldiers' Councils met on January 10 and confirmed this provisional government, but failed to clarify which institution would have ultimate authority. The Spartacists and another new working-class group, the Revolutionary Shop Stewards, supported the revolutionary councils, the SPD and the trade unions the Council of People's Commissars, with the USPD gravitating in between. The parties and groups also disagreed over whether to extend the revolution.

Confusion reigned, except in the ranks of SPD leaders. They pursued stability with a single-minded determination that left little room for concern that they were reinforcing two of their traditional foes and creating a powerful third. Social Democratic labor union leaders met on November

15 with the nation's major employers and signed a far-reaching program of reform. The employers formally recognized the three main trade unions, agreed to bargain with them and disband company unions, accepted the principle of an eight-hour day, and established joint labor-management committees.[13] When the agreement failed to quell the revolutionary ferment among the Berlin working class, Ebert met with Imperial Army Commander General Wilhelm Groener to plan a military offensive against the revolutionary groups. When it became clear that regular army troops were not equal to that task, Ebert and Groener placed Gustav Noske (a Social Democrat) in charge of internal security and provided him with the authority and resources to recruit and train an extralegal army of order, based on the Freikorps, groups that had been spontaneously organized by army officers to protect Germans against Polish insurrections.[14] Industrialists and bankers, notably those from the Ruhr and Berlin, contributed money to support the Freikorps and distribute anti-Bolshevik propaganda.[15]

Luxemburg and Liebknecht, for their part, loudly, clearly, and repetitively stated their belief that the Ebert government was laying the foundation for a counterrevolution. Since the majority of workers were either in the SPD or SPD-dominated unions, and since the SPD commanded a majority in a preponderant number of Workers' and Soldiers' Councils, the Spartacists had no choice but openly to challenge every government move that seemed to place a limit on the revolution and hope they could rally the mass of the workers behind them. The government kept them busy: on December 6, the office of the Spartacist newspaper, *Die Rote Fahne*, was raided and an attempt was made to arrest the Berlin Workers' and Soldiers' Councils; six days later, government forces stormed the People's Naval Division; and on January 3, Emil Eichhorn, the worker-oriented chief of the Berlin police, was dismissed. The Spartacus Union organized a mass protest against each of these actions. When the Eichhorn demonstration of January 5 reached an unexpected amplitude, representatives of the USPD and the Revolutionary Shop Stewards met with Communist delegates to discuss a mass protest. The Communists who attended, Liebknecht and Wilhelm Pieck, without consulting KPD leaders, agreed to proclaim a general strike, resist, by force if necessary, Eichhorn's dismissal, and, if the opportunity presented itself, seize power. A Revolutionary Executive was appointed.[16] It did not endure long; the Freikorps began moving toward Berlin on January 6, marched into the city on the thirteenth, arrested and murdered Luxemburg and Liebknecht on the fifteenth, and for the next few months, enjoyed a free hand in the crushing of Left-wing political opposition to the government.

Among the more notable institutions eliminated in the Freikorps' sweep through Germany was the Bavarian Soviet Republic, an exotic feature even on the peculiar postwar European landscape. The leaders of the revolutionary republic of November 8, headed by Kurt Eisner, had been defeated in a state assembly election on January 12. As he was on his way to relinquish power, Eisner was asssassinated; six weeks of chaos and government paralysis led to a seizure of power on April 7 by a motley conglomeration of Leftists, who proclaimed the Soviet Republic of Bavaria. Lacking a political power base, criticized by the Communists, and the target of an unsuccessful coup attempt, it gave way, on April 13, to a Communist-led Bavarian Soviet Republic. On May 1, Freikorps units entered Munich and commenced a white terror.[17]

The Hungarian Socialist Federated Soviet Republic enjoyed a somewhat longer life—133 as opposed to 24 days—but its grip on existence was equally precarious. Serious economic problems, Allied territorial concessions to the Romanians and Czechs, and political paralysis among the governing parties had created a breach in the ranks of traditional authority. When the Allies ordered the Republican government of Count Mihály Károlyi to evacuate Magyar-populated territory on Hungary's eastern frontier, popular resentment led to Károlyi's resignation on March 20 and a political vacuum. The Hungarian Left, temporarily overcoming its divisions, seized the opportunity. Instead of following the popular mandate, for a revolutionary government of national defense, however, it proclaimed a Soviet government. Although headed by a Communist, Béla Kun, the government was dominated by Socialists, and answerable to the Budapest Workers' and Soldiers' Council, whose main loyalty was to the trade unions.[18] The ministers negotiated a treaty with the Soviet Union, adopted a policy of wholesale nationalization, launched an invasion of Slovakia, and announced their desire for good relations with the Allies. The Allied representatives in Hungary, Romania, and Yugoslavia, however, with French army officers in the forefront, began to plot a counter-revolutionary invasion. The Entente leaders wanted to encircle, isolate, and eliminate the Hungarian Soviet Republic, but U.S. President Woodrow Wilson and British Prime Minister David Lloyd George refused to agree to a military invasion, preferring the maintenance of the blockade and a peace settlement that would, in the latter's words, "constitute an alternative to Bolshevism."[19]

The Hungarian Soviet government, however, faced too many factors outside its control to take advantage of the Allied "restraint." Divisions within the government, mistakes of omission and commission by Kun, the distance of the Red Army, and the failure to receive support from Austria or placate Romania placed the Council of People's Commissars in an impossible predicament.

The proximity of Austria and its Social Democratic government had offered some hope, but the Austrian Social Democratic leaders, Friedrich Adler and Otto Bauer, had made it immediately clear that recognition and friendly intentions were all it could offer. In the *Arbeiter Zeitung* of March 22–24, they wrote, "The Hungarians ask us to break with Paris in order to take up with Moscow; but Moscow is far off, the Soviet armies are still thousands of kilometers away, and Poland and the Ukraine make up a formidable obstacle. We are slaves of Paris because only Paris can supply us with bread."[20] Kun then sent Hungarian Communists to Austria to help plan an overthrow of the Austrian Republic. An April 17 demonstration in front of the Parliament was suppressed by the Volkswehr, a plan to take over the Volkswehr and police on May 1 was canceled at the last minute, and a third coup attempt was anticipated and preempted by the government. During the night of June 14–15, 115 Communist leaders were arrested, the Volkswehr occupied the inner-city area of Vienna, and an attempted Communist assault on police headquarters was bloodily defeated.[21]

When it became clear to the Hungarian Socialists that Kun could neither attract support from without, mobilize it from within, or forge an agreement with the Entente, they decided to drive the Communists from power and form a trade union government. The Right opposition, centered at French-occupied Szeged, learned of the Socialist plan for an armed insurrection and interposed itself on June 24. The Socialists dropped their plans and fought the counterrevolution alongside the Communists. A twenty-hour street fight preserved the Soviet Republic[22]—for another parlous month. On August 1, the Revolutionary Governing Council resigned and handed power over to a caretaker trade union government. Kun and several others left for Austria as the Romanian army advanced on Budapest. The Szeged counterrevolutionaries did not launch any coordinated military actions against the Soviet, moving instead into areas not occupied by the Romanian army. Although the Right did not directly confront the Soviet government in August, it did launch a brutal terror against those who could be identified as its supporters.[23] The Romanians withdrew in early November, and the Hungarian Right, under the direction of Miklós Horthy, assumed full control.

As the more perceptive Communist leaders understood, the failures in Germany, Hungary, and Austria were the direct result of "working-class" actions initiated without the support of a united proletariat. These "revolutions" were, as Paul Levi, the KPD leader, and Karl Radek, the Russian representative in Germany made clear, *putschist* in nature. Obviously, larger parties, closer connections to the masses, and better leadership were needed, but Communists differed over the methods best suited to achieve these ends. As the prospects for spontaneous revolution ebbed in Europe, and the Red Army's efforts to induce it died in Poland, the Communist International issued its prescription in the form of "Conditions of Admission" to the Third International. Formally presented at the Comintern's Second World Congress, July 19 to August 7, 1920, these twenty-one conditions summed up what Russian Communists had been saying and thinking since 1918: the blame for the lack of revolutionary success in Europe lay squarely with Social Democrats, and European Communists lacked the will to disassociate themselves from those counterrevolutionaries. The Conditions of Admission proclaimed the Russians' intent to remove, by schism and expulsion, all the cancers of opportunism, reformism, centrism, and conciliation from the Communist parties of the world. Events in Italy soon demonstrated the immense difficulty involved in custom-building a non-Russian party to Russian specifications and proved that such parties guaranteed neither revolutionary success nor counterrevolutionary effectiveness.

Fascism and Anti-Fascism in Italy

Benito Mussolini had few antecedents or models for the movement he began to build in 1919; no doctrine or tradition awaited his magical touch. He did not invent organized violence by the Right, nor were his programs especially original. He was a gifted improvisator, who understood better than his predecessors and most of his imitators the value of constant demonstrations of vigor, energy, and determination, usually in the form of violence but occasionally as bluff; the use of nationalist rhetoric and symbols as healing, consolidating, and unifying elements; the pose of the willing negotiator; the unscrupulousness of the double-dealer; and the advantages of a fluid, generalized set of demands.

Italian Fascism sought power. People, words, tactics, methods, organizations, all had to conform to that strategic goal. Success, not consistency, was the standard of performance. No one has defined Italian Fascism better, or more succinctly, than Mussolini himself in 1932: "The value of fascism lies in the fact that it is veined with pragmatism, but at the same time has a will to exist and a will to power."[24]

The party program was only a starting point, a vehicle for attracting supporters, that changed as conditions and possibilities changed. Nevertheless, through all the permutations of Italian Fascism, there remained a pronounced core of opposition to conflict, class or party, within the framework of the nation. In particular, and even when Mussolini directed his appeal to workers, Fascists opposed strikes and their fomenters. In one of his earliest speeches, delivered on March 23, 1919, in Milan, he stated: "We declare war on socialism . . . because it has aligned itself against the nation. . . . We wish . . . to separate the proletariat from the Socialist party. . . . We must go toward the workers. . . . However, we must impress upon the workers that it is one thing to destroy, another to build."[25]

Deeds, not words, vaulted the Fascists into the heart of Italian politics. Sensing that there was much greater potential in national reaction to the wave of industrial and agrarian strikes that had washed over Italy for the past two years than in continued national support of Gabriele D'Annunzio's occupation of Fiume, Mussolini turned his armed squads against Socialists, trade unions, and cooperatives. The government did not intervene, King Victor Emmanuel III did not complain, public opinion was not adverse, and the Left failed to muster a systematic response. The Fascists did not participate in the elections of 1920, but their squads were obvious, and by 1921, the Fascist Party had begun the process of making itself seem an indispensible element in the Italian political equation. Movements and parties superior in numbers and power to the Fascists splintered, divided, or floundered, while industrialists, landlords, the army, and, ultimately, the King convinced themselves that they could use Mussolini's party as a malleable instrument for destroying the Left, restoring order, and establishing a strong government.

The Left, for its part, was doing a relatively good job of destroying itself. The Socialists (PSI) had emerged from the war and the elections of 1919 as the largest party in the Chamber of Deputies, it was closely tied to the country's largest labor organization, the General Confederation of Labor (CGL), and the Italian working class was in a militant mood. The PSI failed to take advantage of any of those strengths. It neither used its parliamentary position to support political, economic, or social reforms nor provided a revolutionary direction for workers on strike. The party voted revolutionary platforms, advocated a dictatorship of the proletariat, decried and denigrated reforms proposed in Parliament, but failed to lead or help coordinate the industrial and agrarian strikes that might have led to radical restructuring of Italian society. Italian Socialists seemed unaware of the nature of the parliamentary game to which they had committed themselves, and, lacking a revolutionary tradition and practice of their own, believed they could emulate the Russian experience simply by proclaiming its value loudly and monotonously.

The PSI had several opportunities to form a parliamentary majority with the other large mass party, the Italian Popular Party, and the smaller Left-Center parties, and embark on a program of moderate social and economic reforms, including the goal of the CGL, an eight-hour workday. Alternatively, it could have taken charge of the strike wave of 1919–1920, which engaged four million workers in over 3,600 work stoppages. It is entirely possible that a determined, coordinated push from the Left could have toppled an irresolute and indecisive Liberal-led government that could not influence the Versailles treaty process, dislodge Annunzio from Fiume, stop the strikes, punish the strikers, or legislate reforms. Instead, PSI leaders vigorously opposed the one concrete path toward revolution generated within party ranks, the factory council movement organized by the *Ordine Nuovo* group of Turin.

Within this power vacuum, the Right-wing counteroffensive formed. Employers and landlords organized national confederations. The Fascists merged with older patriotic associations, became increasingly militarized and organized, and began to launch punitive expeditions into the countryside. Socialist attention, though, was focused on an intense intraparty debate over the "Conditions of Admission Into the Third International," to be debated at the Livorno Congress, January 1921. Months before Livorno, the party had divided into factions over the issue of revolutionary activity. Amadeo Bordiga, who believed that the party needed purifying and reshaping into an institution that would abstain from election campaigns and parliamentary participation, formed a Communist faction in July 1919, while the reformists formed their own faction in October. The bulk of the party, however, the Maximalists, as they were called, followed the lead of Giacinto Serrati, who advocated preparing for a violent revolution on the Russian model, using elections and bourgeois institutions for propaganda effects, and joining the Third International. At the party's Bologna Congress in October, the Maximalists received 48,411 votes, the reformists 14,880, and Bordiga 3,417.[26] Bordiga immediately began talking about schism, and his forces were bolstered by the adherence of the *Ordine Nuovo* group in November. Serrati, meanwhile, tried to convince the Russians to allow the PSI to pursue a conditional response to the Conditions of Admission.

He argued at the Second World Congress of the Comintern, and at the Executive Committee meeting following it (July–August 1920), that even though revolutionary conditions were building, the proletariat forces remained weak and the bourgeoisie was organizing its white guards. In the face of cresting reaction, Serrati said, it would be harmful for the PSI to expel part of its membership or force a schism, especially until the Italian masses had come to a clear understanding of its necessity.[27] The ECCI's response put "the question of cleansing the party and all other conditions of admission as an *ultimatum*," and declared, "We are not out for numbers alone—we do not want weights on our feet—we shall not allow reformists into our ranks."[28] The large, seemingly indiscriminate purges required by the Conditions of Admission dissuaded a significant number of Socialists from supporting Comintern adherence. They argued that expulsions should occur slowly and carefully, with full regard paid to the particular circumstances of each country. Expulsions involving differences of opinion over revolutionary potential, they warned, would destroy the organizations and solidarity needed by the working class in a future revolutionary era.[29]

The Comintern sent two representatives, the Hungarian Mátyás Rákosi and the Bulgarian Khristo Kabakchiev, to Livorno to argue the necessity of purging those who denied that the present era was revolutionary in nature; those types, they said, were far more dangerous to the proletarian cause than German Social Democrats, Russian Mensheviks, and counter-revolutionaries. Unity with them meant "unity between Communists and the enemies of Communism. There is no place for this kind of unity in the ranks of the Third International."[30] In addition, Comintern president

Grigori Zinoviev sent a letter to the delegates informing them, in no uncertain terms, that they "must choose between Turati, d'Aragon and co. [reformist leaders], and the Third International."[31] The majority of delegates voted for the unity position (Serrati's conditional acceptance of the Conditions of Admission), giving it 98,028 of the 172,487 votes cast. The delegates who had cast 58,783 votes for Bordiga's unconditional acceptance of the Third International's conditions departed the PSI and formed, on January 21, the Italian Communist Party (PCd'I).[32]

The Livorno schism not only failed to clarify matters on the Italian Left, but measurably weakened it. Prior to the congress, the PSI enrolled 216,000 members; afterward, the two parties had a combined membership of under 100,000.[33] In the May 1921 elections, the combined parliamentary representation of the Socialists (123 seats) and Communists (15 seats) marked a decline from 1919, when the united PSI had won 156 seats. This weakened Left immediately became consumed by inter- and intraorganizational matters, further vitiating the amount of energy and quality of initiatives it directed against the Fascists. The PSI, despite its enhanced reformist plurality, continued to abjure the use of Parliament as a means to strengthen the republic or improve workers' conditions. Within PSI ranks, the reformists sought to end all possibility of enrollment in the Third International, while the Maximalists continued to seek means to accomplish that objective. The Communists, dominated by Bordiga and his ultra-Left, sectarian perspective, opposed alliances with the PSI and systematic use of electoral and parliamentary tactics. Leaders of the PCd'I's Right and Center, not as obsessed with creating a purified revolutionary party, argued for fusion with the PSI Left, while the *Ordine Nuovo* group, no less dedicated than Bordiga to building a pure revolutionary party, urged flexibility in tactical matters.

The CGL Congress, February 26 to March 3, 1921, also paid scant heed to the Fascists, but straddled the questions of internal unity and external linkages more successfully. Though the more militant elements were decisively defeated on the vote of confidence over Confederal leadership of the 1920 strikes and overwhelmingly defeated in their effort to end CGL cooperation with the PSI, there was no schism. The delegates as a whole indicated their sympathy for leaving the reformist trade union international and joining the one the Russians intended to form, if, that is, the Third International and the PSI came to an amicable settlement of their differences over the Conditions of Admission. CGL representatives attended the first Red International of Labor Unions Congress that summer, but the CGL never joined. Nor did Communists exercise decisive influence within the CGL. The CGL leaders pressed the PSI to use its parliamentary strength constructively and attempted to organize armed bands of workers (Arditi del Popolo), but the Socialists rejected both tactics and the Communists called the Arditi a "bourgeois maneuver."[34]

The Fascists, meanwhile, making use of whatever methods would advance their interests, especially countless deeds of violence, increased the number of local squads from 108 in July 1920 to 1,000 in February 1921.[35] At the same time, Mussolini sought alliances with the Socialist, Popular and Liberal parties. Giovanni Giolitti, the Liberal Prime Minister, in an effort to weaken the Left and tame the Right, created a "National Bloc" with the Fascist and nationalist parties for the election of May 1921. That coalition failed to win a majority of the votes or to hold together in the aftermath of the election. The parties of the Left won more votes than the National Bloc, while the combined Socialist and Popular Party total exceeded it by over 800,000 votes.[36] Neither an anti-Fascist governing coalition nor one including the Fascists emerged. The Socialists refused to join a coalition led by Giolitti, and the Popular Party was on the verge of abandoning support for a Giolitti-led government. When the Fascists, who had won 35 seats, were not invited into the government, Mussolini broke the National Bloc by voting with the nationalist parties against Giolitti's position on the Rapallo Treaty (settling the Italian-Yugoslav border and the status of Fiume), and the Fascist squads increased their attacks on working-class institutions and organizations. Indeed, by the November party congress, the *squadristi* elements proved strong enough to derail Mussolini's efforts to replace the Fascist-nationalist–Liberal Party alliance with a Fascist-Socialist-Popular parties coalition; they forced him to renounce the August 2 "peace pact" he had signed with the PSI and CGL.

The CGL, on its own, organized an Alliance of Labor in February 1922, uniting five liberal and Socialist confederations and federations, but the Communists were not invited, and the Alliance of Labor did not immediately demonstrate the will to meet violence with violence or to risk the material gains of the past in open battle. Antonio Gramsci and the PCd'I criticized it as a coalition of leaders lacking a mass base.[37] Then, at their March 1922 Rome Congress, the Communists overwhelmingly rejected a united front with the Alliance of Labor, and spoke as though the main enemy were the non-Communist proletarian organizations. Gramsci spoke out against the concept of a broad-based political bloc, saying: "I am convinced that not just the People's Party, but also a part of the Socialist Party must be excluded from the proletarian united front . . . because to make an agreement with them would mean making an agreement with the bourgeoisie."[38] The Rome Theses, largely the work of Bordiga, demonstrated that his appreciation of the Fascist potential had not increased. "The present Italian situation," it stated, "is in reality a natural and predictable stage of development of the capitalistic order: a specific manifestation of the function and purpose of the democratic state." The theses committed the PCd'I to a campaign "to win ground among the proletariat by increasing its strength and influence at the expense of proletarian political parties and currents with which it disagrees."[39]

When the Fascists began to mobilize their forces directly against the government in Ferrara and Bologna in May 1922, the PSI and PCd'I reacted differently. The parliamentary group of the former, on June 1, voted to support any ministry "which would ensure the restoration of law and liberty,"[40] and when that failed to alter the situation, the PSI began to consider a "strictly legal" general strike as a means of countering the Fascists. A series of local, spontaneous worker strikes against Fascist violence in Piedmont, Lombardy, and the Marches provided the Alliance of Labor with its opportunity. It halted the strikes and told the workers to prepare a general strike to counter the next flagrant Fascist act. The Executive Committee of the Third International responded with an "Appeal" to the Italian workers, blaming the Fascist reign of terror on PSI passivity and urging the workers to break with the reformists and join the Communists in a revolutionary class struggle against the bourgeoisie.[41] The Alliance of Labor launched its general strike at midnight, July 31, following a Fascist attack on Ravenna, but it had delayed too long. Those workers that did respond were smashed by a wave of Fascist counterterror, which broke the strike and the Alliance of Labor.

At the beginning of October, as Fascist forces occupied Trento and Bolzano and the party organized its Fascist Militia, the Socialists split. Serrati's Maximalists and the Terzini, a Left-wing group impatient to join the Third International, voted, 32,000 to 29,000, to exclude the reformists, because one of its leaders, Filippo Turati, had, in June, consulted with the King on the prospect of the Socialists forming a government with the democratic parties to the right of the PSI. The expelled reformists formed the Independent Socialist Party (PSU) and enrolled in the "2 1/2" International (see chapter 2). The CGL then broke its pact of alliance with the PSI and proclaimed itself "independent."[42] Zinoviev hailed the PSI split, proclaiming it "a great and meaningful sign of the times. Despite all obstacles, the world working class movement progresses."[43]

One week later, the Fascists decided to force their way into power by staging nationwide demonstrations culminating in a "March on Rome." Although the authorities remained in control, and capable of halting and breaking the Fascist offensive, the atmosphere of confusion and government weakness convinced the King to appoint Mussolini prime minister on October 30. The day before the appointment, the PCd'I assured its followers that encasing the bourgeois state with armed Fascist guards would not produce a stable regime; "it will be no more successful than the surrendered parliamentary-constitutional mechanism." The workers were urged to build a proletarian united front as the vehicle for the only "solution to the problem of an oppressive state: a government of workers and peasants."[44]

Although Mussolini had to thread his way carefully and slowly, with frequent reversals and side steps, toward the consolidation of absolute state power, his monopoly on violence and the continued hesitations and vacillations of the Left prevented the various crises of his regime from becoming fatal. The CGL took a conciliatory stance toward the new regime, but the two Socialist parties and the PCd'I did not ally against it. When, on December 30, Mussolini ordered the arrest of the PCd'I Central Committee (except for the two who were members of the Chamber of Deputies), the party went underground, and thousands of Socialists and Communists left Italy.[45] Bordiga continued to refuse to initiate a united front with the Socialists, and the Socialists split again. Serrati, following a visit to Moscow, proposed that the Socialists fuse with the Communists, but Pietro Nenni formed an antifusion faction which won a majority at the April 1923 congress. In August, Nenni expelled the leaders of the Terzini, and, in November, categorically refused to join a united front with the PCd'I.

The Communists' insistence on a "socialist revolution" plank, the Pope's refusal to allow the Popular Party to unite with the Socialists, and the defeatism of the CGL blocked the formation of an openly anti-Fascist electoral bloc for the elections of April 1924. The Fascist-nationalist slate won four and a half million votes, the Socialists and Communists, running independently, just over one million. The obvious fraud and intimidation that helped produce those results provoked a harshly critical speech by the leader of the Independent Socialists, Giacomo Matteotti. His disappearance on June 10 and the discovery of his murdered body three days later led to a wave of popular antagonism that profoundly shook Mussolini's government and presented his opponents with a golden opportunity. At first, they responded as though they were determined to force the issue of legality. On June 13, 123 opposition deputies, including the Socialists and Communists, walked out of the Italian Parliament and formed the Aventine Secession. While Mussolini scrambled to overcome the fragmenting effects of Matteotti's murder, the Aventines failed to find a basis for unity or a concrete alternative to the existing regime. Acting as though mass action involving the Left was more fearsome than Fascism in power and that dignified legality could counter Fascist squads, the Aventines allowed popular discontent to dissolve. Turati said on July 13, "We feel that it is essential to do something, but we cannot decide on anything positive."[46] Gramsci accused the Aventines of being afraid of leaving "the purely parliamentary terrain to enter upon political questions," and of failing to give definite political form to their opposition by launching an appeal to the proletariat or intensifying the spontaneous strike movement that had begun to emerge.[47] The Communists returned to the Chamber of Deputies in November, the Socialists and some of the Centrists in 1925, and the Popular Party in 1926.

Outside Parliament, an attempt to resuscitate the Alliance of Labor came to naught, leagues to promote democracy and liberty came and went, and plans for anti-Fascist coalitions soared and crashed. The PCd'I was strengthened, in August, when the long-ordered fusion with the Left Socialists finally occurred and Antonio Gramsci became secretary general of the party. He told the party Central Committee the following February that "the disintegration of the Aventine has strengthened revolutionary tendencies," that the masses must be organized in workers' and peasants' committees, and that the non-Communist Left must be attacked.[48] While party leaders exerted great energy to construct an underground apparatus, the Central Committee ordered the rank and file to mobilize the masses for the coming struggle against Fascism by means of the "tactics of double attack against Fascism and against the treacherous opposition, the denunciation of the Fascist Parliament and the opposition 'quasi-Parliament,' together with a wide propaganda and organisational setting-up of workers' and peasants' committees."[49] But the party's weak base in the deteriorating CGL—Communists had perhaps 15 percent of its members and controlled only three minor federations[50]—and attacks by the Fascist goverment blunted the effect of these exhortations.

The opponents of Fascism consistently overestimated the nature of the internal contradictions of the Fascist regime, and underestimated Mussolini's resiliency and pragmatism, and the striking power of his government. In October and November 1926, following an attempt on his life, Il Duce shattered the base of Italian anti-Fascism: political parties were dissolved, opposition deputies arrested, and a special anti-Fascist police and tribunal established. The anti-Fascists who had escaped the dragnet fled into exile, where they continued their bitter factional struggles.

The "Threat" of Italian Fascism

The corporate state that Mussolini began to construct in the mid-twenties reflected none of the radical promises he had made when he organized the Fasci in 1919. Industrialists and landlords were not dispossessed or even brought under close control. In 1923, the party was ordered to negotiate with the employers' organization, Confindustria; in 1925, employers were given absolute authority over workers, the party was given control over unions, and strikes were forbidden. The 1926 Law on Corporations made class collaboration a national policy, while the 1927 Charter of Labor announced "that private enterprise in the sphere of production is the most effective and useful instrument in the interest of the nation."[51] The law of December 29, 1928, making the Grand Council of Fascism the supreme organ of the Italian state, completed the transformation of Italy into a one-party dictatorship with the working class under tight control. Many Fascisti, however, resented Mussolini's failure to carry through the promised Fascist revolution. Currents of resentment and alienation percolated through party ranks during the thirties, but never actually threatened Mussolini's control of the state.

Mussolini's path in foreign policy was also marked by a policy of improvisation in slow tempo. Although his deeds annoyed Western diplomats, angered those in the Balkans, and drove Yugoslavia into an alliance with France, none of the powers perceived or denounced him as a threat to European peace. Instead, his claim that he represented the only "dike" against the Bolshevik revolutionary tide was widely accepted among European heads of state.[52]

His foreign policy both stabilized and destabilized. By recognizing the USSR and signing a commercial treaty with it in 1924, he helped the West officially end the diplomatic ostracism of the Communist state.[53] On the other hand, he pursued Italian nationalist claims in a disruptive manner. Italians occupied Corfu and seized Fiume in 1923, and provided military support to Albania and arms to Macedonian terrorists, Croat separatists, and other underworld Balkan groups.[54] Mussolini sent arms to the Hungarian government, prepared an arms cache for the Austrian Heimwehr, granted comfortable asylum to Nazis fleeing the failed Munich *Putsch* of 1923, established a pro-Fascist newspaper in France to propagandize against Italian anti-Fascist exiles, and sent spies to infiltrate their ranks.[55]

Mussolini only supported non-Italian radical Right groups that he thought he could dominate and use to advance his nationalist goals. When Fascist parties formed in Bulgaria and Hungary, for example, he ordered the Italian legations in Sofia and Budapest to keep their distance. Instead, he tried to create an international network of Fascist clubs, coordinated by the Secretariat of Fascist Groups Abroad. These clubs found fertile soil only in North America, but even those were not well organized or effective. The Secretariat was reorganized at the end of 1926, but failed to invigorate Italian Fascism abroad or promote unity among the other types of Fascism.[56]

Although Mussolini's pronouncements about Italian national expansion grew increasingly grandiose toward the latter part of the 1920s, his diplomatic behavior did not differ significantly from that of other southeastern European leaders, nor did Mussolini accomplish more than any other Italian leader might have. In fact, by February 1929, when he signed the Lateran Accords with the Vatican, Italy enjoyed a tranquil set of relations with most of the countries of Europe. The Lateran Accords themselves "had enormous repercussions throughout Europe and the Catholic world: the thesis that Mussolini was essentially a moderate and constructive statesman now seemed to have found irrefutable confirmation."[57]

Viewed from the perspective of the 1920s, Mussolini appeared as a successful restorer of order and an architect of stability. Though seven other southern and eastern European countries succumbed to Right-wing offensives during that decade, no other submission was the result of a mass movement or party, indicating that Fascism remained a relatively insignificant factor in European Right-wing politics.

The Marxist Left was equally insignificant as a catalyst for Right-wing adventure. Only in Bulgaria (June 1923), ruled by a radical peasant party (Agrarian National Union), and Albania (December 1924), where a coalition of liberal politicians and peasants tried to introduce a Western constitutional regime, did antagonism to Leftist reform serve as a prime motive for the rebels. All the other overthrows—Greece in 1922 and 1925, Spain in 1923, Poland and Portugal in 1926, and Yugoslavia in 1929—came as the result of political instability and economic problems. Military officers led the coups in Greece, Bulgaria, Spain, Poland, and Portugal; a deposed politician, Ahmed Bey Zog, took control in Albania at the head of a mercenary army he had raised in Yugoslavia; and King Alexander I of Yugoslavia ended his country's constitutional regime, abolished political parties, and inaugurated a reign of personal dictatorship.

In sum, the main problem facing revolutionary movements or parties in Europe in the first postwar decade was not Fascism, but their own weakness, confusion, and disunity, and the strength of conservative and centrist forces. Leaders of Left-wing parties, though, did not seem to understand that and failed to distinguish, in an effective and timely manner, between Fascism and reaction, cure the causes of Left weakness, or impede the sources of Right strength.

Chapter 2

The Foundations of Marxist Anti-Fascism

Italian Fascism was a new form of political reaction, partially disguised by the smoke and ashes of a world destroyed and the haze of a world emerging. Although in significant ways different from the usual form of Right-wing takeover, its effect, at least to outside observers, appeared the same: political stability and social order. Since the great majority of Western statesmen and politicians believed that the main perpetrators of tumult in Europe and the United States were the Russian Bolsheviks* and the Communist parties formed in response to the Russian Revolution, Western leaders did not protest when Italian Fascists and practitioners of the more traditional forms of white terror suppressed Left-wing parties and trade unions.

The Communists, in turn, perceived Fascism as a contemporary form of "bourgeois capitalist" defense and consolidation. Although they discussed, analyzed, and criticized it at length, Fascism did not become the main focus of international Communist activity until the early thirties. Even then, the Communist movement failed to produce a credible analysis of Fascism or an effective strategy or tactical response to it. The leading Marxist thinkers among the Communists had virtually no impact on the practice of anti-Fascism. Rosa Luxemburg and V. I. Lenin died before they could focus on it; Antonio Gramsci and Leon Trotsky were on the periphery (the former in prison, the latter in exile) when their analyses matured to a complex and subtle appreciation; Georg Lukács was hounded from political to aesthetic concerns by fear of expulsion; and Karl Korsch

*The Russian Social Democratic Labor Party (Bolshevik) organized the October 1917 revolution; in March 1918, the party was renamed Russian Communist Party (Bolshevik); in 1925, All-Union Communist Party (Bolshevik); and in 1952, Communist Party of the Soviet Union.

was expelled. Otto Bauer, the leading Social Democratic thinker, developed an insightful analysis—Fascism was a Bonapartist response of the bourgeoisie to its fear of losing social and economic power in a political situation of Left-Right equilibrium—but he neither developed a practical counterstrategy against Bonapartism nor infused Social Democrats with the will to resist it.

Lenin alone had the power and stature to bestow on the international Communist movement a usable set of tactics against Fascism, but he could not have molded the world's Communists into an effective fighting force against it. As he discovered more than once, human elements under his nominal control or influence regularly behaved as if they had not read or understood what he said or wrote. In addition, Italy was far away, the demands of the Russian Revolution were many, and Lenin was far more concerned with the structure, composition, and behavior of Communist parties than the anatomy of Italian Fascism. Nor did he take Mussolini seriously.

Lenin believed that a well-led revolutionary movement in Italy would eliminate all forms of counterrevolution, and so his main focus was on the failure of revolutionary elements within the Italian Socialist Party to rid themselves of the "reformists" and "centrists" in their midst. In June 1920, he wrote: "Any inconsistency or weakness in exposing those who show themselves to be reformists or 'Centrists' means directly increasing the danger of the power of the proletariat being overthrown by the bourgeoisie, which tomorrow will utilize for the counter-revolution that which short-sighted people today see merely as 'theoretical differences.' "[1] Six months later, in an article harshly critical of Serrati's reluctance to break with Socialist reformists, Lenin was much more direct, writing: "Victory in the proletarian revolution *cannot* be achieved, and that revolution *cannot* be safeguarded, while there are reformists and mensheviks in one's ranks."[2]

The appearance of Mussolini "perturbed" Lenin to the extent that he sent urgent messages to "Milan, Bologna, Turin, Rome imploring the comrades to separate themselves from the temporizers and regroup the cadres for militant action."[3] He offered, however, no specific anti-Fascist measures. He placed the problem of Italian Fascism within the context of the Bolsheviks' failure to graft their revolutionary experience and expertise onto the European Left and the inability of the European Left to assimilate the Russian experience. "Just how that will be done," Lenin admitted in his final speech to the world Communist movement, "I do not know. The fascists in Italy may, for example, render us a great service by showing the Italians that they are not yet sufficiently enlightened and that their country is not yet ensured against the Black Hundreds.* Perhaps this will be very useful."[4]

Though he devoted more time to Comintern affairs than Lenin, Leon Trotsky viewed Italian Fascism through a similar prism, as a form of traditional capitalist counterrevolutionary activity. Trotsky, too, underestimated the destructive force and endurance of Fascism in Italy, and much of his early commentary on it was shaped by his belief in Italy's revolutionary potential and his determination to fashion a revolutionary movement to take advantage of it. Mussolini, in Trotsky's estimation, represented a phase of bourgeois reaction to the postwar wave of workers' strikes and the lingering prospect of a Communist revolution in Italy. However, Trotsky lacked Lenin's confidence in Communist parties as agents of upheaval. Trotsky's personal history within the Russian Social Democratic Labor Party and his knowledge of the weakness and ineptitude of the new Communist parties led him to place his confidence in revolutionary united fronts, which would both prepare Communists to lead the coming proletarian revolution and prepare the proletariat to be led.[5] The united front thesis actually developed by the Communist International, before Lenin was incapacitated and Trotsky removed from power, would accomplish neither.

The United Front

The Russian Communists needed some tactic to advance their cause and retard the "bourgeois capitalist counteroffensive." The defeat of revolutions in Germany and Hungary, the foreshortening of mass strikes in Italy and France, and the defeat of the Red Army in Poland had diminished the prospect of a successful European revolution. The working-class movement had been fractured in the war and postwar periods. In each country, numbers of Socialist and Communist parties, groups, and trade unions existed and competed. On the international level, three political and three trade union internationals further complicated matters. In all countries, and at all levels, Communist enrollment lagged well behind that of Socialism.

*Tsarist gangs used in the pogroms against Russian Jews and Leftists.

The main contenders for working-class loyalty were the Second or Socialist International, originally formed in 1889 and reformed in Bern in July 1920, and the Third or Communist International (Comintern), which held its founding congress in Moscow in March 1919. The International Working Union of Socialist Parties (or "2 1/2" International), composed of Socialists who had opposed the nationalist positions of their parties during World War I and who disliked the methods and policies of the Russians, was created by the delegates of thirteen countries in Vienna in February 1921.

The Second and "2 1/2" internationalists merged in May 1923, taking the name Labor and Socialist International. At its peak, in 1928, it contained thirty-six parties, enrolling 6.6 million members, and attracting 25.6 million votes in national elections. Its constitution guaranteed its members maximum autonomy, and the resolutions voted by congresses and executive committees were not binding on the member parties. The accord of 1923, however, represented a poor compromise between parties who could not agree on the questions of exercising power in a bourgeois state and the relationship between bourgeois and Socialist democracy. The member parties maintained unity only by avoiding doctrinal issues and concentrating their efforts on the maintenance of peace in Europe. But their failure to reach a consensus on a strategic alternative to the obviously ineffective League of Nations made LSI peace appeals sound hollow.[6]

Trade union leaders with a Socialist orientation joined the International Federation of Trade Unions, which met at Amsterdam in July 1919. Delegations from forty-three countries formed an organization closely tied to, but not controlled by, the Socialist International. Two years later, in July 1921, the Comintern formed the Red International of Labor Unions (RILU), which it completely controlled. Finally, at the end of 1921, syndicalist and anarchist trade union leaders hostile both to the reformist tendency of Amsterdam and the dictatorial methods of the Russians and their organizations formed the International Workers Association in Berlin. Its membership and influence were limited.

All failed, individually and collectively, to rouse effective resistance to the Right, wherever and in whatever form it appeared. No effective international coalition was built, and no single international rose above the fray to assume or be awarded the mantle of working-class leadership. The LSI and IFTU had the troops, but lacked the central authority to order them into battle. Divisions among the national sections of each insured that their congresses and executive sessions functioned mainly as debate forums or study groups, issuing general warnings and statements of support. The *Bulletin of the Labor and Socialist International* did not focus on Italian Fascism until the disappearance and death of Matteotti, when the LSI Executive sent a letter to the PSI labeling Fascism "the most bestial form of capitalist 'order' " and wishing that Matteotti's death would induce Italian workers to "unite forces."[7]

The Comintern exercised far greater control over its far fewer members, but it did not perform as a highly efficient, streamlined engine. In fact, as a British Communist noted, "for so much of the time it wobbled along in a muddle which was frequently comical but, at the same time, depressing."[8] Aino Kuusinen, who worked for the Comintern for more than a decade, while married to Otto Kuusinen, one of its most powerful secretaries, stated that despite constant reorganization, the Comintern expended enormous energy on fictitious activity and the resolution of internal disputes. Although the Comintern exercised a powerful hold over the national parties, its executive leadership (Kuusinen, Ossip Piatnitsky, and Dmitri Manuilsky) failed to create a state of harmony among them.[9]

In fact, the source of most Comintern inventiveness and international success was the very unbureaucratic Willi Münzenberg, the entrepreneur par excellence of international Communism between the wars. But not even his creative wizardry, his seemingly unending ability to manufacture front organizations, could overcome the fatal flaws of the Comintern: it too faithfully mirrored Russian national interests, and Russian national interests were too often defined in terms of Russian party imperatives and rivalries.

Nevertheless, the Comintern did act more regularly and energetically against Fascism than did the LSI or IFTU, although frequently deepening the hostility between Communists and Socialists in the process. The proclaimed purpose of the Third International and the intense hatred Russian Communists harbored against Social Democrats eliminated the possibility of an anti-Fascist alliance at the international level and made it very difficult at the national one. Angelo Tasca, a leader of the PCd'I during the twenties, claims that the Italian Communists were far more serious about their struggle with the Socialists than with the Fascists.[10]

The "invitation" to the First Congress of the Communist International, dated January 24, 1919, called for "unrelenting struggle" against the "social-chauvinists" (Socialists who had supported the war) and "unsparing criticism and exposure" of "centrists" (Socialists who vacillated during revolutionary periods).[11] One month after the First Congress of the Communist International, Lenin wrote that the Third International had "gathered the fruits of the work of the Second International, discarded its opportunist, social-chauvinist, bourgeois and petty-bourgeois dross," and left it to continue to play "the role of lackey to the world bourgeoisie."[12]

All interwar Comintern tactics contained a badly concealed goal—the destruction of the influence of Socialist parties and trade unions. The united front, proclaimed as a means of rebuilding the workers' revolutionary offensive during an ebb tide of revolution in Europe, became a weapon to bludgeon Socialists, reformists, and Communist "deviationists." The Executive Committee of the Comintern (ECCI) made it into "a policy of pure expediency, in which right and left were no longer actual positions, but errors in timing."[13] Few Communists understood the tactic, most were unhappy with it, and it alienated virtually all non-Communists.

Yet when it came from the minds of its originators, Paul Levi and Karl Radek, it had been a sensible and clear response to German conditions. Radek was the first Bolshevik to grasp that revolutionary possibilities in Germany had ended. In January 1919, he urged KPD leaders to disavow the planned seizure of power and concentrate instead on building a majority following among the workers.[14] Rosa Luxemburg rejected his advice, and the Freikorps crushed the uprising, murdered three KPD leaders (Luxemburg, Liebknecht, and Leo Jogiches), and, one month later, arrested Radek.

He stayed in prison until January 1920, but was allowed to receive visits from Levi and other KPD leaders. Radek argued that the German party should organize the masses for the next revolutionary wave by capturing trade unions and factory councils, entering Parliament and municipal councils, and unifying with the Left wing of the USPD.[15] Levi, who had argued in vain at the KPD founding congress that Communists should participate in Parliament and work within non-Communist trade unions, agreed with Radek on every tactic but one: Levi wanted to expel the ultra-Leftists, whose adventurist outlook and activity threatened Levi's concept of a disciplined mass party. Radek argued against further splits, especially when it involved groups with a revolutionary spirit. Lenin and the Comintern executive agreed with Radek. Levi, however, possessed an independent spirit, and, at the party's Heidelberg Congress in October

1919, maneuvered the expulsion of those he labeled "syndicalists,"[16] costing the KPD nearly half its membership. The Second Congress of the Third International, held in July and August 1920, represented an indirect slap at leaders such as Levi and Serrati, who were, Lenin believed, realistic to the point of pessimism about revolutionary offensives. Since the Russians remained optimistic about the prospects for world revolution, the statutes and Conditions of Admission that were adopted placed severe limits on "rightward" maneuvers, while Lenin's "Theses on the Basic Tasks of the Communist International" authorized only that tactical flexibility that directly promoted the dictatorship of the proletariat. Finally, the ECCI offered the expelled German ultra-Leftists, now calling themselves the German Communist Workers Party (KAPD), a consultative voice in the Comintern.[17] That proved to be only a minor setback for Levi. Shortly after the Second Congress, a majority of the USPD voted to join the Comintern and, in December, merged with the Communists to form the People's Communist Party (VKPD).* Levi had his mass party, albeit 300,000 of the 350,000 members were from the USPD.[18]

Levi now proceeded with his next step, the construction of a united front of German working-class organizations. He and Radek composed an "Open Letter" from the VKPD Central Committee to the Social Democrats, the USPD minority, the KAPD, and the trade unions, proposing joint campaigns to win reforms for the workers, dissolve the "bourgeois organs of defense," and create "organizations of proletarian self-defense."[19] Lenin called the tactics *"perfectly correct,"*[20] but the German organizations rejected the invitation and Levi's position in the Communist movement deteriorated further.

It evaporated two weeks later, at the PSI Congress at Livorno, where Levi placed himself in clear opposition to the Comintern and its delegates, whose splitting tactics would, Levi argued, cost the new Communist Party too many members and the firm core of a mass party.[21] Following Levi's return to Germany, Radek was sent there from Russia, and Rákosi and Kabakchiev came from Italy to arrange the removal of Levi from his position as party leader. When the Central Committee voted, 28–23, to

---

*The USPD majority included the younger, more dynamic trade union members; the minority included most of the leaders, Reichstag deputies, and periodical editors. The latter merged with the SPD in the autumn of 1921. The VKPD was renamed the KPD in August 1921.

condemn Levi's behavior, he and four other members resigned their position. The ECCI hastened to approve, seeing in Levi's criticism of the Italian situation clear proof of "opportunist vacillations," "menshevik-reformist tendencies," and "signs of the formation of a right wing" in the German party.[22] Lenin, on the other hand, was deeply disturbed: "We are so short of tried and tested forces that I am really indignant when I hear comrades announcing their withdrawal, etc."[23]

In March, three Comintern representatives—Béla Kun, Peter Pepper (né Pogany), and August Kleine (né Guralsky)—arrived in Germany. Their mission, probably undertaken at Zinoviev's initiative, was to separate the KPD from Levi's Open Letter. They urged the Central Committee to take advantage of events surrounding a coal strike in Mansfeld and proclaim an armed insurrection against the government, and, when that failed, a general strike. German workers did not respond in large numbers, the police and army killed and wounded hundreds, employers fired thousands, and the KPD lost over half its membership.[24]

In the waning days of what came to be called the *Marzaktion*, Levi wrote to Lenin, describing it not as "a battle of the proletariat against the bourgeoisie, but a battle of Communists against the predominant majority of the proletariat," which had placed the KPD "in open hostility to every large workers' organization and the majority of the proletariat."[25] He then issued a brochure, *Our Path: Against Putschism,* on April 3, containing a harsh critique of the ECCI and labeling the *Marzaktion* a "Bakuninist insanity."[26] The KPD Central Committee expelled Levi from the party on April 15; the ECCI approved on April 26.*

Lenin faced a dilemma. He disapproved of Levi's behavior at Livorno, his decision to write a pamphlet, and, of course, his public criticism of the *Marzaktion.*[27] But Lenin had and still approved the Open Letter, and, after he had informed himself about the March events, agreed that the Comintern delegates had committed "idiocies."[28]

With the Third Comintern Congress about to convene, Lenin had to find a way to criticize Levi's "impermissible and harmful" methods without approving the *Marzaktion* and undercutting the Open Letter. "The crux of the matter," Lenin wrote Zinoviev, "is that Levi in very many respects is *right politically.* . . . Hence: the tactic of the 'Open Letter'

*Levi tried to form a Communist opposition group, and when that failed, he joined the USPD and stayed with it when it merged with the SPD. He died in 1930, by his own hand, it is thought.

should definitely be applied everywhere. This should be said straight out, clearly and exactly, because waverings in regard to the 'Open Letter' are extremely harmful, extremely shameful and *extremely widespread.*"[29]

The Third Congress (June–July 1921) was a bleak affair, overshadowed by the Communist failures in Europe, the Kronstadt rising at home, and persistent reminders of ECCI errors (attacks on Levi and the presence of PSI and KAPD delegates). The Russians had decided to retreat from the revolutionary offensive, stop the splitting, and pursue a path of working-class unity, but too much ground had to be prepared before a forthright announcement of the united front could occur. The ECCI was given full control of international Communist matters, the headquarters of the Communist Youth International was transferred to Moscow, the Red International of Labor Unions was established, the PSI delegates were told that their party could only be a part of the Third International by means of amalgamation with the PCd'I, the KAPD was told to fuse with the VKPD or face expulsion, and the VKPD received a public coat of whitewash for the *Marzaktion.* In the midst of all this activity, Radek's reaffirmation of the Open Letter's appeal for a joint action by all parties of the German Left, including the SPD and USPD, attracted little notice.[30]

The Third Congress, with its ratification of Levi's dismissal, its attacks on Serrati, and its expulsion of the PSI before a fusion with the PCd'I could be arranged, fatally damaged the parties that should have been in the forefront of anti-Fascism in Italy and anti-Nazism in Germany. Serrati and Levi, realistic, intelligent, and independent political activists that they were, probably would have constructed, if left to their own devices, far more formidable united fronts than their Communist successors managed. But the Russians displayed little tolerance for those who did not fit the Bolshevik mode.

The Comintern's united front diverged radically from the spirit and intent of the Open Letter. Zinoviev told the ECCI meeting which issued the united front theses (December 4) that working-class unity meant unity on Communist terms, based on further splits within Social Democratic ranks. United front proposals were to be made with the express aim of exposing the hypocrisy of Social Democratic leaders and "the really reformist tendencies within the Communist parties." The workers, it was claimed, would recognize that the unity efforts of the Communists were sincere, whereas those of the reformist internationals were "a new attempt to deceive the workers and to entice them by new means on to the old road of class collaboration."[31]

Social Democrats rejected this obvious attempt to wreck their parties. Communists, who had just paid such a high price in membership for schisms with Social Democrats, resented the orders to pursue them. The French, Spanish, and Italian sections rejected the united front at the ECCI's first enlarged plenary session, February 21 to March 4, 1922; and the French and Italians renewed their opposition at the June ECCI meeting.[32]

The first serious attempt to build a united front occurred at the international level, when the "2 1/2" International invited the Socialist and Communist internationals to construct a united proletarian response to the "international of capitalist imperialism," which had scheduled a conference at Genoa in mid-April 1922 to discuss war debts and reparations. Lenin considered this meeting "an affair of tremendous practical importance" for the Soviet Union. He ordered a positive response, devoid of criticism of the Socialist internationals, but he told Zinoviev and Nikolai Bukharin:

We must find occasion to declare officially that we regard the II and II 1/2 Internationals only as inconsistent and vacillating participants of a bloc with the counter-revolutionary world bourgeoisie, and that we agree to attend a meeting on the united front for the sake of achieving possible practical unity of direct action on the part of the masses and in order to expose the political error of the II and II 1/2 Internationals' entire position, just as [they] have agreed to attend a meeting with us for the sake of achieving practical unity of direct action by the masses and in order to expose the political error of our position.[33]

An impressive number of the most distinguished Socialists and Communists in Europe gathered at the Reichstag, April 2–5. Among others present were Camille Huysmans, Emile Vandervelde, and Ramsay MacDonald from the Second International; Friedrich Adler, Otto Bauer, and Paul Faure from the "2 1/2"; and Klara Zetkin, Bukharin, and Radek from the Third. In addition, the unaffiliated Italian Socialist Party had been invited and Serrati given the power to speak. The opening speeches by Adler and Zetkin called for united action by the proletariat against the tide of reaction, without imposing prior conditions on proletarian organizations. Emile Vandervelde (Belgium), however, presented three conditions that the Third International would have to meet before the Socialist International would agree to participate in an international proletariat congress: guarantees against Communist burrowing from within, guarantees of the right of self-determination for Ukrainians, Armenians, and Georgians, and guaranteed due process rights for imprisoned members of the Russian Socialist Revolutionary Party. After three days of bitter exchanges, a Committee of Nine was appointed to arrange a compromise. Its members decided to establish an Organization Committee of Nine to undertake preparations for further conferences and call on the workers of every country to organize "great mass demonstrations" on behalf of the eight-hour day, the struggle against unemployment, united action by the proletariat against the capitalist offensive, the reestablishment of proletarian united fronts nationally and internationally, the Russian revolution, "starving Russia," and the resumption by all countries of political and economic relations with Russia.[34] The Comintern delegates offered some concessions on the Socialist Revolutionary issue.

Lenin complained that the Comintern delegates had been outmaneuvered by the "bourgeois diplomats" of the Socialist internationals in this particular united front negotiation, but he continued to believe that the united front was the correct tactic. Once Communists learned how to function more skillfully, Lenin wrote, the united front would offer a splendid battlefield on which Socialists and Communists could compete for the loyalty of the world's proletariat.[35]

The world's workers did not respond to the call for demonstrations, and the Rapallo Treaty signed by Germany and the Soviet Union represented a victory of national interests rather than world proletarian unity. The two "outcast" nations renewed diplomatic relations, renounced financial claims on each other, and pledged future cooperation. When the SPD criticized this new step in German foreign policy, the ECCI lashed out at the "contemptible counter-revolutionary role" played by the two Socialist internationals, which had done "everything possible and impossible to facilitate the efforts of the leaders of the bourgeoisie . . . to despoil the first proletarian republic."[36] Comintern delegates then withdrew from a second conference that the Committee of Nine had scheduled for May 23, and the ECCI urged workers to "fight the leaders of the Socialist International" and "build the united front from below."[37] The Second International accused the Comintern of making a "bad faith" proposal that was "a move in tactics more than anything else," and the Russian government of "imperialism" against the Georgian Republic, unjust treatment of political prisoners, and destruction of proletarian unity.[38]

Results of the United Front in Italy

The growth in size and power of Mussolini's Fascists went unheeded and unappreciated, lost in the Socialists' and Communists' fixation on their internal problems. At a January 1922 meeting of the ECCI, the PCd'I representative, Umberto Terracini, reported on Italian political parties but did not mention the Fascists.[39] Bordiga continued to resist a united front and the idea of fusion with the PSI. Only after the Fascists' "March on Rome" did the Communists suggest that the Alliance of Labor should be reconstructed and a general strike declared.[40]

Even when Mussolini was appointed Prime Minister on October 29 most Communists did not comprehend the gravity of the situation. Terracini told the ECCI that it was not a coup or revolution, that the class situation in Italy was unchanged, and that the events of October were nothing more than a part of the attempt of the Italian bourgeoisie to reestablish state power.[41] According to Victor Serge, the Comintern's leaders regarded it as "a piece of reactionary buffoonery which would soon die away and open the path to revolution."[42] None of the main leaders, Lenin, Trotsky, Radek, or Zinoviev, knew enough about Italy or Mussolini to offer the basis for a serious discussion about Fascism. Lenin admitted, in a letter to Constantino Lazzari, that he had not, because of his illness, followed the activities of the PCd'I since the Third Congress,[43] and his advice to Commissar of Foreign Affairs Chicherin lacked Lenin's usual certitude. Phrases such as "perhaps," "let us," and "I think" displayed Lenin's perplexity.[44]

Nor did any of the main speakers at the Fourth Comintern Congress (November–December) seem worried. Bordiga maintained that Fascism had added nothing new to bourgeois policy and was simply "the embodiment of the counter-revolutionary struggle of all the bourgeois elements combined."[45] Zinoviev did not think that Fascism was similar to traditional reaction; on the other hand, he continued, it was not that distinct from the Social Democracy of people like Noske.[46] All who spoke on the subject agreed that the forces of Fascism were much weaker than they appeared and that the movement itself was rife with destructive contradictions. The Resolutions on the Italian Question stated that "the victory of fascist reaction imperatively demands the widest possible unification of all proletarian revolutionary forces," which meant immediate amalgamation of the PSI and PCd'I.[47] An ECCI manifesto, issued at the end of the congress, optimistically stated that this united Communist Party, applying the tactics of the united front and wielding the slogan of a workers' government, "will be the vanguard of the fight of all workers against cursed fascism; around its banner the best and most conscious elements of the working class and peasantry must rally."[48] But since Lenin had agreed with Trotsky that the Russians could best bolster PCd'I prestige by recommending "insistently," rather than ordering expressly, a PSI-PCd'I merger,[49] inter-Left disarray in Italy was allowed to continue indefinitely.

The Theses on United Front Tactics further confused matters for the Italian Left and weakened the possibility of building an effective anti-Fascist movement in Italy. The theses stipulated that a united front could "come only 'from below,' " meaning through spontaneously organized workers' committees. Communists, however, to demonstrate their sincere desire for proletarian unity, could occasionally attempt to form a united front "from above," by negotiating with leaders of Social Democratic organizations. Nevertheless, no Communist could deviate from the goal of a united front from below—a workers' government, defined as a revolutionary entity distinct from the coalition governments that Social Democrats formed with bourgeois parties following parliamentary elections.[50]

Practically no one on the Italian Left seemed eager for a united front of any type, and those who were criticized the Comintern's orchestration of it. Not even Bordiga's arrest in February 1923 eased the path to fusion with the Terzini or a united front. From prison, Bordiga, who still commanded enormous popularity, went into open opposition against the Third International, issuing a confrontational manifesto in which he questioned how Communists could possibly offer a clear choice to Italian workers by simultaneously attacking Socialist leaders and discussing collaboration with them.[51] While Italian Communists tried to find an answer to that question, Mussolini further entrenched himself in power, and the antifusionists won control of the PSI in April 1923.

The ECCI criticized and commanded the PCd'I for the remainder of the year, to little avail. The Executive dismantled the party's Central Committee in June, removing the Bordiga faction, and bestowing nine of the seventeen seats on the so-called "Center" (led, in Italy, by Palmiro Togliatti). It also ordered the party to initiate a new daily newspaper, symbolically titled *L'Unità*. When the Italian police arrested the PCd'I leadership in September, Gramsci was dispatched from Moscow to Vienna to oversee party matters. Finally, in December, Zinoviev sent the Comintern's main

Latin area expert, the Swiss Communist Jules Humbert-Droz, to Italy. He reported that party leaders were divided, mired in uncertainty, and devoting far more attention to internal matters than to public issues. Only Gramsci had mounted an energetic drive against Bordiga's waning power and popularity, but Gramsci was in Vienna, and the anti-Bordiga factions in Italy had not even organized a worker bloc for the April 1924 elections.[52]

Since the November 1923 election law granted two-thirds of the assembly seats to any party gaining 25 percent of the vote, Bordiga's refusal to head the Communist ticket in the elections and the Left's failure to construct an electoral bloc larger than the PCd'I and the Terzini were not the decisive factors in Mussolini's smashing victory.

Gramsci won one of the 65 seats the Left managed to gain, and he returned to Italy in May to assume his seat in Parliament and take over leadership of the party. He did not, however, assume full control until January 1926. His tasks were Herculean; he had to construct a homogeneous leadership, a mass party, and a united proletarian front on the ruins of the Italian Left and in the face of Fascist state power. During the two and a half years of freedom left to him, Gramsci spearheaded an educational campaign to teach Communists, workers, and peasants about the nature of a revolutionary party, convince them of the primacy of a democratic perspective as the means of creating working-class unity in Italy under Fascist conditions, and delineate the historical factors that created those conditions.

Neither Gramsci's efforts nor the PCd'I-Terzini merger, in August 1924, increased Communist initiative. Its one energetic idea, to desert the inactive Aventine Secession and return alone to Parliament, was prohibited by the ECCI. One Communist deputy was authorized to return expressly to make a short, sharp speech against Fascism.[53] Nevertheless, Communist enrollment increased from 18,000 to 25,000 during 1925, Bordiga's faction was dissolved, and at the Lyons Congress in January 1926, Gramsci's group won a legitimate hold on the party, receiving 90.8 percent of the votes and 19 of the 21 seats on the Central Committee.[54]

Gramsci stressed the primacy of the organizational issue, the need for an alliance between workers and peasants, and a political struggle on several simultaneous fronts. Communists must, he argued, distinguish between Fascists and the non-Communist opposition to Fascism, understand that the masses followed that opposition because they wanted to overthrow Fascism, carry out preliminary political activity alongside that opposition, and then "disintegrate the Opposition, socially and then politically, in order to deprive it of the base it had among the masses."[55] The Lyons Theses did not radically diverge from Comintern tactics and slogans; Gramsci and Togliatti's analysis was more subtle than Moscow's and their leadership would have been more astute and dynamic than Bordiga's had been, but they failed to consider one very important question: would the Fascist government allow them the time to fashion their new party and movement? The answer came in October and November. Exceptional Laws and a Special Tribunal prepared the way for mass arrests of opposition parties' leaders. Gramsci received a twenty-year, four-month, five-day sentence on six different charges of treason.

The Exceptional Decrees and arrests of November propelled a large number of Italian anti-Fascists out of the country and into the politics of exile resistance. The Anti-Fascist Concentration, a cartel of the PSI, PSU, Republicans, General Confederation of Labor, and the Italian chapter of the League of the Rights of Man, formed in April 1927 in Paris. It tried to organize Italian exiles, maintain links with and stimulate activity among Socialists remaining in Italy, and provide aid to refugees from Fascism. Problems caused by the different perspectives of the PSI and PSU leaders created difficulties until July 1930, when the two parties merged. Because of the modesty of its program and its minimal direct communication with the underground resistance in Italy, the Anti-Fascist Concentration exercised almost no influence.

The PCd'I was in such disarray that Tasca and Ruggero Grieco proposed dissolving it, but Togliatti and Humbert-Droz rejected that decision, and an Office Abroad was established in Paris and a new party newspaper, *Lo Stato Operaio*, was created. The Communists did not establish an internal center until 1930, but they had, by 1927, a distribution network, predominantly in the north, for the party's underground newspapers. By spring 1927, the internal party controlled perhaps 7,000 members. It organized clandestine unions, demonstrations of the unemployed, and activities to win over Italian youth. Humbert-Droz claimed that one party underground newspaper, *Battaglie Sindacali*, was selling 30,000 copies a month.[56]

A third anti-Fascist organization, Justice and Liberty, was formed by liberal intellectuals, led by Carlo Rosselli, in 1929. Their goal was to build a mass revolutionary movement to topple Mussolini and replace his Fascist dictatorship with a democratic republic, and they organized a clandestine network that was more violence-oriented than that of the PCd'I. But all internal resistance forces were decimated by waves of arrests, and external intergroup rivalries persisted. Justice and Liberty was militantly anti-Communist, the Socialists did not trust the Communists, liberals and Socialists were antagonistic toward each other, and the Communists scorned all non-Communists.[57]

The PCd'I was the largest party abroad, but it was hardly a mass organization. Only a very small number of the half-million Italian workers employed in France joined,[58] and the party became somewhat of an orphan in the Comintern. It did not form links with other organizations, did not participate in antiwar and anti-imperialist congresses, and branded the Anti-Fascist Concentration "agents of foreign and Italian capitalism."[59]

Togliatti, who, with Gramsci imprisoned, was the party's leading thinker (and would eventually become its leading force and most accomplished survivalist as well), argued that Communists should struggle simultaneously with and against the non-Communist opposition to Fascism, aiming for a "democratic phase" to intervene between the Fascist dictatorship and the dictatorship of the proletariat.[60] The Sixth Comintern Congress (July–September 1928), however, ordered strict noncollaboration with the non-Communist opposition, and Togliatti did not demur. The "democratic phase," according to Grieco, was not only unnecessary but unrevolutionary. Since Fascism could only be overthrown at the same time as Italian capitalism, by means of a proletarian revolution, the Communists had to fight both the Fascists and the supporters of democracy by exploiting general and partial democratic slogans.[61]

Grieco had to admit, though, that the PCd'I was too "weak organizationally, ideologically and politically" to accomplish much in either direction. It became weaker still as internal divisions and quarrels racked the Office Abroad in 1929 and 1930. A series of ECCI-directed expulsions (including Bordiga, Tasca, and Ignazio Silone) consolidated and centralized control of the party, but did not improve its anti-Fascist work.

The LSI made no effort to unify the Italian Left or aid the Socialists' internal resistance effort. In fact, the world's other Socialist parties treated the PSI as a waif in need of occasional handouts. By the end of 1930, then, Italian Left-wing anti-Fascist resistance remained divided and impotent.

The Origins of "Social-Fascism"

The Comintern officially recognized a general Fascist threat in 1923, and made defense against it a part of the united front tactic. But continued confusion over united fronts from above and below, Russian intraparty rivalries, and a third Communist-led revolutionary debacle in Germany confounded Comintern efforts to produce a clear, sensible definition of Fascism or a set of realistic tactics.

In January 1923, the ECCI sent appeals to the Second International and IFTU asking them to join an international committee of action against Fascism, and three days later announced it had established an International Fighting Fund against Fascism.[62] The Socialist organizations refused that invitation as well as one from the KPD and French Communist Party (PCF) to come to Frankfurt-am-Main on March 17 to create a united proletarian resistance to the French occupation of the Ruhr and "organize the fight against war and fascism."[63]

Several days later, in the same city, the KPD convened a congress to launch an international anti-Fascist action committee. There, and at the Third ECCI Plenum in June, Klara Zetkin, who favored united front tactics from above as well as below, provided what could have been the basis for an open, reasonable anti-Fascism. She classified Fascism as a "broad mass movement of petit-bourgeois, small-farmers, and unconscious proletarians." Since the movement resembled a "political asylum for the homeless" and since its leadership made "the most beautiful promises," Fascism did not need aggravated economic conditions in which to grow. Even before the Ruhr occupation, she noted, "Italian fascism was spinning its web in Germany. . . . The Hitler group that dominates Bavaria is now transforming Bavaria into a fascist state." Communists, she concluded, must develop a more nuanced appreciation of Fascism's nationalist appeal to the masses.[64] At the plenum, she warned Communists that Fascism was not merely a form of bourgeois military terrorism, but a "mass movement with deep social roots" which achieved "a political and ideological victory over the worker movement." It would not, she warned, self-destruct. Even though the contradictions of Fascism in power could provide its opponents with an opening to reverse Fascism's political and ideological victory, the military defeat of Fascism would still be necessary, requiring very heavy fighting by the proletariat.[65]

The ECCI resolution voted at the plenum did not refute Zetkin's analysis, but the members did not draw the obvious implications from it. The united front from below remained the vehicle of struggle against Fascism.[66] The plenum also authorized Radek to proceed with his bizarre notion that a front of resistance to the French occupation of the Ruhr could be built on an alliance between German Communists and nationalists. Using the martyred nationalist saboteur Leo Schlageter as a symbol, Radek hoped to gain access to the activists in the national camp. Radek wrote in *Die Rote Fahne* on June 26: "We believe that the great majority of the perceptive national masses does not belong in the camp of capital but in that of labor. . . . We will do everything . . . so that unselfish blood does not flow for the profits of the lords of coal and iron, but for the sake of the great mass of the German working people."[67]

KPD leaders, however, refused to discuss the "Schlageter Front" with the nationalists, the party rank and file turned away from it altogether, and the French Communists rejected Radek's policy of nationalist defense on behalf of a bourgeois-dominated fatherland. German Communists preferred uncomplicated, direct anti-Fascism and pushed the party head, Heinrich Brandler, into ordering a fighting day against Fascism for July 29. A militant demonstration was planned, but police prohibitions and contradictory telegrams from Moscow forced the party to hold its meetings indoors. "Even so, it was an undeniable success. In Berlin alone a quarter of a million people demonstrated with the KPD. The numbers were comparable throughout the rest of the Reich."[68]

That success and the alliance that had developed between the KPD and SPD branches in Saxony and Thuringia evaporated in the backlash from a botched Communist revolutionary try in October. After months of ignoring mounting evidence of spontaneous revolutionary possibilities in the Ruhr, the Russian Party Politburo decided on August 23 that the time was ripe for a "German October." A committee was appointed to oversee events, and the LSI and IFTU were invited to a conference on Germany, where Fascism was "raising its head."[69]

The Socialist internationals did not respond, and rivalries within German and Russian Communist leadership ranks led to confusion over timing and methods. The German federal government unwittingly provided the occasion when it, with the full support of the SPD, ordered the *Land* governments of Saxony and Thuringia to oust their Communist ministers and dissolve the Red Hundreds they had organized and armed. When these orders were ignored, the Reichswehr was ordered to accomplish the task. The KPD called, on October 20, for a general strike, but when the SPD and the conference of factory committee representatives rejected the call, Brandler and Radek decided the situation was not ripe for revolution and cancelled the strike. The Hamburg members did not receive the cancellation message, and launched a strike that was easily suppressed. The federal government deposed the *Land* governments in Saxony and Thuringia, declared the KPD illegal, and arrested numerous party members. Although the party regained its legal status in March 1924, KPD membership fell by over 50 percent.[70] Communist leaders accused the "November Republic" of surrendering "to fascism," blamed the SPD for "fascism's victory over democracy," and promised to liquidate German Social Democracy.[71] SPD leaders swore, in response, that they would never again cooperate with the KPD at any level of government.[72]

The accusations and recriminations within the Comintern over the October debacle in Germany and the simultaneous episode of Bulgarian Communist passivity during the Right-wing overthrow of Alexander Stambolisky's peasant government produced a disastrous concept. Zinoviev, in his preliminary draft proposal for the theses on the German question to be debated by the Comintern Presidium on January 11, stated: "At present the leading sections of German social democracy are nothing but a fraction of German fascism with a 'socialist' phraseology. . . . Fascism is a mixture of the blackest counter-revolution and irresponsible socialist demagogy. . . . In its gradual degeneration, the entire international social democracy has become objectively nothing but a variety of fascism. . . . Who can doubt that the Italian social democracy, headed by Turati and Modigliani, is at present nothing but a fraction of Italian fascism?"[73] The ECCI statement, issued on January 19, basically reiterated Zinoviev's accusation: "The leading strata of German social-democracy are at the present time nothing but a fraction of German fascism wearing a socialist mask."[74] The ECCI had, in sum, decided that the Communist failure to stage a revolution in Germany required the annihilation of Social Democracy. The Fifth Comintern Congress, meeting five months later (June 17 to July 8), would impose the same sentennce on "Right-wing Opportunists" (Communists favoring coalitions with Social Democratic organizations).

That congress, the last where serious debate of political issues was allowed, marked a decided leftward shift to a revolutionary united front.

The theses stated that the "tactics of the united front *from below* are necessary always and everywhere," that a united front only from above is categorically rejected, and that "united front tactics were and remain a method of revolution, not of peaceful evolution." The slogan of a workers' and peasants' government was defined as "the slogan of the proletarian dictatorship translated into the popular language of revolution," and was never to mean "the tactics of parliamentary agreements and coalitions with social-democracy."[75]

Very little discussion accompanied the introduction of the resolution on Fascism. Bordiga and a KPD delegate delivered speeches that went unanswered. The former maintained that Fascism was simply a new form of bourgeois reaction, the latter demanded an all-out war against Fascism, meeting terror with terror. The theses disregarded both, defining Fascism as "the bourgeoisie's instrument for fighting the proletariat," and delineating six political and six organizational/military methods to secure both Fascism's "political defeat and the defense of the revolutionary proletariat against its armed attacks."[76] In addition, the doctrine of "Social-Fascism" was confirmed. Since Fascism and Social Democracy were "the right and left hands of modern capitalism," "the two sides of the same instrument of capitalist dictatorship . . . , social-democracy can never be a reliable ally of the fighting proletariat."[77]

Two months after the congress, in an analysis of the international situation, Josef Stalin confirmed the "Social-Fascist" thesis. "Fascism," he wrote, "is a fighting organization of the bourgeoisie which bases itself upon the active support of Social-Democracy. Social-Democracy objectively represents the moderate wing of fascism. . . . [They] do not negate one another, they complement each other. They are not opposites, but twin brothers." The present condition of "capitalist pacifism" should not, he argued, be interpreted as the liquidation of Fascism, but the "corroboration of fascism in which its moderate, social-democratic wing is advanced to the foreground."[78]

The united front from above did not die, however. It became an instrument of official Soviet foreign policy, useful during a period (1925–27) when Russian leaders appeared more obsessed than usual with the idea that the world's capitalist powers were planning a war against them. Worried about Germany's pro-Entente course, the Russians tried to develop pro-Soviet attitudes and pressure groups in the countries they thought could most effectively block a two-front capitalist offensive:

Great Britain and China. The British Trades Union Congress and the Chinese Kuomintang were assiduously courted as Communist partners in what the ECCI termed "the most important centers of the international revolutionary movement."[79]

The Comintern also pursued a form of the united front from above, when it authorized Willi Münzenberg in early 1926 to organize a League of Oppressed Peoples. Because of the bleak prospects for revolution in Europe, and the existence of only three parties of respectable size (Czechoslovakia, France, and Germany), the ECCI had proclaimed at its Sixth Enlarged Plenum, February–March, that the "rise of the national liberation movement and the gradual strengthening of the labor movement in the East are new factors of the utmost significance."[80] Since the Communist parties in Latin America and Asia were too small to organize serious anti-imperialist movements, they wanted the Comintern to sponsor an international anti-imperialist front that included all organizations opposed to colonization. The International Congress Against Colonial Oppression and Imperialism that Münzenberg convened in February 1927 attracted most of the national independence parties from colonized countries and a representative sampling of the European Left. Most of the non-Communists in attendance knew that this was a Comintern production, but they were nevertheless caught up in the excitement and enthusiasm Münzenberg generated. Fenner Brockway, of the British Independent Labour Party, for example, was scheduled to make a speech demanding that Britain keep its "hands off China." On his way to the podium, he was intercepted by Münzenberg, who whispered: "End your speech by a declaration of unity with the Chinese workers and peasants." Brockway did so "and as the sentences were uttered a Chinese comrade stood at my side with outstretched hand. I took it—and the whole audience, black, brown, yellow, and white, rose and roared its applause."[81] Anti-Fascism received only the slightest nod, when the Italian delegation offered a resolution classifying the battle against Fascism in Italy as a means "to break one of the most dangerous instruments of the politics of imperialism and of colonial oppression."[82] The League Against Imperialism and for National Independence made no further references to Fascism and did not participate in anti-Fascist activities during its two years of meaningful existence. In any event, most of the prominent non-Communists had resigned by January 1929, driven out by the stridency of Communist "Third Period" polemics.

The "Third Period"

During the "Third Period" (1928–1935), Stalin ceased regarding the Comintern as a significant factor in world politics, and it ceased paying attention to the objective situations of its national sections. By the end of 1929, the member parties had become, to a large extent, reflecting screens of the Stalinist worldview. The ongoing ideological and power struggles within the All-Union Communist Party forced national leaders, on pain of expulsion, to distort their country's conditions to fit Russian forms. "It was as if," Isaac Deutscher wrote, "the giant figure of an athlete engaged in a homeric fight had thrown around itself twenty or thirty shadows, each mimicking the tense wrestling and the violent gestures of the real body, each pretending to shake heaven and earth."[83]

The events surrounding Zinoviev's removal from the presidency of the Comintern in October 1926 set the stage for a new interpretation of international events. Facing a strong attack from Zinoviev and Trotsky on the Left and the impatience of several national sections, Stalin had "to rationalize an incipient left turn" without surrendering his basic belief that the world was in a state of partial capitalist stabilization. He erased Zinoviev's Third-Period analysis of 1925 and formulated a new one, in which the "internal contradictions of the process of the stabilization of capitalism are coming out in ever sharper form," leading, if the parties did their duty, to "an immediate revolutionary situation."[84] Though the new party line met the needs of the Stalin-Bukharin faction, it meshed badly with the requirements of the national parties.

As a result, the reorganization of the Comintern hierarchy and Bukharin's leadership of it (as head of a newly created Political Secretariat) did not improve Comintern performance. According to Humbert-Droz, the work had largely fallen on four people. He wrote Togliatti, in early 1927:

Very few non-Russian comrades remain here who can work effectively. . . . Bukharin is always too occupied with Russian matters and he scarcely appears regularly at the sessions of the Political Secretariat and Presidium. . . . [Otto] Kuusinen, the one of us most in contact with the Russians, has withdrawn more and more into the secretariat of his country [Finland] and the editing of *The Communist International,* and he is striving not to be held politically responsible for the overall work. In other words, we lack an effective political direction.[85]

The deteriorating international struggle against Fascism soon received another seismic jolt in December, as Stalin turned against Bukharin.

While the latter continued to argue that the era of capitalist stabilization showed no signs of ending, Stalin spoke of "collapsing stabilization" and a "new revolutionary upsurge."[86] They also differed on the question of Fascism, Stalin wanting to apply it as a universal label for all forms of reaction, Bukharin holding out for more subtle distinctions. The Fourth RILU Congress, April 1928, marked Stalin's ascendancy. The resolutions identified six "fascist" countries (Bulgaria, Spain, Portugal, Lithuania, Italy, and Poland), accused the Western democracies of using Fascist methods to suppress workers' movements, and branded the League of Nations and the International Labor Organization as allies of Fascism.[87] Stalin told the Leningrad party organization in May that Fascism was a means of stabilizing the "capitalist hinterland" so that the West could prepare its war against the Soviet Union.[88]

The member parties were not aware of the split or its cause, but something was obviously amiss. When the delegates to the Sixth Comintern Congress arrived in July 1928, neither the Theses on the International Situation nor the draft program was available for discussion. As the congress dragged on to September 1, and the theses appeared, their extreme crudity, harshness, and stridency indicated a new course. Imperialist war obsessed the writers of the discussion material; they devoted seventy-six paragraphs of the Theses on the International Situation to the topic. It opened with a summary of the "various phases of the general crisis of the capitalist system": the First Period, that of acute capitalist crisis, ended with the German defeat in October 1923; the Second, the period of gradual and partial stabilization of the capitalist system, had just ended; the Third Period was now in full force. "This third period, in which the contradiction between the growth of the productive forces and the contraction of markets becomes particularly accentuated, will inevitably give rise to a fresh era of imperialist wars among the imperialist States themselves; wars of the imperialist States against the USSR; wars of national liberation againnst imperialism; wars of imperialist intervention and gigantic class battles."[89]

Fascism received very short shrift in this very long program: a three-paragraph, near parody of the Fifth Congress' analysis. "Alongside social-democracy," it began, "which helps the bourgeoisie to oppress the working class and blunt its proletarian vigilance, stands fascism." It is the form in which, under certain historical conditions, "bourgeois-imperialist reaction conducts its offensive." Its "chief function is to annihilate the revolutionary vanguard of the working class, i.e. the communist strata of the proletariat and their leading cadres." During critical moments for capitalism, this section concluded, Social Democracy "not infrequently plays a fascist part."[90]

The final section of the program, "The Strategy and Tactics of the Communist International in the Struggle for the Proletarian Dictatorship," contained the "class-against-class" tactic* that Communist parties were to follow during the Third Period. It mandated a total campaign to eliminate all traces of bourgeois influence from the working class, even when the source of the taint was found within the Communist movement.

The delegates, even though they had been hand-picked by their respective Politburos, expressed clear hostility to this new line, but mainly in the small committee meetings. Few objections were heard in the plenary sessions. The Fascist thesis, however, drew tepid admonitions from Togliatti and Pierre Sémard (France) against overgeneralized use of the Fascist label, and a much stronger warning from Bukharin against anti-Fascist tactics that cordoned Communists away from the very masses they needed to address and win.[91] Trotsky, from exile, called this congress "the turning point in the life of the Communist Party of the Soviet Union and the entire Comintern."[92]

It certainly altered the direction of Italian anti-Fascism. Togliatti had been arguing for an anti-Fascist struggle that was to be both proletarian and popular, a parallel struggle for socialism and democracy. Wages and freedom, he wrote, "are two aspects of the same situation which cannot be separated, the starting-points of a single struggle against fascist tyranny and against the dictatorship of the bourgeoisie and capitalism." When the Tenth Plenum of the ECCI ordered the PCd'I to accept the "class-against-class" approach, Togliatti is reported to have said: "If the Comintern says that [our analysis] is not correct, we shall refrain from posing these objectives. We shall think these things, but we shall not say them. We shall only say that the anti-fascist revolution shall be the proletarian revolution."[93]

---

*The phrase was devised by Jules Humbert-Droz in march 1927, to justify the ECCI's order that French Communists must break with the Left bloc in the April 1928 elections, and refuse to withdraw losing candidates in the second round of voting. PCF leaders only acceded after a seven-month debate. Stalin and Bukharin fully supported this tactic, which helped the French Right regain control of the government. Theodore Draper, "The Strange Case of the Comintern," *Survey* (Summer 1972), 18:110–115.

Another theorist who fell afoul of the Comintern's switch to the "class-against-class" tactic was Georg Lukács, who had been criticizing the Hungarian Communist Party for failing to form, in 1928, "a left-oriented workers' front" to take advantage of the current political situation in Hungary. In his "Theses Concerning the Political and Economic Situation in Hungary" (the so-called "Blum Theses"), Lukács wrote that since there was no chance of re-establishing a Soviet Republic in Hungary, the party should focus its efforts on replacing the incumbent semi-Fascist regime with a bourgeois democracy, and lead a "struggle for total democracy, for the republic headed by a government of workers and peasants, a struggle against the democratic liquidation of democracy."[94] Although he did not argue for alliances with other parties or approve reformist trade unions, and carefully distinguished his democracy—the democratic dictatorship of the working class—from the Western or parliamentary variety, he was branded a "liquidationist." He avoided expulsion by writing a self-critical recantation.

The LSI also held an international congress that summer, its third, in August. It, too, denounced Fascism, but offered no method to combat it. Instead, it heaped invective on the Soviet Union ("dictatorship by a terrorist minority") and the Sixth Comintern Congress, for setting "all its hopes on a world war which would give birth to a revolution of violence."[95] Several months later, the LSI Executive urged its members "to think of our comrades in the countries in which a Fascist dictatorship prevails."[96]

Willi Münzenberg attempted to overcome the inactivity and division by means of an international congress, designed to attract all parties into a revolutionary united front against fascism. This International Anti-Fascist Congress was scheduled for Berlin in March. The prospects for unity, however, were severely jolted when LSI secretary Friedrich Adler labeled it a Communist maneuver, and the Communists responded by accusing Adler of marching at the head of the saboteurs of the workers' united front against reaction. At the congress, the French Communist writer Henri Barbusse presided over a gathering of Communists and fellow travelers who approved resolutions faithful to Third Period policies, and established an International Anti-Fascist Committee to plan a day of demonstrations against Fascism and war. The committee set the date, August 1, and never met again.[97] International Red Day failed to attract significant support.

Münzenberg's other international front, the League Against Imperialism, fared no better. The ECCI criticized it for its "incorrect and opportunist estimation of left social-democracy," and its lack of a mass workers' and colonial base.[98] The ECCI, in turn, was thoroughly purged of its "Right Deviationists," including Bukharin, and the All-Union Communist Party's security apparatus penetrated further into, and assumed greater power over, the Comintern.

Therefore, on the eve of the Great Depression, and a new period of crisis, Communists and Socialists lacked, separately and mutually, the means to meet new challenges from the radical Right. The Social Democratic organizations had been nonfeasant (failing to take or formulate any practical steps against Fascism or reaction), while the Communists had been malfeasant (diffusing the specific demonism of Fascism by applying it indiscriminately, and denaturing the one tactic—the united front—that offered some protection against it).

Chapter 3

The Nazi Phenomenon

The Reichstag election of September 14, 1930 changed the nature of the radical Right's threat to German democratic and republican institutions and weakened the capacity of the parliamentary system to meet the new challenge. On that day, the National Socialist German Workers party (NSDAP) became the second-largest party in the Reichstag. Voter turnout increased four million over 1928, fueled by farmer and middle-class reaction to the deepening depression and general public anger with the government for accepting the Young Plan continuation of war reparation payments and failing to alleviate the social effects of the economic crisis. Although Hitler's speeches and Nazi propaganda had obviously attracted a large number of these voters to the NSDAP, the Nazi's vote total was swelled as much or more by voters' dissatisfaction with the conservative parties.

The 6.4 million votes (18.3 percent) and 107 seats won by the NSDAP represented an astonishing gain over the 810,000 votes (2.6 percent) and 12 seats it had won in 1928. Among the other parties, the KPD substantially improved its parliamentary position as well, adding 23 seats to the 54 it had won in 1928. The Catholic Center Party also increased its vote total (by 400,000) and now held 68 seats. Every other party lost ground, some badly. The Nationalist People's Party (DNVP) lost the most (1.9 million votes and 32 seats), while the SPD, despite losing ten seats, remained the largest Reichstag party.[1]

Suddenly, a radical Right party stood on the threshold of political power in Germany. Although radical Rightists had been active in the chaotic aftermath of the war and revolution, their movement had been too fragmented to represent a significant threat to the government. But the SPD-dominated provisional government, more concerned with revolution from the Left than counterrevolution from the Right, failed to remove or weaken the traditional foundations of Right-wing power. The Social Democrats did not, that is, tamper with the established elites in the army, bureaucracy, and corporate trusts, and did not organize a democratically based army to maintain order. The Weimar constitution did not dissolve the states (*Länder*) or seriously weaken their independence, and it gave the President of the republic, in Article 48, full power to issue decrees and exercise dictatorial power during states of emergency.

Caught between extremes, the Social Democrats paid a dear price in the Reichstag election of June 1920. Identified with the revolution and the Versailles treaty by the Right and with antirevolutionary activity by the Left, the SPD lost over five million votes and 42 seats. Although it remained the largest Reichstag party throughout the twenties, it would not lead another government until June 1928, and only participate in two others, between 1921 and 1923.

The conservative-centrist coalition that governed Germany during most of the decade was, however, sufficiently in control of events to keep in check a radical Right that more often than not undermined its own progress. The Freikorps lacked a program of political and social change to match its armed strength. The various nationalist groups could not unite, could not get control of the Freikorps, could not organize a sizable militia of their own, and could not win the army to their side. Nevertheless, elements of the radical Right demonstrated, between 1921 and 1923, considerable talent for disruption.

The first attempt to seize power, the Freikorps *Putsch* led by Wolfgang Kapp and General von Lüttwitz in March 1921, marked the apogee of working-class influence in the Weimar Republic and displayed the huge divisions in the ranks of working-class organizations. The *Putsch* was defeated by a general strike called by the General Federation of German Trade Unions (ADGB). The USPD and KPD were invited to join, but the former refused to work with SPD-influenced unions and formed its own strike committee; the latter intended to stand aside from this interbourgeois quarrel. The KPD only became involved when a significant number of rank and file Communists from the Ruhr and central Germany joined. The SPD members of the government first tried to stop the strike, then refused to accept the strike settlement program proposed by the ADGB, and finally approved the use of local Freikorps troops to crush the workers' defense battalions the Ruhr Communists had helped organize.[2]

Yet when Right terrorists assassinated Foreign Minister Walther Rathe-

nau in June 1922, workers again rose to defend the republic, demonstrating nationwide and demanding stronger laws to protect the republic. The
SPD supported the demand, and the Reichstag passed the Law for the
Protection of the Republic. State governments and federal judges, however, would blunt the law's impact on the Right, and, in the later years of
the republic, would use it against the KPD.[3]

France's invasion and occupation of the Ruhr in January 1923 (to coerce
continued reparations payments) set the stage for the radical Right's last
serious, violent effort to overthrow the Weimar Republic. The occupation
caused economic distress and provoked intense feelings of nationalism.
Several far-Right groups in Bavaria formed, in the spring of 1923, the
Kampfbund to organize an armed uprising, but their opportunity did not
come until autumn. In October, the Bavarian government and the Bavarian division of the Reichswehr defied the federal government's state of
emergency that accompanied the termination of state-approved resistance
in the Ruhr. When the federal government hesitated to use loyal troops
to end this Bavarian "separatism" and the Bavarian government hesitated
to force the issue, Adolf Hitler pushed the NSDAP into the breach and
launched a "national revolution" in Munich on the night of November 8.
When the badly organized *Putsch* failed to seize key positions or attract
Bavarian ministers, police, and army units, General Erich Ludendorff proposed, the next morning, a march on Reichswehr headquarters. The
Bavarian state police blocked the streets, shots were exchanged, sixteen
Nazis were killed, many others were wounded, and the rest of the demon-
strators, with the exception of Ludendorff, who continued to march, fled.
Hitler was soon arrested, tried, and sentenced to five years in prison.[4]

Though the radical nationalists had failed in their immediate goals,
neither the KPD nor the SPD discounted the danger from the Right, even
though the Marxist parties did not fully comprehend the nature of the
threat. As early as December 1922, a German Communist writer had
identified a "Fascist Danger in South Germany," and labeled the NSDAP
a petty-bourgeois-based, anti-Semitic, nationalistic, anti–big capital, reactionary, militarily organized, highly centralized group.[5] Several days before the Munich *Putsch*, a KPD conference accused the SPD of delivering
"the entire area of unoccupied Germany to fascism."[6] Then, following
Hitler's imprisonment, a Communist writer concluded that Hitler was "a
conscious swindler of his followers," acting on behalf of big capital to
restore bourgeois order.[7] The SPD responded to the Bavarian coup by

joining with its former coalition partners, the Center and Democratic parties, to form the Reichsbanner Schwarz-Rot-Gold, a paramilitary self-defense organization.

The failed *Putsches* of the Right, the failed uprisings of the KPD, and the failure of the government to devise a coherent social and economic program, protect Germany from the Ruhr invasion, and maintain order created a crazy-quilt electoral pattern in 1924. German voters swung dizzily from one extreme to another. In May, the SPD lost 71 seats, the Communists won 62 (up from 4), the nationalist parties won 106 (up from 15), and the extreme Right 32; but in December, the SPD won back 31 of the seats it had lost, the KPD lost one-fourth of those it had won, and the extreme Right lost one-half.[8] These electoral swings, and the economic and social conditions that provoked them, weakened the moderate parties and widened the gap between the middle class and the SPD. The Social Democrats, caught between two hostile factions—the Center-Democratic parties and the Communists—slid further into a purely defensive orientation, trying to block the formation of Right-wing ministries and prevent the erosion of past victories. Unable to win majority votes for financial measures to strengthen the republic, the Social Democrats began to vote for enabling measures that bolstered Weimar in the short term but, by strengthening the Executive at the expense of the Reichstag, weakened it in the long term.

The republic was further weakened by the presidential election of 1925, when the man who eventually would bestow power on Hitler, Paul von Hindenburg, was elected. Even in the face of precipitously declining membership figures (a loss of two-thirds), the Communists refused to unite with the SPD behind a single candidate. The KPD's refusal to withdraw its candidate, Ernst Thälmann, from the second round allowed Hindenburg to eke out a victory over the liberal-Socialist candidate, Wilhelm Marx.

Perversely, the far less significant issue of a referendum later that year to strip German princes of their wealth, produced KPD-SPD unity and impressive results. The Marxist parties' position captured 14.6 million votes (or 50 percent more than they had in the Reichstag elections of 1924),[9] but the coalition did not endure. The SPD did not want to be part of an ongoing united front, and its Reichstag deputies believed the party could reap greater political benefits by protesting against the recently exposed secret agreements that the Weimar government had negotiated with the Soviet Union in 1922 and 1923. (German airplane, poison gas, and ammunition factories were built in Russia, aircraft and tank schools to train German soldiers were established, and the Germans provided technical assistance to manufacturers of Russian ammunition.)

The KPD, harassed by the SPD and the federal government, and distracted by internal struggles, schisms, and Comintern interference, ceased to be a serious factor in German politics for the remainder of the twenties. The SPD, on the other hand, became a veritable Republican institution. Millions of members were directly enrolled and millions more were in Socialist-oriented trade unions; it controlled 203 journals and numerous auxiliary organizations, including the Reichsbanner with its several hundred thousand veterans. Although it played no part in Weimar governments between 1923 and 1928, it shared in the government of Prussia, governed alone in Baden, Hesse, and Hamburg, controlled one-third of the seats in the *Land* diets, and administered many cities.[10] Its leaders became so dependent on the republic, they began to feel responsible for maintaining it. That proved difficult, since three of the other four major Weimar parties were not interested in the compromises on economic and social issues necessary for stable, energetic government.

The NSDAP, however, was unable for many years to exploit the situation. Hilter, pardoned and released in December 1924 (after serving nine months of his sentence), no longer believed that he could overthrow the republic by force. He first tried to build a mass party of industrial workers, but when that approach did not significantly increase party membership, the NSDAP Congress of August 1927 shifted the focus to the middle class, and began to recruit students and veterans. The election of 1928, however, confounded the party by demonstrating that its new super-patriotic slogans evoked significantly greater vote totals from farm and rural areas than cities. Hitler, then, intensified party efforts to build electoral victories on rural and small town votes.[11]

The 1928 election also altered the fortunes of the SPD. It won a plurality of seats (153 of 491), and the Social Democrat Hermann Müller became Chancellor of a shaky coalition government. But the parties could not agree on the financial and economic programs needed to restore economic health to an increasingly desperate country, and President Hindenburg refused to allow Müller to use Article 48. When the issue of funding unemployment benefits could not be resolved, the SPD, bowing to ADGB pressure, resigned from the government, but agreed to support the new one. This decision cost the Weimar Republic its last representative ministry, and the SPD its tiny Left wing. They formed a Socialist Workers Party in 1931.

The new ministry, headed by the Catholic Center Party's Heinrich Brüning, tried to act as if it were above partisan politics and relied on emergency presidential powers to govern. The Reichstag, however, voted to repeal the emergency decreees. Brüning refused an SPD offer to negotiate a compromise settlement of the issues dividing them, and scheduled new elections for September 1930. The NSDAP, invigorated by a two-year-long successful voter registration drive, hammered away at the need for a broad front of all classes against Weimar criminals, Jewish liberals, and Marxist parties. Millions of new voters and dissatisfied old voters, hurt by the state of the economy and fearful of social disorder, trooped to the polls in record numbers, and launched the NSDAP into political significance.

Brüning remained Chancellor, still determined to govern by decree. Communists castigated his government as a vehicle for Fascism, and joined with Nazis to overturn the decrees, support no-confidence motions, and sponsor increased social welfare spending. Social Democrats, though calling the Brüning government a paver of the Nazi road, still voted against the decree-repealing and no-confidence measures. SPD politicians, under attack from the Communists and seeing Weimar politics degenerating into violent street demonstrations, feared that the alternative to the republic was Fascism. This *sauve qui peut* strategy dimmed the SPD's image. In the Left-wing intellectual milieu of Berlin, Marta Feuchtwanger remembered that "the Social Democrats were considered a little bit weak and indecisive. . . . [They were] not very much respected. They were considered too weak, already in the hands of the military." She and her friends thought the Communists acted more decisively.[12]

Indeed, the KPD could not be accused of inactivity, but many of its actions did seem ill-advised and misdirected. One of its more militant members then, Gustav Regler, has since written of the party: "Never in a time of extreme social upheaval was a great popular movement afflicted with such ineffective leaders,"[13] or, he could have added, with such a jerry-built organization. By 1931, the party had assembled a rickety conglomeration of militias. The proletarian hundreds of 1923 had been channeled into the Red Fighting Front League. It had been banned by the government in 1929, sent underground, and replaced by Proletarian Self-Defense groups. The Red Fighting Front's youth counterpart, the Red

Youth Front, was replaced by the Anti-Fascist Red Guard, which the government banned in 1930. There also existed Red Factory Guards and the Fighting Committee of Red Berlin. In the wake of the September 1930 elections, the KPD tried to consolidate its anti-Fascist and defense organizations into a Fighting League Against Fascism, designed to hold on to the new KPD voters, combat the influence of the Nazis in working-class areas, and challenge the new SPD formations.[14]

The Nazi electoral victory and the Harzburg Front of radical Right organizations, formed in October 1931, convinced the SPD to see to its own defenses. The Reichsbanner organized an elite militia, the Schutzformationen, and the SPD, ADGB, and workers' sports organizations created the Iron Front for Resistance Against Fascism.[15] Neither were used. SPD leaders, feeling trapped in the increasingly narrowing space between them and the radical extremes, only grew more hesitant.

The Communists continued to act without inhibition, but the party remained divided over tactics. The Central Committee and the ECCI wanted collective, cadre-controlled violence in the name of revolutionary anti-Fascism, while party members, especially in Berlin, where unemployment and frustration had reached dangerously high levels, were using individual terrorist acts to protect their neighborhoods against Nazi invaders. On several occasions, but without noticeable success, the Central Committee and the ECCI condemned individual acts of terrorism and tried to redefine the tactic of the "armed struggle against fascism" and its slogan, "Strike the fascists where one finds them," into elements of a mass struggle.[16] KPD leaders also tried to direct some of the violence against the SPD; according to Richard Krebs, all units of the KPD were ordered "to sabotage the enterprises of the Iron Front at every turn."[17]

Under the desperate economic circumstances, the militant Third Period tactics of the KPD worked on one level: party membership doubled (to almost 300,000). But on the more important plane of keeping the Nazis out of power, Third Period tactics failed. Communists contributed to the political and social disarray of the last years of the Weimar Republic, and failed to provide a realistic or positive alternative to the institutions they helped undermine. On two key occasions, the Communists even worked side by side with the Nazis. Between August 1931 and July 1932, the two supported a referendum against the SPD government of Prussia and then combined on a no-confidence motion in the *Land* Parliament that toppled the ministry. Then, in November 1932, the KPD's new labor federation, the Revolutionary Trade Union Opposition, organized a strike to oppose a wage cut by the Berlin Municipal Transit System. The ADGB and a majority of the transit workers opposed the strike, but the NSDAP supported it. When the ADGB refused to grant strike relief funds, Communists and Nazis stood side by side in the streets of Berlin rattling their relief collection boxes, picketing, and demonstrating.[18]

These bizarre activities by the Communists weakened the impact of the KPD's more logical decisions. Shortly after Hitler had received over thirteen million votes in the June 1932 presidential election, the KPD formed Anti-Fascist Action "to provide a framework in which people from all walks of life could be brought together in loose coalition to fight economic, social and legal repression, and above all a basis on which Social Democrats and Communists could join in self-defence against Nazis." It fought against high rents, evictions, and confiscations, demonstrated in front of welfare offices, and fought against NSDAP presence in working-class neighborhoods.[19] Klara Zetkin, in her capacity as honorary president of the Reichstag, opened the summer 1932 session with a speech calling for a "United Front of all workers to turn back fascism," and broadly defining workers to include women, youth, intellectuals, and white-collar "salary and wage slaves."[20] And when, in July, Brüning's successor as chancellor, Fritz von Papen, deposed the caretaker government of Prussia (with its SPD ministers), the KPD called on the SPD to form a united front of resistance.

The Prussian Social Democratic leaders refused, deciding unanimously "not to depart from the juridical foundations of the Constitution regardless of what may happen."[21] The palpable fear and passivity that motivated that decision eliminated the SPD as a political factor in Weimar. The party failed to propose or pursue serious obstacles to the rapid rightward course of German politics, and thereby drained the spirit of resistance from its followers.

At the same time, the astonishing number of major elections in 1932—four: two Reichstag, a presidential, and a *Land*—exhausted German voters and their reservoirs of goodwill for Weimar governments. Ministries neither reflected the electoral strength of Reichstag delegations nor improved economic or social conditions in Germany. The governments of Weimar's last months evolved from the machinations of a few individuals: President Hindenburg and his small circle of advisers; General Kurt von Schleicher, the Minister of Political Affairs in the Defense Ministry;

and Fritz von Papen, Hindenburg and Schleicher's choice to carry out their plans for a conservative ministry governing by presidential decree. All were personally ambitious, all overestimated their political ability, and all underestimated the dynamism of the NSDAP and Hitler's drive for power. Hindenburg and Schleicher forced Brüning from the chancellorship in May, but the newly elected Reichstag immediately, and overwhelmingly, approved a KPD-sponsored no-confidence motion in Papen. A new election was scheduled for November 6.

The Nazis suffered a momentary setback in that election. Their association with the KPD in the bus strike plus a general revulsion of middle-class voters from Nazi-instigated violence cost the party a substantial loss of votes (4 percent). Papen urged Hindenburg to prorogue Parliament and suppress all political organizations, beginning with the Communists and Nazis. Schleicher, maneuvering to become Chancellor, told the President that such a plan would provoke a civil war that the army would be unable to control. If he were head of the government, Schleicher claimed, he could split the NSDAP, secure the support of a large majority of Nazis, and then win the toleration of the other parties by building a political front of trade unions and occupational organizations. To avoid having to use the army, Hindenburg gave Schleicher an opportunity to govern, appointing him Chancellor on December 2.

Schleicher failed to deliver on his promises, and on January 4, Papen met secretly with Hitler. To strengthen his bargaining position, Hitler ordered the NSDAP to contest the Lippe *Land* election, scheduled for January 15, as if it were a national campaign. The Nazis used their slight gain in votes (over the November election) to trumpet their national power and organize a massive demonstration in front of KPD headquarters in Berlin. Schleicher banned a Communist counterdemonstration, but allowed the Nazi militia to parade on January 22. Unable to secure support from the parties situated between the NSDAP and the KPD, Schleicher asked Hindenburg for authority to dissolve Parliament, proclaim a state of emergency, postpone new elections, and ban the KPD and NSDAP. Hindenburg refused; Schleicher resigned on January 28; and on January 30, a cabinet headed by Chancellor Adolf Hitler and Vice-Chancellor Fritz von Papen and including three Nazi ministers was apppointed. Neither the SPD, the KPD, nor the trade unions made a move to block the appointment.[22]

The supineness of the Marxist Left did not persuade the Nazis of its harmlessness. When the Reichstag burned on February 27, Nazi party leaders believed it was the start of a Communist uprising. KPD parliamentary deputies and officials were arrested, party offices closed, and the party press indefinitely banned. The Decree of the Reich President for the Protection of People and State, issued the next day under Article 48, was subtitled "A defensive measure against Communist acts of violence endangering the State." Article I of the decree suspended the civil liberties protection clauses of the constitution until further notice, stating that "restrictions on personal liberty, on the right of free expression of opinion, including freedom of the press, on the right of assembly and association, and violations of the privacy of postal, telegraphic and telephonic communications, and warrants for house-searches, orders for confiscations as well as restrictions on property rights are permissible beyond the legal limits otherwise prescribed."[23]

During the following months, a vast dragnet of Communists ensued; SPD civil officials were sacked; trade union offices and property were seized; all political parties were dissolved; workers were brought under firm control; and the property and persons of Jews came under attack. There were few structural changes—the army, the government bureaucracy, and heavy industry remained substantially unchanged.

Fascism in Other Countries

The Great Depression and Hitler's success provided impetus and inspiration to a broad variety of radical Right groups and movements in Europe and the United States. Many governments countered with restrictive legislation: between 1931 and 1936, Finland, Czechoslovakia, Sweden, Norway, Denmark, the Netherlands, Belgium, Great Britain, and the Irish Free State passed varying laws prohibiting uniforms, incitement to sedition or disaffection, and private armies.[24] Poland dissolved its Fascist groups and Austria proscribed its Nazi Party in 1934; Romania outlawed its extreme reactionary group, the Iron Guard, in 1938, and executed over 1,000 of its leaders the following year; and the leader of Hungary's Party of National Will (Arrow Cross), Ferenc Szálasi, was arrested in 1938. But the German experience had demonstrated that laws and acts alone could not halt Fascism; the Reichstag, at various times, had banned uniformed demonstrations and paramilitary organizations and arrested radical Rightists. Only a combination of government determination, sometimes ruthless and bloody, and native Fascist ineptitude prevented any other Fascist movement from achieving power in Europe without the direct intervention of the German army.

The traditional Right, however, continued to enjoy successes similar to those of the 1920s: a military coup in Bulgaria in 1934 was followed by a royalist dictatorship under King Boris III; the assassination of King Alexander I of Yugoslavia that same year with the aid of Italian Fascists did not dislodge the traditional ruling classes, and a regency maintained control; the Spanish army, church, and monarchists combined forces to overthrow the republic during the course of a three-year civil war (1936–39); General Ioannis Metaxas was voted decree powers by the legislature and then was given dictatorial powers by the King of Greece in 1936; and in 1938, King Carol II of Romania abolished the constitution. Critical Fascist and proto-Fascist threats did, however, take full shape in France, Austria, Hungary, and Romania.

Paris, on February 6, 1934, was the scene of a violent melee involving radical Right-organized demonstrators and the police. Right-wing leagues, building on the discontent generated by the depression, the impotence of Parliament, the instability of governing ministries, and the Stavisky scandal cover-up, mobilized their forces in the Place de la Concorde, a bridge span away from the Chamber of Deputies, to protest the reign of the "robbers." No evidence has come to light indicating that a seizure of power had been planned or contemplated, but the surge of the excited crowd against the police barriers strung across the Pont de la Concorde frightened the forces of order. The police responded with bullets and tear gas, Prime Minister Edouard Daladier resigned, and the thoroughly shaken Left organized a series of counterdemonstrations. (See chapter 6.)

Six days later, claiming that the Social Democrats had launched a *Putsch* against it, the Austrian government loosed its police and military forces to crush what had been the best-organized and appeared to be the most solidly entrenched Socialist party in Europe. At the war's end, Austrian Socialists (SPÖ) had ridden a wave of worker strikes and worker discontent toward a republic, but had made every effort to keep the radicalism of the workers within firm limits. Although the SPÖ had the largest delegation in the new Parliament, it lacked a majority and governed for several years in coalition with two conservative parties (Christian Socials and German Nationals). The latter two, convinced that the danger of revolution had passed and that economic and international affairs had stabilized, broke the coalition in June 1920. The voters followed suit in the October election, giving the Christian Social Party a plurality. From then until the Anschluss, the Christian Socials governed Austria in coalition with varying combinations of the Greater German, Land League, and Heimwehr parties. This Bürgerblock pursued an anti-Socialist, ultimately antirepublic policy.

Despite its loss of ministerial power, the SPÖ remained a potentially powerful political force in Austria. It continued to win a large percentage of the national vote, control Vienna, advocate revolutionary theories, enjoy a substantial influence in the trade union movement, and possess a militia (the Schutzbund). Appearances, however, proved deceptive. The steady increase in its popular vote totals did not translate into effective influence over national policy, and its influence among workers and soldiers dwindled. As the Right grew stronger and more confident, SPÖ passivity increased. When the more militant workers and the party's Left-wing called for action, SPÖ leaders responded with more words and theories. The Linz Program of 1926 issued a stern warning to the bourgeoisie that if it should try to block the transition from capitalism to socialism, "the working class would be forced to smash the opposition of the bourgeoisie by means of dictatorship."[25] The Linz Program was a bluff; the vast majority of Austrian Social Democrats "abhorred violence and were a truly humanitarian party."[26]

They demonstrated in 1927 just how reluctant they were to engage in violence, even of a defensive nature. In July, just three months after the SPÖ won 42 percent of the popular vote in the parliamentary election, Social Democratic workers launched a spontaneous demonstration to protest the acquittal of Heimwehr members who had been accused of murdering a Schutzbündler and a child. The demonstrators set fire to the Palace of Justice, and ninety-four of them were killed by the police. Social Democratic leaders refused to sanction an armed response, fearing it might lead to civil war and the need for an SPÖ dictatorship, and chose instead to respond with a general strike. "Not a wheel moved for four days. . . . Yet it was practically of no avail," wrote Julius Braunthal, because the Austrian government was sure the SPÖ would go no further.[27]

Feeling isolated and weakened, SPÖ leaders became increasingly self-protective. They clamped tight control over the Schutzbund and tried to ignore their Leftists' insistent demands for militant activity. When the government of Chancellor Engelbert Dollfuss decided to govern without

Parliament in March 1933, the Social Democrats, in Otto Bauer's words, "shrank back, dismayed, from the battle. . . . We postponed the fight because we wanted to spare the country the disaster of a bloody civil war."[28] Nor did the party respond to the laws dissolving the workers' councils, trade union newspapers, and Schutzbund that followed. The only initiative demonstrated by the SPÖ leadership in the waning days of its existence involved allowing the party's "realpolitik" Rightists, led by Karl Renner, to approach the "democratic elements" among the Christian Social Party and even the Dollfuss government itself.[29] When the Left wing demanded actions more in line with Social Democratic revolutionary theories, the last SPÖ Congress, in October, approved resolutions bristling with militant terms, but did nothing to implement them.

Nor did the tiny Austrian Communist Party (KPÖ) support the Social Democratic Left's campaign for a united front. In January 1934, the Comintern accused the SPÖ Left of obfuscating the process of "facsization" in Austria.[30] Thus, when the Dollfuss government launched its attack on the Austrian Left on February 12, Social Democrats and trade unionists lacked effective leadership and coordination. Pockets of workers fought bravely to defend what they had built since the war, but they were no match for government forces.

The shooting ended after four days; the SPÖ was outlawed and its leaders jailed or forced to flee. Many Social Democrats joined the Communist Party (which had been banned in May 1933). More than two-thirds of the seventy delegates to the KPÖ Congress held in September 1934 had joined after February, and one-half of the party's new Central Committee consisted of former Social Democrats. They obviously influenced the resolutions, which pleaded for a united front, not as a maneuver, but as "a necessary condition for the proletarian class struggle."[31]

The destruction of the Austrian Left, however, did not lead to Fascism. In fact, Dollfuss had launched his forces as part of his campaign to undermine internal Fascist demands and external pressures from Hitler and Mussolini. He had brought the Heimwehr into the government coalition in May 1932, imposed an authoritarian government in March 1933, created a single party—the Fatherland Front—in May 1933, and promulgated a Christian Corporative constitution in April 1934. At the same time, he had attacked the National Socialists. During 1933, a series of suppressive measures had culminated in the proscription of the Austrian Nazi Party and the arrest and deportation of thousands of its members.[32]

The Nazis retaliated with a *Putsch* attempt on July 25, 1934, that ended with Dollfuss assassinated, Mussolini sending four divisions of Italian troops to the Brenner Pass to warn against an invasion from Germany, and the ruin of Austrian Nazism for two years. It was not until mid-1936, following Mussolini's rapprochement with Hitler, that Chancellor Kurt von Schuschnigg broke with the Heimwehr, signed an agreement with Germany, and allowed the Austrian National Socialists to become active again. Although at the time of the Anschluss, March 12, 1938, the Nazis perhaps had the same number of supporters as the government, the former could not have toppled the latter on their own.[33]

Hungary was also the scene of a fierce competition between an authoritarian regime and an active radical Right. There was, however, one notable difference: in 1932, Gyula Gömbös, who had proclaimed himself a National Socialist as early as 1919, became Prime Minister. He moved slowly, because his predecessors had instituted many of the policies he favored, the Left did not present even a remote threat, Horthy would not have tolerated radical measures, and Gömbös had not been able to create a unified, broad, popular mass movement. He introduced the trappings of a Fascist state—party militia, propaganda—and appointed to official positions supporters of his "unitary Hungarian nation" and "one party corporate state."[34] After his death in October 1936, no leader of charismatic quality emerged and no program of radical nationalism appeared that had the power to shape native Hungarian Fascism into a substantive threat to the Horthy regime.

Several efforts to achieve unity among radical Right groups and several plots to seize power failed. When the government cracked down in 1938, the German goverment sent money to aid the radical Right groups, but Ferenc Szálasi, the leader of the largest radical nationalist group, the Arrow Cross Party, did not approve Hitler's plans for Hungary. German money, therefore, underwrote the coalescence of smaller radical Right parties into a Hungarian National Socialist Party–Hungarist Movement. It claimed to have enrolled over 200,000 members as of July 1939. Neither party did well in the May 1939 legislative election; avowed Fascists won only 49 of 259 seats.[35] (An Arrow Cross government, under Szálasi, would be placed in power by the German army in October 1944, only to flee before the advancing Russian army six months later.)

The Romanian Fascist equivalent, Corneliu Codreanu's Legion of the Archangel Michael and its militant auxiliary, the Iron Guard, grew in size and electoral appeal during the early 1930s, but on the eve of the December 1933 elections, it was dissolved and 18,000 of its members were jailed. It was renamed the All for the Fatherland Party, and, in the November 1937 elections, became the third largest party with nearly 16 percent of the vote.[36] King Carol II, who had tried to co-opt Fascist sentiment in 1934 with his own youth organization, the Guards of the Fatherland, attempted to do the same in early 1938 by means of a nationalist concentration government. When Codreanu refused to join, the King suspended the old constitution, promulgated a new one awarding the monarchy vastly increased power, submitted it to a referendum, and arrested Codreanu and most of his party's leadership. Codreanu was murdered in prison, his followers reacted violently, and the government bloodily suppressed the Iron Guard. At the end of 1938, King Carol borrowed some of the symbols of Fascism—uniforms and rituals—and clothed his monarchical dictatorship in the raiments of the Front of National Rebirth.[37]

The Attempt to Extend Fascism

Several months before the Nazis' pivotal election victory in September 1930, Benito Mussolini delivered a series of revisionist foreign policy speeches during an extended speaking tour of northern Italy. On October 27, he proclaimed: "Yesterday, it was Italy, today it is the world, because everywhere there are people fighting for or against fascism."[38] Although no overt Italian activity followed, Mussolini allowed Nazis to train in Italy, shipped arms to the Austrian Heimwehr, and pressured Austrian Chancellor Dollfuss to eliminate his Socialist opposition.

He also tried, unsuccessfully, to create a universal Fascism. He co-opted the idea from young Italian intellectuals, who, concerned with the stagnation of the doctrine in Italy, wanted to revitalize it and use it to cleanse the West of its corruption. Aware of the problems left unsolved by his regime and the currents of Italian discontent, Mussolini had, in the same October 27 speech containing his expansionist theme, announced that "Fascism, as idea, doctrine, and realization is universal: Italian in its particular institutions, and universal in spirit."[39]

It proved difficult, however, to identify authentic Fascist movements and even more difficult to band them together or control them to any degree. Reactionary movements as diverse as the Austrian Heimwehr and the Belgian Rexists received money from Italy, while the Nazis were scorned as "pagan" racists and German expansionists.[40] The first effort to achieve unity in these disparate ranks was taken by the Fascist Royal Academy, which sponsored an International Congress on Europe, named after Alessandra Volta (the great Italian physicist of the nineteenth century). Academic and political dignitaries from the European Right were invited to Rome in November 1932, but could only agree on such general themes as the need for spiritual revivification of Europe, unity against Bolshevism, and guidance from Italy.[41]

Early in 1933, young Fascist intellectuals, inspired by the success of the Volta conference, called for the creation of a "Young Europe," to be launched by a European youth congress. Mussolini quickly co-opted this enthusiasm by creating Action Committees for Roman Universality (CAUR), charged with the task of uniting foreign Fascist movements to Italy. The CAUR promised full independence and integrity for each movement that enlisted in the campaign to solve Europe's economic crisis by means of a continent-wide corporatism and to prevent Fascist theory from being corrupted by racist principles. Under the auspices of the CAUR, an International Fascist Congress was held at Montreux in December 1934. Radical Right and reactionary organizations from fourteen countries appeared, including the Heimwehr, the French Françistes, the Spanish Falange, the Romanian Iron Guard, the Irish Blue Shirts, and Vidkun Quisling's National Unity Party. They agreed on the need to reconstitute states along corporate lines, to recruit youths to transmit the corporatist faith, and to relegate the Jewish issue to the status of a national problem. A Secretariat was established to aid in the future exchange of ideas and propaganda, but it only met twice, and made no noticeable mark on European affairs.[42] The Montreux Congress had shown that Mussolini's expansionist program could not be advanced by a motley collection of small, badly led, politically powerless groups.

Nor, as events during the first half of the thirties seemed to indicate, could Italian nationalism be advanced by Mussolini's posturing. He made himself Foreign Minister in July 1932, took over the Ministries of the Army, Navy, and Air in 1933, and brought an end to Libyan resistance in January 1932, but his overblown rhetoric could not disguise his lack of achievement in European affairs. All his schemes failed or rang hollow: disarmament, supported as an economy move; naval parity with France, deemed necessary for status purposes; and the Four Power Pact signed in Rome in June 1933, designed to replace the League of Nations with an

Italian-brokered great power alliance. Hitler's foreign policy, beginning with his abrupt withdrawal from the League of Nations in October 1933, threatened to overshadow entirely Mussolini's star.

At first, Hitler's appointment as Chancellor had been welcomed by Italian Fascists, as evidence of the impending triumph of Fascism in Europe, and by Mussolini, who believed he would be the senior partner in a Fascist enterprise to revise the Treaty of Versailles. Austria, however, became a bone of contention: Hitler wanted to annex it; Mussolini wanted it to remain *de jure* independent and *de facto* dependent on Italy. Mussolini also began to worry that Nazi imperial designs would aggravate the European situation to a degree detrimental to his goals. Therefore, he began, in early 1934, a balancing act, using the specter of German aggression to convince France and Great Britain to support Italy's Austrian and colonial policies.

Mussolini also pursued an active campaign to restrict German influence in Austria. He urged Dollfuss to annihilate Austrian Social Democracy as a means of weakening the appeal of Austrian Nazism, and concocted a tripartite agreement in March 1934 between Italy, Austria, and Hungary. These Rome Protocols explicitly concerned Yugoslavia, but contained an implicit anti-German character. Nor did the cordial meeting between the two dictators in June deter Mussolini from mobilizing troops at the Brenner Pass and unleashing the Italian press to denounce German adventurism in the wake of the assassination of Dollfuss. In an attempt to block future German threats, Mussolini signed an agreement with French Foreign Minister Pierre Laval in Rome on January 7, 1935. They agreed the two countries would consult periodically, jointly guarantee Austrian independence, and arrange some territorial concessions for Italy in North Africa.[43] Mussolini decided that same month, perhaps because of something Laval said or omitted to say, perhaps because he sensed the need for a resounding foreign policy triumph, to launch his long-contemplated acquisition of Abyssinia, as soon as an incident could be found or manufactured.

Before the Wal-Wal episode occurred, however, Hitler, again without warning, stole Mussolini's Fascist thunder by announcing in March that Germany was rearming. Helpless and consternated by the Führer's unilateral defiance of the Versailles treaty, the leaders of Italy, France, and Great Britain met at Stresa, April 11–16, to don a mask of bravado. They declared their intention "to oppose, by all suitable means, any unilateral repudiation of treaties which is liable to endanger the peace of Europe," confirmed their intention to maintain Austrian independence and integrity, and promised to push the League of Nations to condemn Germany's attitude. The "Stresa Front" crumbled almost immediately, as Mussolini chose to ignore Britain's clear warning that it would oppose him if he started a war in Africa.[44] When the war began in October, the British supported economic sanctions and a gulf opened between the two countries. Within the year, Addis Ababa fell to the Italians and Germany advanced its nationalist program by reoccupying the Rhineland.

Several months later, in July 1936, the Spanish army launched a rebellion against the legally elected Popular Front government of republican Spain. The Spanish Civil War was neither Fascist-inspired nor did it bring a Fascist regime to power, but the victory of the forces under the command of Generalissimo Francisco Franco could not have been accomplished without the men and matériel sent him by Mussolini and Hitler. Troops and supplies flowed to Spain from both countries, even though they had signed a general European Nonintervention Agreement in early September. Franco repaid the underwriters of his victory in March 1939, when he joined the Anti-Comintern Pact (with Germany, Japan, and Italy) and signed a friendship pact with Germany.

Shortly after they, individually, began aiding Franco, Mussolini and Hitler signed the October Protocols (Axis); it was not an alliance but a mark of the tightening link between them. They moved closer together the following year, when they signed the Anti-Comintern Pact of November 1937. All the advantages of this Fascist advance, however, favored the Nazis. Italy gained little from its costly involvement in the Spanish Civil War; instead, by further isolating itself from France, Great Britain, and the League of Nations, Italy became increasingly dependent on Germany.

When, in 1938, Hitler fully displayed the extreme radical nature of his designs (at the expense of German Jews and countries with a German population), Mussolini could only trail behind, picking up the leavings from Hitler's unilateral, unannounced moves. A few months after Hitler deprived Italy of its one solid foreign policy chip by annexing Austria, Mussolini, striving to gain parity, enacted racial laws against Italian Jews. The Munich Conference in September further illustrated the vast contrast between the dangers represented by each dictator: Hitler won strategic territory, while Mussolini gained some prestige as a conciliator and peacekeeper. Der Führer was displeased (he wanted war); Il Duce was delighted (he feared war).

Matters did not improve in 1939, either for non-Fascist countries or Fascist Italy. Germany swallowed the rest of Czechoslovakia without noti-fying Mussolini, and following the Italian invasion of Albania in April, Hitler coaxed the Italian leader into signing a formal military alliance, the Pact of Steel. It unconditionally tied Italy to Germany's agenda and timing.

The "Fascist threat" to European peace, identified by the European Left almost twenty years earlier, had now fully emerged, albeit clothed in the garb of German militarism. Leftists, however, had proved unequal to the task of meeting the threat themselves or convincing others of the need to check it.

Chapter 4

The Contradictions of Marxist Anti-Fascism

As the German variant of Fascism grew in strength between 1929 and 1933, and hovered on the threshold of political power, anti-Fascists failed to mobilize effective counter-measures. In the countries that could have blocked the aggressive international activities of Fascist Italy and Nazi Germany, the Left did not offer popular alternatives and enjoyed only three short-lived electoral victories during the decade. The stunning successes of Social Democracy in the Scandinavian countries (heading governments in Denmark from 1929, Sweden from 1932, and Norway from 1934) were not replicated on the Continent. British Labour's plurality in the May 1929 election and party unity shattered on the rocks of budget disagreements. The September 1931 elections that resulted reduced Labour to forty-six seats in the new Parliament and sharply reduced its political influence for the remainder of the decade. The Popular Front elected in Spain in February 1936 was almost immediately involved in a civil war it would lose, and the French Popular Front, victorious in the May 1936 elections, spent its force before autumn of that year.

The political coloration of the administrations that governed the three major democratic powers in the critical years, 1937–39, varied from conservative (Great Britain) to center-left (France) to liberal (United States). None responded to the promptings of the Left to assume an active, open anti-Fascist foreign policy, mainly because public opinion did not demand such a stance. Leftist propaganda failed to persuade more than a small minority of the people in those countries that an anti-Fascist campaign had direct relevance to their immediate concerns: recovery from the effects of the depression and maintenance of peace. The incessant squabbling of Left-wing parties, and their failure to build stable, broad-based mass organizations, also weakened their appeals. Communists refused to join or remain in organizations they could not control, and Socialists stayed away from organizations controlled by or susceptible to control by Communists.

During the early thirties, the Communist International continued to pursue the vagaries of its Third Period sectarian course. Georgi Dimitrov, head of the ECCI's West European Bureau (Berlin), told German Communists that no German took Hitler seriously and that the Communists' "foremost task is to liquidate [Social Democratic] influence. Afterwards, we'll sweep Hitler and his *Lumpengesindel* [rabble] into the garbage can of history."[1] Several months later, in June 1930, the KPD Politburo called for "the sharpest struggle against the leadership of the Social Democratic party, which serves as a critical arm of the fascization of Germany."[2] Each new cabinet was condemned as either a "conveyor belt" to a Fascist dictatorship (Brüning's) or "a form of Fascist dictatorship" (Papen's). Richard Krebs claims that Dimitrov issued a secret memo in January 1931, calling for "united action of the Communist Party and the Hitler movement to accelerate the disintegration of the crumbling democratic bloc which governs Germany."[3]

The Socialist International committed much less harm, mainly because it attempted so little. Instead of formulating and promoting substantive anti-Fascist tactics, the LSI delivered morale-boosting speeches: on May 1, 1931, it asked workers in democratic countries to turn their thoughts "in brotherly solidarity toward their persecuted class comrades . . . who are groaning under the yoke of Fascism and untiringly fighting for their liberation"; the Fourth (and last) LSI Congress, in July 1931, expressed its "complete confidence that the German workers will defeat German fascism"; and an LSI-IFTU Disarmament Conference in May 1932 urged the world's workers to "fight unceasingly, untiringly and unmercifully for the re-establishment of democracy, for its defense and for its development."[4]

Only the international peace movement grew during the early thirties, attracting youths and intellectuals in all countries to a variegated, frequently divided enterprise. But its course did not run parallel to that of the Communist antiwar campaign: the former was pacifist, the latter protective of the Soviet Union. In April 1932, Henri Barbusse, who had been, reports his long-time companion, Annette Vidal, "obsessed" during the winter of 1931-32 "by the thought of a war," decided to organize an antiwar congress—"an immense gathering of all the world's antiwar forces, a gathering above parties, above concepts, philosophies, or reli-gions."[5] He secured the cooperation of France's other renowned antiwar activist, Romain Rolland, who was not a Communist but who was sympa-thetic to the Russian Revolution, and they established an organizing com-mittee, sent letters to prominent Left-wing personalities in Europe and the United States requesting the loan of their names as sponsors, and tried to prevent the congress being labeled a Münzenberg enterprise. When, however, Münzenberg had the League Against Imperialism issue a sup-porting manifesto, Rolland wrote Barbusse: "The Anti-Imperialist League of Münzenberg has annexed itself to our congress. This is not simply an abuse of power, it is the most unworthy of blunders, something of which an *agent provocateur* would be proud. It gives substance to all the accusa-tions of Adler, Vandervelde, etc. I protest with the most extreme energy."[6]

When the French Socialist newspaper *Le Populaire* attacked the con-gress as a Comintern front, Barbusse claimed that Münzenberg was sim-ply publicizing it on behalf of a German committee supporting the con-gress, while Rolland insisted that the congress would be open to all parties and that no one party would be allowed to dominate.[7] Nevertheless, Münzenberg assumed control, arranged for Comintern funding, and laid plans for a permanent antiwar committee.[8] (Barbusse, a devoted Com-munist, undoubtedly knew of Münzenberg's participation from the start—may even have requested it or been ordered to solicit it—and simply acted the role of an innocent in order not to alienate Rolland.)

In any event, the LSI Executive refused to participate unless the Social-ists were given a number of seats on the congress' organizing committee commensurate with LSI enrollment. Barbusse told Friedrich Adler in July that the congress was not designed as a party gathering and that Com-munists and Socialists would have to attend as individuals or delegates of antiwar or workers' groups; he urged the LSI secretary not to oppose the attendance of trade unionists attached to Socialist parties or unions. The LSI Executive, however, condemned the congress as a Communist maneu-ver to create a united front at Socialist expense.[9]

The World Congress Against War attracted over 2,000 delegates from twenty-seven countries to Amsterdam, August 27–29. The majority rep-resented workers' groups and Communist organizations, and the need to defend the Soviet Union dominated the speeches and resolutions. Fascism received little attention, only the closing pledge mentioned it as one of the war-causing evils the delegates swore to fight. But an Italian anti-Fascist provided, according to the American report, the "most stirring, breathtaking" moment of the congress. The incident bore all the signs of a Münzenberg production: an Italian sailor suddenly appeared on the rostrum during the final session, warned the delegates that Fascist Italy was preparing a war, and departed shouting, "Abasso il Fascismo! Viva la rivoluzione sociale!"[10]

Münzenberg then created a permanent committee, the World Committee Against War and Fascism, located in Berlin, and gathered the impeccable names that covered its letterhead: Barbusse, Rolland, Albert Einstein, Heinrich Mann, Bertrand Russell, Havelock Ellis, Maxim Gorki, Theodore Dreiser, John Dos Passos, Upton Sinclair, and Sherwood Anderson. Rolland strenuously objected to the World Committee's location and Münzenberg's tight control over it. The ECCI, itself uneasy about Münzenberg, particularly his independence and lack of enthusiasm for Third Period tactics, decided to give control of the World Committee to Dimitrov.[11] Münzenberg regained control early the next year, when Hitler's appointment as Chancellor of Germany forced the World Committee and Münzenberg's enterprises to relocate in Paris, and Dimitrov was arrested and charged with the Reichstag fire.

Comintern leaders were determined not to allow antiwar committees to develop into interparty coalitions susceptible to control by non-Communists, who might undermine the united front from below. Believers in disarmament and the League of Nations were scorned as dupes, Socialists were condemned for supporting war preparations against the Soviet Union, and Trotskyists were accused of fomenting provocative incidents. The attacked responded in kind. The pacifist, pro-disarmament League of the Rights of Man* objected to the congress' focus on imperialist war and the Soviet Union, and protested: "Not one word about the war that is overtly preparing the path for Fascism! Not one word on the peril directed at Europe and us by the Nazi movement and the accession to power of German barons and generals representing the pre-war imperialist and militarist spirit of Prussia."[12] Socialist leaders labeled the World Committee an instrument in the service

---

*Founded in France in February 1898, by the ardent Dreyfusard, Ludovic Trarieux, to defend the principles of the Revolution of 1789, the league had become, by the 1930s, anti-colonial, pro-peace and disarmament, and critical of all oppressive regimes and laws (including the Soviet Union). It enrolled over 100,000, most of whom were on the moderate Left.

of the Communist united front, a "Bolshevik maneuver," and part of the Comintern's "fratricidal war against the LSI."[13] Trotskyists and Trotsky spurned it as a Stalinist instrument and a spurious, confusing united front.[14] Independent Leftists agreed with a group of French revolutionary syndicalists that the congress was "a facade" for unity.[15]

Within the Comintern during 1932, only a small group of Czech Communist leaders spoke openly for anti-Fascist coalition building. At the Ninth Plenary Session of the ECCI in April 1931, Josef Guttmann had criticized the anti-Nazi policies of the KPD.[16] One year later, the Czech party's Central Committee discussed moving toward a united front from above with the Socialists, and at the Twelfth ECCI Plenum in August and September, Czech representatives argued against "Social-Fascism" and demands for Communist Party domination of united fronts, urged the abandoment of tiny Communist trade unions for work within the much larger Social Democratic ones, and criticized Communist activity in Germany. The ECCI responded negatively. By October, the Czech party Central Committee was once again parroting the approved Comintern line.[17]

Outside the Comintern, and, of course, attacked by it, Leon Trotsky analyzed German Nazism and criticized Comintern anti-Fascism more incisively than any other writer or thinker of the era. He had been banished to Alma Ata in January 1928 and deported from the USSR one year later. He was not widely read, however, and some of those who tried to read him with an open mind felt confused and helpless. André Gide, for example, wrote: "Dreadful confusion after reading the Trotskyite manifestoes that Pierre Naville lent me. But, however well founded certain criticisms may seem to me, it strikes me that nothing can be more prejudicial than divisions within the [Communist] Party."[18] In addition, Trotsky's anti-Fascist strategy, social revolution, appealed far more to a small group of middle-class intellectuals than to the mass of workers.

Comintern hegemony over anti-Fascist activity and its control over a significant number of workers and militants forced Trotsky to carry on a dual struggle and polemic, which further complicated his analyses and tactics. He repeatedly argued, after 1928, that Comintern theories and strategies were devastating the anti-Fascist struggle. He criticized the Comintern's Draft Program of that year for its "senseless and over simplified contention on the *identity* of the social democracy with Fascism."[19] In September 1930, he wrote that *"Fascism in Germany has*

become a real danger," and that "one necessary element" in the effort to
fight National Socialism "is an irreconcilable ideological struggle against
the centrist leadership of the Comintern."[20] The Comintern version of the
united front could not, he wrote one year later, be used to fight Fascism
because it was not designed for that purpose; it was, instead, designed to
expose Social Democratic conservatism. By making the united front seem
a "cunning maneuver" rather than a fighting tactic of the proletariat, the
Comintern was preparing the path for the victory of National Socialism.
Since, he wrote, workers in Social Democratic and reformist organizations
would only fight with and through those groups, an effective working-
class front could only be constructed on serious, definite conditions openly
presented to the leaders of Socialist organizations.[21] Despite his acumen,
Trotsky could neither make over nor take over the Comintern or its
troops, and his critical hammer blows chipped off fragments from the
existing parties, further complicating the anti-Fascist situation.

Hitler's appointment as Chancellor of Germany and the lack of KPD
response to it made no discernible impact on Comintern anti-Fascist
thinking or rhetoric. The Social Democrats were blamed for the Nazi
success, and Wilhelm Pieck, speaking on February 6, said the KPD saw no
reason for pessimism, that in fact it was "winning the confidence of the
masses."[22] The events of January 1933 did, however, make the LSI more
amenable to discussion of an international anti-Fascist front, if, that is,
Communists ceased criticizing Social Democrats and abandoned the united
front.[23] Even though French, British, Czech, Polish, and German Communists argued for acceptance of these conditions, the ECCI rejected them
because, it was claimed, the Comintern "did not believe in the sincerity of
the Second International Bureau's proposal, and could not believe in it, in
view of all their past behavior."[24] The ECCI did, however, authorize the
national sections to negotiate anti-Fascist committees of action with their
Social Democratic counterparts and to refrain from criticism during "the
period of the common struggle against capitalism and fascism."[25] No immediate pacts resulted, and the ECCI accused the LSI of preferring a
united front with Fascism to a united front of the working class.[26]

The LSI Executive responded in March by prohibiting its member
parties from negotiating with Communists. By August, however, when a
conference of Socialist Party leaders convened in Paris, a three-way split
had become evident. British Labour and the Netherlands and Scandinavian parties demanded a complete break from Communists and the

launching of a campaign to defend democracy. Jean Zyromski (leader of a Left-wing faction of the French party) and Pietro Nenni pushed for the adoption of revolutionary tactics to fight Fascism. Taking the middle ground, Otto Bauer and Léon Blum (the leading spokesperson of French Socialism) argued that Social Democrats could, without surrendering their democratic character, ally with Communists. The final resolution straddled the issue by taking no official position on alliances between Socialist and Communist parties, and calling for international working-class unity, a unified response by democratic governments to Fascism, opposition to war, and faith in the League of Nations.[27]

The continued rigidity of the ECCI, even in the face of Hitler's devastation of one of its most important sections, stemmed not from internal division, but from bureaucratic inertia and Stalin's failure to provide the Comintern with new guidelines. The unpredictability and fluidity of the international situation bred caution in the Soviet Union. The general secretary virtually ignored the international for several years, and Comintern officials did not dare to essay a new path. The leaders of the national parties were simply left to flounder around the corpse of the united front from below. Only the Czechs and Willi Münzenberg displayed any initiative.

A series of articles in the Czech party newspaper, Rudé Pravó, by Josef Guttmann, blamed the KPD for the fall of the Weimar Republic. Then, Guttmann refused to print the ECCI's resolution blaming the SPD,[28] Communist trade union leaders published an appeal for unity with the Socialist unions, and the party's Seventh Plenum authorized Klement Gottwald to propose collaboration with the Socialists. The Czech Socialists refused. The ECCI repudiated the offer, convinced Gottwald to issue a partial self-criticism, and placed full blame for the "deviation" on Guttmann.[29]

Guttmann, the second most powerful figure in the Czech party and a member of the ECCI's Presidium and Secretariat, refused to retreat. On December 7, he issued a memorandum to the Czech party Central Committee, criticizing KPD and Communist use of the united front tactic. If, he concluded, Communists continue to

speak of the United Front tactic by condemning all compromise or association with Social Democratic workers as opportunistic, to stigmatize as disreputable Social Democratic workers who do not separate themselves from their leaders (instead of blaming ourselves for not knowing how to win them and not learning to do it), we will find ourselves on a precipitous slope. From there it is only one step toward the idea that a fascist dictatorship is inevitable because the working masses are not sufficiently mature to understand us, a single step toward that fatalistic opportunism which, to a large extent, contributed to the defeat of the KPD.[30]

He was expelled from the Czech Communist Party on December 31.

Münzenberg, moving in approved channels, fared much better. He brought to fruition the efforts of a committee of workers' groups from Germany, Italy, and Poland, which had established an office in Copenhagen in March 1933 to plan an anti-Fascist congress. They had been joined by Left wingers from the French schoolteachers' unions and Henri Barbusse, but they could not find a city that would allow them to hold their congress. Münzenberg arranged for it to meet at the Salle Pleyel in Paris on June 4–6.

Preparatory Left-wing unity congresses proliferated that spring. Antiwar congresses in London and Montevideo and workers' congresses in Scandinavia, the Netherlands, and Belgium were held between March and June. André Gide wrote in his journal on June 6: "I have received, since the Hitler crisis has been acute in Germany, a dozen solicitations from different groups whose objects, as it would appear from their declarations, are the same, so it is appropriate to wish them to get together and not let their efforts be scattered."[31] The Trotskyists, too, urged unity, but not on the basis of the Salle Pleyel appeal; they wanted an agreement between the internationals and demanded the scrapping of the united front from below tactic and the "Social-Fascist" slogan.[32]

Nearly 3,000 delegates, including about 200 Socialists, attended the Workers' Anti-Fascist Congress at the Salle Pleyel. Familiar names spoke familiar words,[33] and a European Workers' Anti-Fascist Union was duly formed. It merged, two months later, with the World Committee that had been formed at Amsterdam the previous year. Barbusse and Münzenberg headed the World Committee for the Fight Against Imperialist War and Fascism (or, as it was popularly known, Amsterdam-Pleyel). It launched a broad appeal couched in narrow limits: "We call across all party boundaries for a common fight! Apart from this movement any other independent movement setting itself the same or similar aims can only *hinder or disturb* our social work."[34]

Another spate of "unity" congresses followed: in 1933, there was a World Youth Congress in Paris, and antiwar congresses in New York, Shanghai, and Australia; the following year, there were youth, students', women's, and workers' congresses against Fascism and war in Paris, Switzerland, Mexico, the United States, and Brussels. Communists diligently organized national sections and local chapters, and the World League became the largest Communist front group of the thirties. It included pacifists, but was not pacifistic. Its aim was to mobilize workers to promote collective security against aggression.

Münzenberg also organized international anti-Fascist demonstrations to protest the Nazis' imprisonment and trial of Dimitrov and three other Communists for conspiring to burn the Reichstag. Münzenberg matched fabrication with fabrication, publishing *The Brown Book of the Hitler Terror* and transforming his World Committee for the Victims of German Fascism into a Commission of Inquiry Into the Burning of the Reichstag. An International Committee of Jurists and Technical Experts, composed of eight non-Communists from seven countries, met in London on September 14 to stage a countertrial. Three days prior to its opening, Münzenberg organized a mass demonstration in support of Dimitrov at the Salle Wagram in Paris. Otto Kuusinen coordinated a wave of similar demonstrations in other countries, and Communist periodicals were filled with pleas to save Dimitrov. The German court and the International Committee exonerated the four Communists in December; but the former also exonerated the Nazis, while the latter found them guilty.[35]

The LSI, meanwhile, appealed to workers to unite on a program of defense of democratic institutions, aid to victims of Fascism, a moral and material boycott of Hitlerism, and the war danger.[36] The International Committee of Independent Revolutionary Socialist Parties* tried and failed to fuse the LSI, Comintern, and League Against Imperialism into a unified workers' front against Fascism.[37] Trotsky declared Social Democracy disintegrated and the Comintern collapsed, "the one through base treachery, the other through bankruptcy," and called for discussions between his followers (the Bolshevik-Leninists) and the independent revolutionary Socialist organizations to prepare the ground for a new workers' international.[38] Although the "Fourth International" became a regular feature of Trotskyist discourse, the organization was not officially founded until September 1938, and contributed little to international anti-Fascism.

It required the bloody events of February 1934 in Paris and Vienna to

*An informal grouping of independent Left groups from Great Britain, Norway, Poland, the Netherlands, and Italy, which had first met in 1930 to condemn the lack of revolutionary content in the two Marxist internationals.

stir the stagnating waters of Marxist anti-Fascism. The energy, direction, and alliances that formed, however, came not from above but from below. The workers of France made it impossible for Communist and Socialist leaders to avoid unity talks, and Austrian Social Democrats flowed into the Austrian Communist Party, forcing its leaders to present a more inviting united front proposal. Given their respective domestic political situations, French unity heralded potentially seismic changes, while Austrian unity signaled unified rather than divided impotence.

Since the Austrian Communist Party had been banned nine months before the Austrian Socialist Party had been crushed and since the KPÖ had been so small (2,600) as compared with the SPÖ (600,000),[39] the February events in Austria did not provoke serious rethinking in Moscow. *Pravda* simply noted on February 14 that the "Austrian social-democrats, like their German friends, helped to prepare the triumph of fascism."[40] Soviet writers in the West, like Ilya Ehrenburg, focused on the "great example, the courageous epic, the romantic struggle" of the Austrian workers.[41] The LSI, however, having lost one of its main linchpins, ceased to be a serious international, and became, according to two of its members, "little more than a loose federation of the British and French parties with those of certain small states of Western Europe," whose influence "declined very rapidly."[42]

As the course of world events began to strengthen national anti-Fascist trends and weaken international Social Democracy, Stalin finally, albeit still grudgingly, began to remove the hobbles on Communist anti-Fascist activity. He approved a gradual opening of the Communist door to "bourgeois coalitions." He did not foreclose the option of pursuing mutual understandings with Fascist Italy and Nazi Germany, but he allowed Commissar of Foreign Affairs Maxim Litvinov and Comintern secretary Georgi Dimitrov to broaden, respectively, the concepts of collective security and workers' fronts. In addition, two voices that had been silenced in the late twenties were allowed to speak out against Fascism and the need for a collective security accord with the Western democracies. Nikolai Bukharin was appointed editor of *Izvestia*, and he assigned Karl Radek to write articles for the newspaper on the subject of war and Fascism.

Dimitrov, the Comintern's outstanding symbol of resistance to Fascism, had arrived in Moscow at the end of February 1934. He appeared at a Politburo meeting on April 4 to press the case for Communist cooperation with Social Democrats against Fascism. Stalin doubted the value of it, but he allowed Dimitrov to proceed, assuring him of Politburo support and placing him on the Political Secretariat of the ECCI and at the head of its Central European Bureau. Dimitrov also headed the committee assigned to prepare resolutions for the long-delayed Seventh Comintern Congress. In the outline he sent to the Politburo on July 1, Dimitrov argued for an end to "Social-Fascism," alteration of the Third Period united front tactic, and more autonomy for the national cadres. The Secretariat was divided over his proposals, Togliatti and Manuilsky approving, Piatnitsky, Kun, and Wilhelm Knorin (Dimitrov's predecessor on the Central European Bureau) opposing.[43]

Dimitrov did not confine his activities to the corridors of the Comintern. In April, he held a press conference to acknowledge the role Social Democratic workers had played in the campaign to free him and their sympathy for the Soviet Union. He urged them to join "an active struggle against the bourgeoisie and fascism . . . conducted by Socialist, Christian and non-party workers, side by side with Communist workers."[44] He had not, however, secured the right to scrap the united front from below. His November warning to Communists, that success in united front efforts required an intensified struggle against Social Democratic ideology,[45] indicated that Third Period ideologues still retained influence in the ECCI and Soviet Politburo.

While Moscow's leading cadres maneuvered for position, anti-Fascism began to solidify as a doctrine and movement in Europe and the United States. Hitler's destruction of the Weimar Republic, the demonstration of the French Right leagues and the smashing of the Austrian Social Democrats in February 1934, and the crushing of a general strike in Spain that October spurred a chorus of concern, greater activism, and new studies. German voices dominated this new surge. Two Marxist scholars, Arthur Rosenberg and Herbert Marcuse, identified Fascism as an antiliberal or irrational seed within capitalism that developed as capitalist production methods became increasingly monopolistic. In terms of strategy, Rosenberg's analysis convinced him that bourgeois-Marxist coalitions to fight Fascism would be exercises in delusion,[46] while Marcuse pessimistically concluded that "the fate of the labor movement, in which the heritage of [German] philosophy was preserved, is clouded with uncertainty."[47] The Institute of Social Research, with which Marcuse was associated, moved to New York from Frankfurt in the summer of 1934, but the bulk of its analysis of German Nazism did not begin to appear until 1939, virtually ignored Italian and other national variants, and made no attempt to for-mulate political responses to it.[48]

German writers in exile, however, proved much less pessimistic. They had been calling, since the summer of 1933, for a world conference of anti-Fascist writers; other Western writers made similar demands at the First All-Union Congress of Soviet Writers, held in Moscow in August 1934. Their plea for a broad anti-Fascist front and a writers' anti-Fascist organization did not bear immediate fruit, and the resolution on interna-tional literature used typical Third Period rhetoric to phrase the tasks of "the revolutionary writers of the whole world."[49] Radek's argument, that anti-Fascist writers should submit to Communist Party discipline if they wanted to fight Fascism effectively, was countered by Jean-Richard Bloch's assertion that such narrow dogmatism served only the interests of Fascism. Back in Paris, Bloch discussed, with Russian novelist and *Izvestia* correspondent Ilya Ehrenburg, the convening of an anti-Fascist writers' congress. Ehrenburg dispatched a proposal to Moscow, and was sum-moned to return and discuss it with Stalin, but the events surrounding the assassination of Leningrad party boss Sergei Kirov prevented the meeting. Ehrenburg was ordered to return to Paris and organize the congress.[50]

But these were movements in a minor key, and most Communists found it difficult to follow the cues. As a result, backing and hauling continued in the European parties and the Comintern. The Spanish Com-munist Party (PCE), after three months of negotiation, agreed to join the Socialist-organized Workers' Alliances, but, following the defeat of the October general strike, blamed the Socialists for needlessly postponing and inadequately preparing it.[51] At a Czech Central Committee meeting in November, Jan Sverma proposed a rapprochement with the Social Demo-crats, and the committee adopted a resolution calling for the formation of a "workers and peasants government . . . which will assure the broadest liberties to the oppressed nationalities and suppress the fascist gangs, defend the independence of the Czechoslovakian nation and the fraternal union of all the nations of Czechoslovakia." It was harshly criticized by the ECCI.[52]

Closer to home, Togliatti, in a series of lectures on Fascism delivered at the Lenin School,* carefully criticized Third Period strategy in the guise of examining PCd'I actions against Italian Fascism. He argued that the

---

*It had been founded in 1925, to train Western Communists in revolutionary methods.

greater the ability of the working class to defend democratic institutions, the less chance a Fascist dictatorship had to succeed; that during a Fascist era a proletarian dictatorship could only be achieved if the proletariat fought "in defense of all its democratic rights"; and that Communists could no longer "remain turned inward on [themselves] like a sect, cut off from the masses, incapable of wide-ranging political action to tie up with them, to direct them."[53] On the other hand, when French Communists allied with Socialists and Radical-Socialists in 1935, Togliatti accused them of ignoring the base, negotiating only at the top, and leaving too much room for the Socialists and Radical-Socialists to obstruct Communist mass activity.[54]

International Socialists remained unimpressed by what they saw and heard coming from Moscow. On October 10, 1934, the ECCI asked the LSI to meet with two Comintern representatives (Maurice Thorez and Marcel Cachin) to plan a joint action in support of striking Spanish workers. They met in Brussels, but the LSI executives refused to commit their organization until they could poll the member parties. The Executive met in November, but only the French party responded positively; the others claimed that association with the Communists would compromise Social Democracy in the eyes of the rest of the world. Though unable to reach a compromise, the Executive did lift the ban on coalitions with Communist parties and told each party it could make its own arrangements to fight Fascism.[55]

The International Federation of Trade Unions proved no more eager to arrange joint activity with its Communist counterpart, the RILU. The reformist federation would, in the following years, reject a working-class united front because "democratically-minded Socialists" could not be harnessed together effectively with "dictatorially-minded Communists." Instead, Social Democrats were told to fight Fascism by liquidating capitalism, establishing a planned economy, and countering Italian and German expansion by disarmament and nationalization of armament factories.[56]

Given this international vacuum, even hesitant Comintern activity seemed energetic. The ECCI, on January 16, 1935, formally approved the efforts of the French Communist Party to arrange a unity pact with the French Socialists, and accelerated the planning for the Seventh Comintern Congress. While the theses and resolutions were being prepared, the Communist umbrella opened wider. In February, on the eve of an international anti-Fascist art exhibit (due to open in Paris and then move to

London), the Comintern proclaimed: "A new ally has joined the ranks of the anti-fascists—the left-wing intelligentsia. . . . The intellectuals are overcoming their petty-bourgeois individualism."[57] Dimitrov told an "Anti-Fascist Evening" of the Moscow Writers' Club on February 28 that "creative art must be placed at the service of the proletarian revolution, and employed in the struggle against fascism."[58] And Ehrenburg's International Congress of Writers for the Defense of Culture would open shortly.

Change of some magnitude appeared obvious, but lacking a clear announcement or statement of principles, the member parties were forced to grope through the murk of Comintern rumors and official pronouncements on other subjects to distinguish the shape of the new tactic. British party leaders, for example, thought that the united front would continue to be built on a network of locally organized worker, factory, and street committees, not a system of electoral coalitions or supraparty unity organizations, and that the new united front would be distinguished from the old only by the cessation of interparty polemics.[59] Although such a formulation would have nullified the French and Spanish Popular Fronts, the British had not missed the point by much. The united front against Fascism would not alter basic Communist goals—defense of the Soviet Union, domination of the world's working-class movement, and revolutions leading to dictatorships of the proletariat—but simply cause them to be pursued more quietly and under the rubric of anti-Fascism.

As they prepared to move toward a moderate-seeming political position, Communists had to fortify their Left flank against the assaults of Trotskyists and other Leftists who advocated social revolution as the only means to defeat Fascism. An "Against Trotskyism" column began to appear regularly in *International Press Correspondence,* collectively branding as "Fascists" all Left-wing critics of Comintern strategy and Soviet diplomacy.

Finally, the grand showcase for the new tactic, the Seventh World Congress, convened on July 25, 1935 (and continued until August 20). Dimitrov delivered the keynote speech on August 2. Jules Humbert-Droz called it "a gust of fresh air . . . in the great tradition of·Lenin at the Second and Third Congresses."[60] Dimitrov began routinely, defining Fascism as "the open terroristic dictatorship of the most reactionary, most chauvinistic and most imperialist elements of finance capital," but hit a new note when he blamed both Social Democrats and Communists for allowing it to succeed. He proposed a two-track method to block its further progress. First, a proletarian united front would be built, dedicated to fighting Fascism and reaction by defending "every inch of bourgeois liberties" and "the immediate economic and political interests of the working class." It would consist of "class bodies of the united front chosen irrespective of party, at the factories, among the unemployed, in the working class districts, among the small townsfolk and in the villages." The second tier, a people's front, would recruit the unorganized working masses (peasants and urban petite bourgeoisie). This "wide, popular anti-fascist front" would also be composed of local action committees.[61]

Eleven days later, following a lengthy, mostly laudatory, and generally tedious discussion, Dimitrov delivered a second major address, demonstrating the dialectical connection of the two tracks:

They are interwoven, the one passing into the other in the process of the practical struggle against fascism. . . . For it cannot be seriously supposed that it is possible to establish a genuine anti-fascist People's Front without securing the unity of the working class itself. . . . At the same time, the further development of the united proletarian front depends, to a considerable degree, upon its transformation into a People's Front against fascism.[62]

Dimitrov, in sum, restated, to meet current conditions, the traditional Bolshevik tactic of maneuver. Implicit in all his remarks was the belief that Communism represented the dynamic, militant, revolutionary element of the working class and the conceit that, for a variety of historical reasons, the workers had not yet grasped that essential truth. The combination of a nonrevolutionary united front and a nonpartisan people's front, he seemed to believe, would endow Communists with the respectability they needed to enter the heretofore closed ranks of the liberal and Socialist masses, and lead them, first, to victory over Fascism, and then toward the dictatorship of the proletariat.

Practical applications were left to the national parties, but only a few eagerly grasped the new nettle. Two KPD opponents of the new tactic had to be removed from its Central Committee, while Béla Kun and the entire Hungarian Central Committee were purged for resisting the people's front. Earl Browder (CPUSA) and Harry Pollitt (CPGB) applied it without hesitation, mainly because they had the least to lose (their parties were very small and they had no other practical means of attracting new members). The previously reluctant Maurice Thorez, in France, placed all hesitation behind him, and moved well beyond what the Russians deemed advisable (see chapter 6). The result, an electoral alliance with Socialists and Radical-Socialists, was only tolerated because it seemed to fortify the national defense posture of this new Soviet ally (see chapter 5). Czech Communists, however, were not allowed similar latitude, even though the Russians had just signed an alliance with their country as well. When Czech Communist deputies voted for the foreign affairs budget, proclaimed the priority of national defense, and supported Victor Beneš' presidential campaign, the ECCI called the party leaders to Moscow to criticize their lack of restraint, and then sent Klement Gottwald back to liquidate the opening to the Right, "parliamentary cretinism," unity with Social Democrats, and national defense thinking; he also purged the party press and Secretariat.[63]

Thus, from the outset, Communist unpredictability undermined the potential reach of the people's front. Although people's front congresses multiplied (Canada, South Africa, the United States, Australia, Brussels, Paris), and pamphlets poured from Münzenberg's presses, Socialists kept their distance and Trotskyists showered criticism on it. The LSI rejected, on October 13, an ECCI request for joint action in support of Abyssinian resistance against the Italian invasion, and an invitation from the World Committee to unify all international workers' organizations. Socialist parties and factions also behaved unpredictably: some responded to the worsening political and diplomatic situation with heightened revolutionary rhetoric, while others became more reformist, legalistic, and pacifistic.

Trotsky delivered a blistering attack on the Seventh Congress, charging that "it marks—after a period of vacillation and fumbling—the final entry of the Communist International into its 'Fourth Period' which has for its slogan—'power to Daladier!' [the leader of the French Radical-Socialists]; for its banner—a tricolor; for its hymn—the *Marseillaise*, drowning out the *International*." It represented, he continued, an "opportunistic and patriotic turn" that "consolidates the social-patriotic camp."[64] Several months later, Trotsky wrote: "The more leaders of the People's Front 'reconcile' the class antagonisms and dampen the revolutionary struggle, the more explosive and convulsive character will it assume in the immediate future, the more sacrifices it will cause, the more defenseless the proletariat will find itself against fascism."[65]

The people's front, though it mobilized far more people on behalf of anti-Fascism than any other approach, proved, as Trotsky predicted, destructive. Its rigid alignment with Soviet national interest allowed the

Communists, in the name of anti-Fascism, to attack and even destroy, as "agents of Fascism," opponents or critics of the USSR or the Comintern. Unfortunately for the anti-Fascist movement, the most potent symbol of people's front anti-Fascism, the Spanish Civil War, also became the showcase of flagrant Communist fabrication and violence in the name of anti-Fascism.

Nevertheless, before disillusion exacted its full cost, the Loyalist cause attracted thousands of previously nonpolitical people in Europe, the United States, and Latin America. The pamphlet literature was enormous, and innumerable meetings and fund-raising events were held as people's front committees of every description and title and spokespeople from all points on the political spectrum expended a prodigious effort to save the Spanish Republic from "Fascism." The more courageous and determined began to trickle across the Pyrenees to defend the republic bodily. On July 23, two Italians joined an Anarchist militia and eleven Germans joined the Socialist fighting forces; several more Germans and some Englishmen, on vacation in Spain, joined the militias in early August; fifteen Frenchmen arrived on August 8. Several British arrivals took part in an unsuccessful attempt to capture Mallorca, and Nat Cohen (from London's East End) was elected to lead this mostly Spanish group, which took the name of the Tom Mann Centuria.[66]

By September, enough foreign volunteers had arrived and enough were planning to arrive to induce the ECCI to organize recruitment. When foreign Socialist and Anarchist parties did likewise, Spanish Prime Minister Largo Caballero agreed to the formation of the International Brigades. The volunteers were, for the most part, organized into foreign-language battalions, each bearing the name of a renowned freedom fighter (Lincoln, Garibaldi, Mickiewicz, Louise Michel). Nearly 60,000 military volunteers from two dozen countries served in Spain: 15,400 from France, 5,411 from Poland, 5,108 from Italy, 4,294 from Germany, and over 3,000 each from the United States, Great Britain, Belgium, and Czechoslovakia. Nearly 75 percent were workers and over half were Communists. The international support network, organized and administered mainly by Communists, raised funds to finance seventeen permanent hospitals, forty mobile field hospitals, and 170 ambulance and transport vehicles. They were accompanied by some 2,500 medical volunteers. The volunteers suffered heavy losses: 9,934 dead, 37,541 wounded, and 7,686 deserted, imprisoned, or not found.[67]

The Spanish Civil War also attracted unprecedented attention from intellectuals and artists. Stephen Spender probably spoke for most of those who supported the Loyalist side when he wrote: "It became possible to see the Fascist/anti-Fascist struggle as a real conflict of ideas, and not just as the seizure of power by dictators from weak opponents."[68] Many young writers and poets, especially from Britain, fought and died; Louis Aragon toured the frontlines broadcasting his poetry from a loudspeaker van; André Malraux flew airplanes and wrote a novel, *L'Espoir*; Vaughan Williams stopped writing symphonies in order to compose folk songs about the volunteers. A few lost their illusions.

Philip Toynbee, for example, did not hate Fascism or military dictatorships less after his trip to Spain, but people's front activities now seemed dreary and dishonest:

An infinite number of committees lasting for an infinite number of hours and achieving infinitely little; the same ranting speeches from platforms all over the country; cunningly devised pamphlets which always told so much less even than the truth we already knew. . . . And certain appalling ladies who recruited young men to fight in Spain with as much zest as those martial ladies on the plinths of Trafalgar Square had shown during the First World War.[69]

George Orwell, on the other hand, had few illusions to lose. He returned with a throat wound and a powerful contempt for Communists and people's fronts. He accused the former of taking revolutionary gains from workers and jailing people "whose opinions were too Left"; the latter, he charged, had "about as much vitality, and about as much right to exist, as a pig with two heads or some other Barnum and Bailey monstrosity."[70] British Leftists, in his opinion, lied about the war on the dubious "ground that if you tell the truth about Spain it will be used as Fascist propaganda."[71] Orwell's truth was not palatable to two staunch supporters of the Loyalist cause: Kingsley Martin of *The New Statesman* rejected two of Orwell's articles, and Victor Gollancz, who had published all Orwell's previous books, refused even to consider the one on Spain Orwell was preparing to write.*

Even the *apparat*-toughened Togliatti sounded disappointed when he arrived in Spain and discovered that the Frente Popolare lacked connections to mass activity. He reported to Moscow on August 30, 1937, that

---

*It would be titled *Homage to Catalonia*, and be published by Secker and Warburg in 1938.

popular front committees have virtually ceased to exist, factory committees are appointed from above, there is little democracy in the trade unions, and the "political parties, except for our own, conduct scant political activity among their own members."[72]

The fact remains, however, that for all the disappointments, lies, and purges, it is unlikely the Spanish Republic could have lasted as long as it did without Soviet aid and Communist volunteers. The democractic countries adhered faithfully to the farce of nonintervention, the League of Nations did not vote sanctions against the supporters of the rebels, and the LSI and IFTU wrote Spanish Foreign Minister Alvarez Del Vayo that they were relying on the League of Nations to resolve the conflict, although they understood that "the slow procedures of the League did not provide Spain with the complete satisfaction it has the right to expect."[73] Nevertheless, the Communists' brutal suppression of the Marxist Workers' Unity Party (POUM)* in June 1937 further worsened the prospects of international assistance.

Even before the republic's northern front collapsed in the spring of 1937, and the French Popular Front government headed by Léon Blum had resigned (in June, after one year in office), it had become evident to Russian leaders that the people's front movement would not be able to mobilize a sufficient number of people to further Soviet objectives. Not only had the Popular Front governments of Spain and France failed to stem the tide of reaction and align the two countries more solidly with the Soviet Union, but people's fronts in Great Britain and the United States had failed to alter their respective governments' appeasement and neutralist foreign policies, and proletarian united fronts at the national and international levels had failed to emerge.

As German and Japanese words and moves became more aggressive in tone and nature, Dimitrov began to move the Comintern away from the people's front against Fascism and toward the united front of peace, "which will not only include the working class, the peasants, the intellectuals and other toilers, but also the oppressed nations and the peoples of countries whose independence is threatened by warmongers. A peace

---

*The Partido Obrero de Unificación Marxista was formed in 1935 from small groups of former Communists. Centered in Catalonia, its few thousand members were more revolutionary than the Spanish Communist Party, but though its leaders corresponded with Trotsky, he considered them too conciliatory. The POUM had closer ties to the independent Left Socialists than to the Fourth International. George Orwell fought in a POUM unit.

front is required which would extend to all parts of the world." This front, he said, cannot be content simply with protests, resolutions, and declarations, it must practice "concrete mass action."[74] By early 1937, the peace front—to protect the Soviet Union against Fascist-initiated wars—had replaced the people's front in the rhetoric of Comintern speakers and writers. Several months later, in July, Togliatti met with LSI executives at Annemasse, and reported to the ECCI that the Socialists "refused any new formulation that might signify a precise commitment to concrete joint action" and that he noticed no great weakening of "the positions of the reactionary elements in the LSI, the enemies of the united front."[75]

The people's front had not aided, and may in fact have seriously weakened, Communist parties in Southern and Eastern Europe. In the wake of the Seventh Comintern Congress, the Hungarian Central Committee was replaced, the Polish party was dissolved after a murderous purge of its leaders, the Greek party was outlawed by the Metaxas government in 1936, and the Bulgarian government expelled the Communist deputies from the legislature in 1938. Only in Yugoslavia did the people's front, because of its multi-ethnic dimension, improve the fortunes of the Communist Party.[76]

The people's front also failed to improve the fortunes or influence of the Italian and German anti-Fascist movements. Long before the Seventh Congress met, Italian Left-wing exiles had been moving toward consolidation of their forces. The Socialist Anti-Fascist Concentration reached a short-lived accord with the liberal Justice and Liberty in July 1931, but in early 1933, Socialist leader Pietro Nenni, irritated by the liberals' ideology, made overtures to the PCd'I. The Anti-Fascist Concentration split over this issue and dissolved in May 1934, and in August, the Socialists and Communists signed a unity pact based on very general principles.

Though this pact did not create a united front, it did open the path to a Congress of Italians Abroad (Brussels, 1935), joint opposition to Mussolini's war against Abyssinia, recruitment of the Garibaldi Battalion for Spain, and a Popular Italian Union for Italian workers abroad. With the exception of the followers of Justice and Liberty, whose offer to create a united Italian corps to fight against Franco was rejected, the unity pact encompassed the majority of Italian anti-Fascists in exile. But the movement was too small to make an impact on Mussolini's powerful state apparatus, it received little support from the internationals, and its members and agents in Italy were regularly arrested. Nevertheless, on July 26,

1937, Socialists and Communists signed a new charter proclaiming their "unity in action as a first step toward the united party of the working class, which will be the most powerful weapon of the proletariat in its struggle against fascism and capitalism."[77] Justice and Liberty, however, disintegrated following the assassination of Carlo and Nello Rosselli on June 9.

German refugees, coming much later and spreading much wider than the Italians, failed even to achieve formal unity. Many of the most prominent emigrated to the United States, and a significant number went to the Soviet Union. Although the intellectuals among them produced numerous articles, books, pamphlets, journals, speeches, and letters, they failed to arouse world opinion to act against Hitler, and they did not have a marked impact on the anti-Fascist movements of the democratic countries or the Marxist internationals. Thomas Mann, in January 1934, noted: "My behavior and my views are in no way formed or influenced by the emigré 'front.' I stand on my own feet and am not in touch in any way with the German emigrés who have been dispersed around the world. Furthermore, those German emigrés simply do not exist in the sense of a spiritual or political unity. Individual fragmentation is complete."[78]

He could just as easily have been describing the condition of the German Left; poorly united before January 31, 1933, it shattered into fragments in the following months and years, and then the shards fragmented further. Two men devoted an enormous amount of time and energy to heal these fractures. Heinrich Mann wrote dozens of articles for *La Dépêche de Toulouse*, supported his nephew Klaus' journal of cultural resistance and unity, *Die Sammlung*, wrote many books, essays, pamphlets, and forewords to other writers' books, presided over the German Freedom Library in Paris, and chaired the Committee for the Establishment of a German Popular Front.[79]

"The grey eminence and invisible organizer" of that committee was Willi Münzenberg.[80] He also established the World Committee for the Relief of the Victims of German Fascism, the Institute for the Study of Fascism, Editions du Carrefour (an anti-Fascist publishing firm), the international network to raise money and supplies for the Spanish Loyalists, and a Committee of Inquiry Into Alleged Breaches of the Nonintervention Agreement.

Neither Mann's labors nor Münzenberg's inventiveness could overcome the deep disunity of the German Left, both inside and outside Germany.

A unified internal resistance movement did not appear, and the diffuse network of small oppositional cells proved highly vulnerable to the Nazi police apparatus. Dissident SPD and KPD members, mainly from the ranks of young workers and students, tried to transform themselves into a revolutionary opposition. Such groups as the Red Patrol in Berlin, the Socialist Front in Hanover, and New Beginning tried to organize illegal activity against the Nazi state.[81] The exiled party organization sent literature and money—the Social Democrats to maintain control over their membership, the Communists to launch strikes and demonstrations and rebuild a Communist trade union organization. Systematic and brutal repression destroyed, by the end of 1935, any hope of effective internal resistance. "After 1936, all that remained was the self-sacrificing resistance of individuals and minute groups, mutual help, close contact with reliable friends, exchange of information, and the strengthening of one's own position with the aim of surviving the regime."[82]

Abroad, anti-Fascists were safer, but less effective, realistic, and practical. Impotence provoked witlessness among exiled German Marxists. The Socialists did not officially go into exile until early May, following Nazi seizure of trade union property. During the intervening four months, the SPD Executive had tried to carry on a legal struggle against Hitler and avoid precipitate activity. Two weeks after the party sent six representatives abroad (first to Saarbrücken, then Prague), SPD deputies voted to approve a highly nationalist speech of Hitler's. The Social Democratic Representation Abroad repudiated the approval and formed a new party headquarters at Prague, issued a newspaper declaring open war on Nazism, and appointed itself the Executive of the German Social Democratic Party (Sopade). The Prague group insisted that since it incarnated the German Social Democratic tradition, it should lead the anti-Nazi resistance. Sopade leaders refused to negotiate with the various Socialist splinters and dissenting groups that formed. When the SPD leaders who remained in Berlin repudiated Sopade, the once-powerful German Social Democratic movement lay in three small fragments: the SPD in Germany (officially banned on June 23, 1933), Sopade in Prague, and a Marxist-Leninist-oriented Left in Germany.[83]

The KPD Central Committee divided over Dimitrov's move toward a broader united front. As a result, it was not until January 30, 1935, following a bitter meeting in Moscow, that the KPD, under ECCI pressure, issued a resolution calling for the creation of the broadest possible anti-Fascist front, and not until February 11 that the Sopade was invited to issue a joint declaration calling on German workers to form unity committees. The Sopade Executive and the dissident Socialist groups all declined,[84] thereby stiffening the resolve of the KPD's "class-against-class" supporters. The intraparty fight over the people's front ended not with the Seventh Congress, but with the "Brussels" Conference (actually held on the outskirts of Moscow, at Ruhlevo, in October). Two of the staunchest opponents of the people's front were removed by the ECCI from the Central Committee, and a resolution was voted declaring that the KPD would now "proceed to the fulfillment of its tasks with a new adjustment to Social Democracy."[85] But when Walther Ulbricht and Fritz Dahlem traveled to Prague on November 23 to explain this "adjustment" and appeal to the Sopade "to act together in a spirit of comradeship," they were rejected.[86] Wilhelm Pieck, meanwhile, established the KPD's official exile base in Paris, and Dimitrov invented his "Trojan horse" tactic for party work inside the Third Reich. KPD members were ordered to infil-trate Nazi organizations and convert them into mass bases. The arrest rate of these "horsemen" was prodigious, probably around 300,000 by 1939.[87]

Communist efforts to create a German people's front fared superficially better in Paris. There, on February 2, 1936, a Committee to Prepare a German People's Front was formed; it met again on April 10–11, attract-ing eighty writers, intellectuals, journalists, Communists, dissident So-cialists, and nonpolitical refugees. According to Albert C. Grzesinski, a once-prominent Social Democrat, the committee "never became really active. Discussions took place, meetings were held, resolutions were adopted. It took one whole year to agree on and draw up a joint manifesto on the aims of the German opposition."[88] The "Appeal of the German People's Front for Peace, Freedom, and Bread" was published in January 1937. It called for an alliance of all German parties and groups dedicated to the overthrow of Hitler, and was signed by twenty Social Democrats, fifteen Communists, ten members of the Socialist Workers' Party (includ-ing Willy Brandt), and twenty-nine intellectuals (Heinrich Mann, Lion Feuchtwanger, Stefan Zweig, Ernst Toller, and Egon Kisch among them).[89] It was formally adopted at a People's Front Congress held in Paris in April.

By then, however, German intellectuals in general, and Willi Münzen-berg in particular, had come under an ominous cloud of suspicion in the minds of the highest officials in the Kremlin. Münzenberg was recalled to

Moscow in September 1936 and subjected to tough questioning by Comintern officials about his independence and rumors that he had criticized the ECCI's KPD and German People's Front policy. Only his deep involvement in the cresting international support network for the Spanish Republic, and the intervention of Togliatti, spared him from detention in the Soviet Union.[90] Two months after Münzenberg returned to Paris, the NKVD, at Stalin's orders, commenced a large-scale roundup of foreign exiles in the Soviet Union; nearly 70 percent of the German intellectuals who had fled from Hitler to the Soviet Union were eventually arrested.[91] The ECCI was equally decimated in 1937 and 1938, reducing its services to a bare minimum, and forcing the closure of the Lenin School. Many foreign Communists who had been resident in the Soviet Union disappeared,[92] as did many Russians who had served in Spain.

Münzenberg refused to surrender the people's front idea to the Russian offensive against it. At the German People's Front Congress, he urged all anti-Hitler forces to unite and criticized the obstacles created by Communist equivocation and petty scheming. He was expelled from the KPD on May 23, 1937, for "intriguing against the People's Front policy and refusing to carry out party directives."[93] Non-Communists streamed from the committee, as Communists dropped even a pretense of democratic behavior or tolerance of the opinions of other ideologies.[94] Before the committee succumbed, its non-Communist remnant sent to the KPD Central Committee a message that went unheeded:

You are discrediting the united and popular front movement. . . . You are strengthening in the proletarian camp the position of those who . . . [argue] that comradely and beneficial cooperation is impossible with the Comintern and its sections. You are encouraging countless enemies by your attitude and weakening the popular front movement at a time when its establishment within and outside Germany is more necessary than before.[95]

The Sopade proved equally unyielding. It had been forced, by German pressure on the Czechoslovakian government, to transfer its headquarters to Paris in the spring of 1938. Many unity meetings were held, and many unity proposals offered, including a union of Austrian and German Social Democrats, but the Sopade leadership refused to participate in any group that included Communists or that threatened to dissolve Sopade into a new party.[96]

Only the ex-Communist Willi Münzenberg proved flexible and energetic. He criticized the Comintern's anti-Nazi policies, tried to build a non-Communist united front against Fascism and for a democratic and socialist Germany, and continued to create interparty front groups, including a relief committee for Spanish Civil War refugees interned in French camps.[97] His activity infuriated the KPD Central Committee. In a report entitled "The Ruin of Münzenberg," it was stated: "The 'theoretical' machinations that Münzenberg is using in an attempt to clothe his 'resignation' with the mantle of 'everyone for unity' will not fool a single anti-fascist, *neither today nor in the future*. All Doriots [see chapter 6] have assumed this disguise to cover their *path to the enemy*."[98]

The LSI remained virtually inactive, and the Comintern approved relations only with those organizations that unequivocally and uncritically stood for defense of the Soviet Union. Stalin labeled critics of the USSR "Trotskyists" and "German-Japanese agents," and Dimitrov called them "spies, diversionists, terrorists and police provocateurs in the service of German fascism and the Japanese militarists."[99] Little was now heard of people's fronts. *World News and Views** publicized the peace front, and *The Communist International* promoted a united front of the working class.

The Munich settlement in September 1938 turned the Comintern further from people's and popular fronts and back to attacks on Social Democrats, pacifists, and "capitulationists." Workers were urged to replace "governments of national treachery" with governments of "real national salvation," and form "a defense cordon of armed peoples" to "doom fascism to impotence and hasten on its defeat and inevitable ruin."[100]

The shell of the LSI was shattered by the Munich settlement. Two Socialist parties, those of the Sudetenland and Czechoslovakia, were doomed, and the remainder divided, preventing the Executive Committee from reaching an agreement on a resolution. British Labour condemned the pact; the majority of the French party preferred it to war; the parties of Belgium, Holland, Switzerland, and the Scandinavian countries declared their neutrality; and the Hungarian and Polish parties welcomed the territory their countries had gained at Czechoslovakia's expense.[101] Following the unsuccessful LSI Executive session in Brussels in October, the Scandinavian parties tried to distance themselves from the international in the hope "they could take refuge in their neutrality and escape from the com-

International Press Correspondence had changed its title, on February 7, 1938, as an indication that it planned to cover foreign affairs and events in a broader, less sectarian manner.

ing world war. The British considered the rump of the International useless and their contributions to its budget a total waste."[102]

The once eagerly anticipated rupture of the Socialist International provoked no discernible reaction from Moscow. Stalin had ceased thinking about parties and fronts. He told the Eighteenth Party Congress in March 1939 that the Soviet Union was in a *sauve qui peut* situation, and would deal with *any* country that offered concrete guarantees of Soviet security. Only a few, Trotsky among them, understood that Germany was included in that group of countries. During the following months, Communist and Comintern publications focused their attention on Russia's well-publicized negotiations for a mutual assistance pact with France and Great Britain. Though Communist writers had expressed harsh skepticism of British and French intentions, they, along with the rest of the world, learned on August 23 the stunning news that the Socialist Fatherland had signed a nonaggression treaty with Nazi Germany. *World News and Views*, not fully comprehending the alteration that had taken place in Stalin's thinking, called it "A Blow at the Head of Hitler's Fascism," which breached the anti-Comintern front and made it easier for France and Great Britain to oppose Fascist aggression in the West.[103]

Those Communists, like Jules Humbert-Droz, who understood what had occurred, seethed at the complications this treaty would cause them: "Merde! This is the last straw. . . . I felt this new turnabout by Stalin represented a betrayal of all our political struggles against fascism and for peace."[104] Others, like Enrique-Castro Delgado, recently arrived at Comintern headquarters from the Spanish Civil War, kept rereading the treaty "once, twice, three times. . . . And I thought. While I thought, I seemed to hear a soft, but firm voice that ceaselessly repeated: 'Stalin is right . . . Stalin is never wrong.'. . . I am sure that in 299 offices, 299 other functionaries are reading the treaty, looking at *Pravda*, and hearing what I hear: a soft, but firm voice ceaselessly repeating, 'Stalin is right . . . Stalin is never wrong.' "[105]

The exiled Austrian Social Democrats understood how thoroughly the Nonaggression Pact evidenced the utter bankruptcy of Marxist anti-Fascism. In a letter to the LSI Executive meeting, August 26–28, they wrote: "The LSI lacks that which an international workers' movement urgently needs in this historic situation: an international strategy and an international will to fight fascism that is shared by all its members." Since, the letter continued, the Third International has not been a true international for many years, "the working class finds itself faced with the most terrible of wars lacking its principal weapon, an international organization."[106]

Several months after the signing of the Nonaggression Treaty, with the Red Army ensconced in Poland, Estonia, Latvia, and Lithuania and about to begin a war with Finland, the Comintern ordered its national sections to build united fronts of struggle against "war and reaction," to fight "against the imperialist bourgeoisie, against the top leaders of the social-democracy and other petty-bourgeois parties."[107]

The Executive of the LSI, at its final meeting on April 3, 1940, also remained true to its interwar form, doing little to help or harm. It criticized the war, called for a lasting peace, and established a committee to prepare a program for the reconstruction of Europe.[108]

Chapter 5

Pragmatic Anti-Fascism in the Soviet Union

Soviet citizens were not allowed to express spontaneously any anti-Fascist sentiments they might have harbored. The All-Union Communist Party leadership allowed only occasional, carefully controlled demonstrations of anti-Fascism, such as at Klara Zetkin's funeral in 1933 or during the first few months of the Spanish Civil War. Otherwise, mass activity or mobilization against "Fascist aggression" did not occur. Nor did the Commissariat of Foreign Affairs (Narkomindel) promulgate or practice a foreign policy that could legitimately be labeled anti-Fascist.

Lenin and Stalin, the makers of Soviet foreign policy during the years when Italian Fascism and German Nazism were in power, pursued the same objective: security of the revolutionary state. Lenin's determination to have peace at almost any cost at Brest-Litovsk in 1918, and Stalin's decision to sign a nonaggression treaty with Hitler in 1939, stemmed from the same impulse, that of saving Russia from a war that offered her little in the way of revolutionary or national security.

The twists of Soviet foreign policy in the years between those two treaties resulted from the efforts of its leaders to mesh revolutionary ideology with national defense in a world that appeared to them to be counterrevolutionary until 1921, and antirevolutionary, procapitalist, and predatory thereafter. Disputes within the Politburo over the question of how best to meld revolutionary and national pursuits, power struggles within party and state organizations, and Stalin's secretiveness and reclusiveness further sharpened the turns that were made. Nevertheless, with avoidance of war *the* dominating concern of Soviet leaders between 1917 and 1939, several diplomatic themes achieved relative constancy. Russian foreign policy makers endeavored to keep Germany and Japan friendly, or at least unaligned with other potential enemies; they tried to prevent or undermine other potentially hostile alliances; and they avoided any agreement that could automatically involve the Soviet Union in a war. All "threats" to Soviet national security during the interwar period—from "world capitalism and the Entente" of the post-World War I years to "Western imperialism and reaction" of the pre-World War II years— involved objective and subjective considerations, reflected internal and external factors, and thus generated a range of responses, sometimes contradictory in nature. Fascism, the most complex of the interwar threats, inspired the most conflicting range of responses.

Since Lenin died before he could develop an analysis of Italian Fascism and before Mussolini and Hitler had become international menaces, it would be anachronistic to speak of the anti-Fascist element in Lenin's foreign policy. Stalin was an occasional anti-Fascist, utilizing it only when no other policy seemed available to forestall or overcome German hostility. He never pursued a consistent or pure anti-Fascist foreign policy. Anti-Fascism, in the form of collective security, was simply one of the counters he used in his diplomatic contest with the capitalist world. As long as it functioned as a more effective instrument than the Comintern or nonaggression pacts to keep the Soviet Union free from war, he remained faithful to it; as soon as it ceased to enhance Russian national security, he dropped it.

With the exception of the Treaty of Riga (with Poland) and a trade agreement with Great Britain, both signed in March 1921, the Soviet Union remained isolated from the international diplomatic network in the immediate postwar world. Bolshevik leaders had hoped that the Versailles treaty would transform Germany into an immediate ally, but the Germans hesitated to challenge the Entente so readily or openly. Germany became more amenable as a result of the prodding of the Reichswehr and the diplomacy of Ulrich Count Brockdorff-Rantzau, the German ambassador to Russia from November 1922 to his death, in September 1928. This Junker conservative had argued in July 1920 that the Bolsheviks were less of an evil "than the consequences of the undignified helotism into which our vengeful and rapacious enemies have forced us for generations to come."[1]

The Allied Supreme Council inadvertently provided the occasion for the German-Soviet rapprochement. The two "pariah" countries received an invitation to attend an economic and financial conference at Genoa on

April 10, 1922, to help unsnarl the war loan-debt-reparation tangle, settle relations between the Soviet Union and the capitalist countries, and open the road to European reconstruction. One week after the conference opened, the Russians invited the Germans to complete a mutual cooperation agreement that had been discussed on previous occasions. The Treaty of Rapallo, signed on April 16, contained mutual renunciations of all accumulated claims and counterclaims and the outlines of future economic relations. In Lenin's estimation, the treaty eliminated the possibility of Germany becoming part of an international anti-Russian scheme, and he wired Commissar of Foreign Affairs V. I. Chicherin to "start a highly circumspect flirtation with Italy separately."[2]

Mussolini's "March on Rome" in October altered Lenin's plans, and indications are that, had he not succumbed to the effects of a second stroke, he would have pursued an anti-Mussolini tack. He wrote Chicherin in early November: "Perhaps we should kick at Mussolini and have *everyone* (Vorovsky and the whole delegation) *leave Italy*, starting to *attack* her over the fascists? Let us stage an international demonstration. This provides a very convenient pretext: you have beaten our men, you are barbarians, diehards *worse than those in Russia in 1905*, etc., etc. I think we should do this. Let us give the Italian *people* some serious help."[3]

Lenin's successors did not follow his advice. A Narkomindel press release dated September 22, 1923, on the Italian-Greek conflict and Fiume, contained no mention of Fascism, and was much more critical of Greece and Yugoslavia (for failing to enter into *de facto* relations with the Soviet Union) than of Italy.[4] Then, in February 1924, Italy formally recognized the USSR and signed a commercial agreement with it. Five months later, Konstantin Yurenev, the Soviet representative in Rome, horrified Gramsci, the Central Committee of the PCd'I, and Jules Humbert-Droz by hosting a banquet for Il Duce. When Gramsci learned about plans to host a similar banquet on the seventh anniversary of the Russian Revolution (November 7), and Humbert-Droz discovered that Yurenev had been ordered to propose a political and military alliance to Mussolini, they protested in strong terms. Gramsci published an "Open Letter to Comrade Yurenev" in *L'Unitá*, and Humbert-Droz wrote a stinging letter to the ECCI, demanding that orders be given to rescind the invitations. The July banquet, he wrote, had already hurt the Communist cause among Italian workers, and November 7 offered the prospect of "demonstrating workers being beaten and arrested in great numbers while Mussolini is hosted at the Russian Embassy!" He wanted Yurenev replaced with someone who would pay more attention to Italian workers than to Fascist officials.[5] In a second letter, he criticized USSR leaders:

One of the Italian party's weaknesses, and not the least, is the opinion, generally spread and cultivated by Fascists and reformists, that the Communist party is philo-fascist. . . . The repeated interviews of Yurenev, of [Aleksei] Rykov [chairman of the Council of People's Commissars], of [Avel] Yenukidze [secretary of the Supreme Soviet], with signatures, photographs, and dedications to *Popolo d'Italia*, where they speak of Mussolini as a great man and of the order that reigns in Italy . . . have given credence to the legend among the workers that an Italo-Russian, communist-fascist friendship and collaboration exists.[6]

It was Mussolini's reluctance, however, not the protests of Humbert-Droz and the PCd'I, that prevented closer ties between the two countries.

Faced with an ongoing cavalcade of Right-wing successes and Left-wing failures, Soviet foreign policymakers concentrated their efforts on securing recognition, signing nonaggression treaties, preventing German reconciliation with the Entente powers, and denouncing British imperialism and warmongering, while the Comintern harshly criticized member party errors and Social Democratic perfidy. By the January 1925 plenum of the Russian party Central Committee, Stalin had decided that in case of war, Russia could not rely on the Western Left to offer much assistance. The strength of the Soviet army, he said, had become the "burning question in the event of complications arising in the countries around us." Should war come, he warned, the Red Army would be the last to take action. "And we shall do so in order to throw the decisive weight in the scales, the *weight* that can turn the scales."[7]

Italian Fascism seemed to elicit no concern, and Italy was rarely mentioned in the annual foreign policy reports delivered by Chicherin and his deputy, Maxim Litvinov. Nevertheless, Mussolini had clearly cooled on the relationship by 1926, and the Italian Foreign Ministry ignored two Soviet protests that year. One concerned a mob demonstration in front of the Soviet embassy in April, following an unsuccessful attempt on Mussolini's life; the other was provoked by the Italian-Romanian treaty, signed in September, implying support for Romania's claim to Bessarabia. When Italy added its signature to the Bessarabian Protocol, formally ratifying Romanian possession, in March 1927, the Italian-Soviet détente, at least from the Adriatic perspective, no longer was in force.[8]

Litvinov, who had been the effective head of the Narkomindel since 1926 (and would officially become Commissar in 1930), did not profess undue concern, however. He assured the Central Executive Committee of the Supreme Soviet on December 10, 1928, that "our relations with Italy provide an example of the possibility of normal and extremely correct relations despite the difference in our social and political systems." The following year, he stated that "relations with Italy are wholly correct."[9] In fact, Litvinov was convinced, as late as November 1930, that he could negotiate a nonaggression pact with Mussolini.[10]

The increased volume and stridency of nationalist rhetoric in Germany, the electoral success of the NSDAP in 1930, and Japan's invasion of Manchuria in November 1931 radically altered Soviet foreign policy makers' perceptions of the world's danger zones. Efforts to tighten relations with Germany continued, and Stalin ordered the Comintern to cease planning revolutionary or *putschist* activity in Germany.[11] A flurry of countervailing nonaggression pacts, notably with France and Poland (but also with Lithuania, Latvia, and Estonia), were initialed or signed between May 1931 and May 1932.

Although the Soviet leaders took Hitler seriously, they underestimated the speed with which he would gain power and the damage he would do once in power. They seemed more secure after a large group of German industrialists visited the USSR in February 1931, Germany renewed the Berlin Treaty promise (of 1926) that neither country would join an alliance directed against the other, and Marshal Pilsudski tried to arrange an accommodation between Romania and Russia. Litvinov told the Central Executive Committee on December 29, 1933, that "Japanese policy is now the darkest cloud on the international horizon."[12]

Despite portentous diplomatic moves provoked by the new Third Reich—mainly the shattering of the Reichswehr–Red Army connection—Stalin told the Seventeenth Russian Party Congress in January 1934: "We are far from enthusiastic about the fascist regime in Germany. But fascism is not the issue here, if only for the reason that fascism in Italy, for example, has not prevented the USSR from establishing the best relations with that country."[13] Gustav Hilger, a high-ranking counselor in the German embassy (1923–41), wrote that Soviet diplomats "never tired of pointing out how well Moscow got along with Italy and Turkey, even though the Communist parties there were completely outlawed," and that "such persons as [Deputy Commissar of

Foreign Affairs Nikolai] Krestinsky, Litvinov, and [Prime Minister Vyacheslav] Molotov went out of their way to assure us that their government had no desire to reorient its foreign policy."[14]

The Politburo, in 1933, was more concerned with Japan and with Russian isolation in Europe. The Four Power Pact signed by Britain, France, Italy, and Germany on June 7, and the world economic conference scheduled for June 12, seemed to indicate a Western capitalist reconsolidation and the possibility of a revision of the Treaty of Versailles in a manner unfavorable to the USSR. Party leaders were not yet disposed, though, to focus on a single "enemy," and turned a deaf ear to Litvinov's "German danger" thesis. But events during the last six months of 1933 apparently altered their perception. Poland's and Finland's rejections of Radek's proposal that the Soviet Union and Poland jointly guarantee the security of the Baltic states, German withdrawal from the world disarmament conference, and Polish-German negotiations for a nonaggression treaty were followed on December 29 by Litvinov's annual state of foreign affairs speech to the Central Executive Committee of the Supreme Soviet, signaling a new direction in Soviet foreign policy. The era of "bourgeois pacifism" has ended, he said, but since some capitalist states were less belligerent than others, the Soviet Union, though continuing to seek friendly relations with all countries, would "devote particular attention to the strengthening of relations and maximum rapprochement with those countries, which, like ourselves, furnish proof of their sincere desire to preserve peace."[15] Thus began Litvinov's quest for collective security against the spector of the USSR having to face, alone, German or Japanese aggression.

France, its Eastern European security system undermined by the announcement of the German-Polish Nonaggression Treaty (January 26, 1934), responded favorably. In May, Litvinov and Foreign Minister Louis Barthou met in Geneva to draw up an Eastern European security pact which would, it was hoped, provide a region-wide guarantee of borders similar to that provided in the West by the Locarno treaties (1925). The USSR also agreed to join the League of Nations. When this "Eastern Locarno" collapsed in the wake of German hostility and Barthou's assassination (in October), the League of Nations became Litvinov's main forum for the promotion of Russian collective security proposals. But, wrote Hilger, "underneath the seemingly unambiguous front of Litvinov's foreign policy . . . constant and never ceasing efforts were made by Soviet representatives to improve their country's relations with the Third Reich."[16]

The USSR was not alone in either attempt; by the end of 1934, almost all European countries sought some form of collective security and an understanding with the Third Reich. Russian collective security efforts suffered because the leaders of small countries feared it, and the leaders of large countries either distrusted it (Great Britain), discounted its military value (France and Great Britain), or hated it (Germany). Given that situation and the Russians' determination to sign only those treaties that allowed them maximum autonomy, a satisfactory system of reinforcing guarantees could not be constructed.

Hitler's announcement in March 1935 that Germany would rearm despite the prohibitions in the Treaty of Versailles provoked sharp rhetorical responses from the Russians. Marshal Mikhail Tukhachevsky, in a *Pravda* article, bluntly analyzed Hitler's aggressive designs; Litvinov, in a speech to the League of Nations on April 17, called it "a menace to peace"; and the lead editorial in *The Communist International* edition of April 20 labeled Germany "the chief instigator of war in Europe," and accused Great Britain of channeling German aggression toward the Soviet Union and *"playing the role of chief inspirer of a counter-revolutionary war against the Soviet Union."*[17] The Seventh Comintern Congress labeled German National Socialism "the most reactionary, the most aggressive form of fascism," warned that Nazi "war provocations have spurred on the war parties . . . to fight in all countries more vigorously for power and to intensify the fascization of the state apparatus," and accused "the fascist states—Germany, Poland, Hungary, Italy—[of] openly striving for a new repartition of the world and a change in the frontiers of Europe."[18]

The sharpness of the rhetoric reflected the deepness of the anxiety Russian leaders felt watching Germany rearm, Italy invade Abyssinia, and Japan attack China, while the Western democracies and the League of Nations failed to organize a firm, collective opposition. Bilateral Soviet efforts—a five-year economic agreement with Germany based on an RM200 million credit, formal signing of the Franco-Russian treaty of mutual support, and the signing of a similar treaty with Czechoslovakia—did not, in Russian eyes, adequately rebalance the power scales in Europe. Therefore, on five occasions between May and December 1935, and four others in 1936, Soviet representatives made offers to high-ranking Germans to find ways to improve the political relations between the two countries. Russia even replaced its Jewish envoy in Berlin, Jacob Surits, with a non-Jew in November 1936.[19] But Nazi officials refused to contemplate any but commercial ties.

The Soviet Union's response to the Italo-Abyssinian war reflected the fear of isolation pervading Russian minds in 1935. At first, the Russians acted along parallel lines with French Prime Minister Pierre Laval, hoping as he was to arrive at a peaceful settlement that would leave the League of Nations untarnished and prevent a confrontation between Italy and Great Britain.[20] The terminology used by the ECCI at the Seventh Congress clearly marked the Russian effort to balance itself between the democracies and the Fascist dictatorships. Not Italian Fascism but "Italian imperialism is directly proceeding to the seizure of Abyssinia, thus creating new tension in the relations between the great imperialist powers."[21] The PCd'I and the French Communists were allowed to promote popular opposition to the invasion, but the ECCI did not attempt to mobilize its own international protest. The obligatory telegram to the LSI simply urged joint action to maintain peace. There was no mention of Fascist aggression. Finally, not only did Litvinov, in his addresses to the Council of the League of Nations, treat the invasion strictly as a threat to international peace, he told the Italian ambassador in Moscow that the Soviet Union "trusts that its fulfillment of its international duty will not reflect on the future friendly relations between the Soviet Union and the Kingdom of Italy."[22]

Although Soviet rhetoric and its public position at Geneva stiffened early in 1936, the Russians obeyed only the letter and not the spirit of the sanctions finally voted by the League of Nations, applying sanctions only to the specific commodities on the embargo list. Exports of the three (out of twenty-four) commodities on the embargo list that the USSR traded with Italy (iron ore, manganese, and chromium) immediately ceased, but shipments of oats, phosphates, wood, pig iron, and coal continued. The volume of oil shipped increased in January and February 1936 by 27.8 percent and 33.6 percent respectively over that of December. Total Russian exports to Italy in the period December 1935 to March 1936, when compared with December 1934 to March 1935, declined far less (16.5 percent) than those of Britain (91.4 percent) or France (60.6 percent). Finally, though the USSR displayed near-perfect observance of the import sanctions, so did Britain and France, with far larger losses.[23] The moment

Abyssinian resistance ceased, the Soviet representatives at Geneva voted to lift the sanctions.

Since the Italian invasion of Abyssinia did not represent a direct threat to Russian national security, Soviet leaders tried to use the war as an occasion to strengthen the principles of collective security, urge stronger sanctions, and argue against appeasement or conciliation. They had no intention of separating themselves from the Council of the League of Nations and the democracies at a time when Germany and Japan loomed much more menacingly than Italy.

Molotov, in January 1936, reported that the German Fascists had transformed their country "into a military camp," that the Fascist leadership was "preparing to act in the immediate future," and that its position in the very center of Europe made it "a menace not only to the Soviet Union."[24] Stalin, in a March 1 interview with Scripps-Howard correspondent Roy Howard, identified the "Japanese zone" as the center of world war danger, the "German zone" as a second danger spot, and the Italian-Abyssinian war as "an episode."[25]

Despite the need to use Russian troops on two occasions in 1936 to repel Japanese-supported forces on the Sino-Russian border, Germany's reoccupation of the Rhineland in March had much more ominous portents. Hitler's move cut France's access to her Eastern allies, and left the latter without the backing of a major power they could trust. France's failure to respond to this violation of the Versailles treaty demonstrated her complete dependence on Great Britain. The matter was turned over to the League of Nations which did nothing, despite Litvinov's demands that collective measures, mainly full, obligatory economic sanctions, be imposed on violators of international obligations and aggressors.[26]

Since the French alliance no longer seemed of much value, Litvinov tried to construct a peace front of regional pacts, designed "to protect particular sectors from aggression" and supplement the League Council.[27] Narkomindel officials defined their efforts as anti-aggression, not anti-Fascist, in nature. In June, for example, Deputy Commissar for Foreign Affairs Krestinsky had told the Polish ambassador to the USSR, "At the present time we are pursuing an anti-German, anti-Italian, and anti-Japanese policy."[28] On November 28, Litvinov told the Eighth (Extraordinary) Soviet Congress that the peace front was not a "call for the creation of an international bloc to struggle against fascism. . . . We, as a State, are not concerned with the internal fascist regime of this or that country. Our collaboration with other countries and our participation in the League of Nations are based on the principle of the peaceful co-existence of two systems—the socialist and the capitalist—and we consider that the latter includes the fascist system."[29]

The military responses of the Soviet Union, in northern China, Outer Mongolia, and Spain, to the aggressive moves of Japan, Italy, and Germany seemed to contradict Litvinov's words. But those responses were clearly limited, localized, and not meant to inhibit rapprochement with the aggressors. During 1936, then, Stalin tried to find a means to demonstrate Russia's will and capacity to defend her borders and international interests, and win the friendship of both the democracies (by demonstrating the USSR's bona fide commitment to peace, freedom, and democracy) and the aggressors (by enticing them to sign nonaggression pacts). The Spanish Civil War temporarily tipped the Russian balance away from the aggressors, but not toward the West. Ivan Maisky, Soviet ambassador to Great Britain and its representative on the Nonintervention Committee, harshly attacked the West's refusal to enforce the Nonintervention Agreement and was attacked in turn for his country's shipment of war supplies to the Loyalists. But even as Maisky presented his evidence of Italian, German, and Portuguese violations of the agreement, he continued to maintain that "the great dividing line of our time is not that between communism and fascism, but that between peace and war."[30]

The purge trials, conducted simultaneously with the Spanish Civil War, further widened the gap between the USSR and the Western democracies. The purges of the "Trotskyite-Zinovievite Center," the "Anti-Soviet Trotskyite Center," the "Counter-Revolutionary Military Fascist Organization," and the "Anti-Soviet 'Bloc of Rights and Trotskyites' " staged between August 1936 and March 1938 eliminated what little trust and confidence non-Fascist countries had in Russia as a dependable ally. They also devastated Soviet foreign policy making and military capability. At least 62 percent of the top-level diplomats and Foreign Commissariat officials (and 34 percent of the entire staff) disappeared, while in the armed forces, $\frac{3}{5}$ of the marshals, all 11 Deputy Commissars for Defense, 75 of 80 members of the Military Soviet, all the military district commanders and the heads of political administrations in military districts, 13 of 15 army commanders, 57 of 85 corps commanders, 110 of 195 divisional commanders, 186 of 406 brigade commanders, and $\frac{1}{4}$ to $\frac{1}{2}$ of all officers from the rank of colonel down were removed.[31]

Nor did the USSR's material commitment to the democratically elected government of Spain weigh heavily in the minds of Western leaders. Certainly, as far as the British and American governments were concerned, Soviet intervention only threatened to prolong or spread a war on behalf of a Socialist government neither British nor American foreign policymakers favored. France, when apprised of British concerns, retreated quickly from the offers of support it had made when the Spanish republican government first came under attack. When it became evident that Western foreign policies would not change, that shipping losses were very high, and that without a massive infusion of men and matériel the Loyalist side could not win, Soviet enthusiasm and support for the republic waned noticeably.

Stalin had not, in any event, leapt immediately into the Spanish fray, despite pressure from Comintern and RILU members. Exactly when and why the decision to send arms was taken is not known, but the first Soviet shipload of rifles arrived in Spain on October 4, a shipload of fifty tanks followed on October 14,[32] and more than 50 percent of the airplanes flown by republic forces between August 1936 and April 1937 came from the Soviet Union. The Spanish paid in gold for the matériel, and Spain became, for a period, the USSR's second-best export customer. But direct shipments peaked in the spring of 1937, and had virtually ended by August.[33] During that period, ninety-six Soviet merchant ships were captured and three others sunk by the Italian navy.[34] Thousands of advisers were sent from Moscow, but no Russian was permitted to join the International Brigades.

It was not concern for the democratic-loving people of Spain that motivated Communist aid, but the fear that an early collapse of the Frente Popolare would undermine a main prop of the collective security branch of Soviet foreign policy, anti-Fascist popular fronts. In addition, the rapid overthrow of the republic would have removed an anti-Fascist counterweight in the West, made France feel more encircled, vulnerable, and hence dependent on Britain, and bolstered the prestige and confidence of Mussolini and Hitler. That said, Soviet investment in the shaky Loyalist enterprise had obvious limits.

Even as Litvinov was delivering a blistering anti-Fascist speech to the Eighth (Extraordinary) Soviet Congress on November 28, citing Spain as the test case for "the first large-scale sortie of fascism beyond its borders,"[35] Italian ambassador to Russia Augusto Russo was telling Foreign Minister Galeazzo Ciano "that the Bolsheviks are slowly preparing for a red defeat in Spain and . . . Litvinov is looking for a sort of alibi under the guise of an international agreement."[36] In fact, the signing of the Anti-Comintern Pact in November 1936 by Germany, Japan, and Italy had refocused Soviet attention on the Far East, and Soviet leaders became far more concerned with building a Chinese popular front than supporting a Spanish one. Here, too, a gap opened between the USSR and the democracies when Great Britain and France refused to support Russia's call at Geneva and China's proposal at the Brussels Conference (November 1937) for economic sanctions against Japan.[37]

As Soviet feelings of isolation grew, in 1936–37, its foreign policy pronouncements grew in shrillness. Peril in the form of "Trotskyite agents, spies, and saboteurs" seemed to lurk in every corner, and warmongers around every turn. A rapprochement between Poland and Romania, symbolized by visits of Polish Foreign Minister Józef Beck to Bucharest and King Carol of Romania to Warsaw in June, was treated by the Russian press as a sinister prologue to closer relations between them and Germany.[38]

Any last collective security hopes Soviet leaders might still have harbored, disappeared when Neville Chamberlain became Prime Minister of Great Britain in June 1937. He preferred conciliation to sanctions, and harbored such distrust for the Soviet Union that he failed to consult it about or include it in his peacekeeping moves. France, for the most part, followed where Chamberlain led. Neither country reacted strongly to the Anschluss, Germany's invasion and annexation of Austria, on March 12, 1938. Litvinov, however, treated it as if it were a watershed event in European history. He told the Soviet Politburo on March 14 that the "seizure of Austria represents the most important event since the world war, fraught with the greatest dangers and not least for our Union."[39] He issued a press statement on March 17, stating that the Soviet Union was ready "to proceed immediately to discuss practical measures, dictated by the circumstances, with other powers in the League of Nations or outside it,"[40] but received no positive responses.

Count Werner Friedrich von der Schulenburg, from his vantage point as German ambassador to the USSR, told his superiors in Berlin that although the Russians would not break publicly with collective security, they would henceforth "decide in each case whether its own interests require cooperation with England and France." He also predicted that in the impending test case, Germany's conflict with Czechoslovakia over the Sudetenland, Russia would only intervene "if she herself is attacked, or if it becomes manifest that the outcome will be favorable to the side hostile to Germany."[41] Schulenburg then suggested to Soviet foreign policy officials that, as a token of mutual goodwill, the two sides stop slinging mud at each other's leaders. Discussions in Berlin and Moscow led to an agreement to tone down the rhetoric and ease the tense atmosphere.[42]

Although Litvinov solemnly swore that Russia would fulfill its mutual aid commitment to Czechoslovakia, none of the foreign representatives in Moscow and few of the foreign ministers abroad believed that the Soviet Union would intervene. Beck, for example, wrote that "the most attentive observation of Russia did not show any military preparations for that intervention."[43] No concrete initiative was taken by Soviet diplomats to overcome the lack of a common border between the USSR and Czechoslovakia and the adamant opposition of Poland and Romania to Soviet troops crossing their territory. The Soviet press maintained total silence on the question of Soviet intervention.[44]

Military intervention became a moot point when appeasement triumphed at the Munich Conference—at the expense of one-third of Czechoslovakia and every Russian belief in the possibility of a peace front. Maisky in Britain and Surits in France reported that Chamberlain and French Prime Minister Edouard Daladier were firmly committed to pursuing a policy of "capitulation" and allowing Hitler a free hand in southeastern Europe.[45] No credible evidence supports the latter accusation, but Britain and France had clearly decided to pursue their diplomatic goals with only minimal regard for Soviet interests. Georges Bonnet, the Foreign Minister of Russia's ally France, wrote on August 11 that it was "a definite goal of his to come to a full understanding with Poland, eliminating Soviet Russia as a partner in current policy, retaining with it only the contact necessary to counteract Soviet-German rapprochement."[46]

Trotsky from his exile in Mexico, warned of the effect Munich would have on the Soviet Union. It represented, he wrote, "the collapse of Stalin's international policy of the last five years. . . . The military alliance between France and the USSR from now on loses 75% of its value and can easily lose the entire 100%. . . . We may now expect with certainty Soviet diplomacy to attempt rapprochement with Hitler."[47]

Unquestionably, Munich had deprived the Soviet Union of even the figment of reliable allies and an effective collective security arrangement.

Since Stalin's purges had also completed the decimation of most of the important European Communist parties that various Right-wing dictatorships had begun, there also existed no realistic possibility of Communist-induced mass activity on behalf of Soviet interests in any country save France. The full measure of isolation felt by Soviet leaders in 1938 is preserved in the official party history written that year. It declared that "a second imerialist war has actually begun," distinguished by its "one-sided character": the stronger "democratic" powers retreat before the Fascist aggressors, scolding and "asserting that they are preparing to resist," but neglecting to build "a united front of the 'democratic' states against the fascist powers." The "so-called democratic states" fear the working-class movement in Europe and the national liberation movements in Asia more than they fear Fascist "excesses." In response, the *History* continued, the USSR had strengthened its frontier defenses, improved the fighting efficiency of its armed forces, joined the League of Nations, signed mutual assistance pacts with Czechoslovakia, France, and the Mongolian People's Republic, and signed a nonaggression pact with China.[48] By the time the book appeared in print in 1939, the League and the nonaggression treaties with France and Czechoslovakia were worthless.

Stalin, therefore, had few options; he could only exploit whatever small openings occurred, while he awaited Germany's next move and Britain's response. A Trade and Payments Agreement with Italy was signed on February 7, including a secret protocol in which the Soviet Union agreed to renew its 1932 agreement to supply the Italian navy with oil, secured a special clearing account in Rome for "certain specified purchases," ordered a destroyer for its navy, and agreed to buy and sell certain commodities.[49] Twelve days later, a trade agreement was signed with Poland. But neither of these pacts even approximated what Stalin wanted and needed: either an ironclad mutual aid pact with Great Britain and France or a nonaggression treaty with Germany and Italy.

Movement toward both began in March 1939, following the Nazi seizure of the remainder of Czechoslovakia. Chamberlain, admitting that "the Germans have not acted in accord with the spirit of the Munich agreement,"[50] gave in to cabinet pressure and began talking about a policy of containment, the keystone of which would be a firm guarantee to Poland. The Soviet Union was not advised or consulted, nor was she to receive a guarantee of her security. An obviously angry Maisky wrote to Moscow: "What can Britain (or even Britain and France together) actually do for Poland and Rumania if Germany attacks them? Very little. By the time a British blockade becomes a serious threat to Germany, Poland and Rumania will have ceased to exist."[51] Although Chamberlain repeatedly assured his ministerial colleagues and the members of the House of Commons that he had an open mind toward the Russians and considered them as serious participants in his policy of containment, he wrote to his sister on March 26: "I must confess to the most profound distrust of Russia. I have no belief whatever in her ability to maintain an effective offensive, even if she wanted to. And I distrust her motives."[52]

Stalin distrusted Chamberlain just as thoroughly. At the Eighteenth Party Congress (March 10–21), Manuilsky, the single Russian representative to the Comintern who had not been purged, stated: "The plan of the English reactionary bourgeoisie consists of sacrificing the small states of South East Europe to German fascism and thereby directing German aggression against the East—against the USSR."[53] Stalin then condemned the democracies' nonintervention policy, because it would not obstruct either a Japanese or German attack on Russia, and outlined his "clear and understandable" foreign policy:

Firstly, we stand for peace and for the strengthening of businesslike relations with all countries. . . . Secondly, we stand for peaceable, close and neighborly relations with all neighboring countries which have a common frontier with the U.S.S.R. . . . Thirdly, we stand for the rendering of support to nations which have fallen prey to aggression, and are fighting for the independence of their countries. Fourthly, we are not afraid of threats from aggressors, and we are ready to retaliate with two blows for one against the instigators of war who attempt to infringe the integrity of Soviet borders.[54]

In sum, Stalin offered no concrete promise of support to any country, and promised to deal with any country willing to provide firm guarantees of Soviet national interests.

Britain and France stepped forward first, on April 14, offering to negotiate an alliance agreement. Three days later, Alexei Merekalov, Soviet ambassador to Germany, called on Ernst von Weiszäcker, German Secretary of State for Foreign Affairs, and suggested they discuss normalizing and improving relations.[55] But it was not until May 30 that Weiszäcker informed Ambassador Schulenburg that Germany had decided to undertake "definite negotiations with Moscow."[56] At that point, Molotov, who had replaced Litvinov as Commissar of Foreign Affairs on May 4, told the world that even though the Soviet Union preferred a trilateral mutual security pact between the USSR, Britain, and France to promote peace and end further aggression, it would not allow itself to "be drawn into conflict by war-mongers who are accustomed to have others pull their chestnuts out of the fire for them."[57]

British and French negotiations with the Soviet Union foundered on the rocks of Soviet insistence that the democracies commit themselves to "all manner of assistance, including that of a military nature," should Russia or any of her bordering Eastern European states between the Baltic and Black seas be attacked.[58] The Soviet Union refused to contemplate involvement in any international crisis that threatened to place it face-to-face with Germany, without the clear, written commitment of France and Britain to launch an immediate attack against Germany. The British and French, however, refused to make offensive commitments of any kind.

Herbert von Dirksen, the German ambassador to Britain, wrote his Foreign Office on July 20 that negotiations between the democracies and Russia would fail, that the British were not really interested.[59] Maisky and Surits voiced similar thoughts to the Narkomindel in early August, when they learned the names and ranks of the members of the Anglo-French delegation sailing for Moscow.[60] And Charles Bohlen of the United States embassy in Moscow noted that British embassy staff members "were appalled by this low-level delegation"; it was, he wrote, a "half-hearted" approach with "the mark of failure on it right from the beginning."[61]

Schulenburg broke the diplomatic impasse in the East on August 15. He informed the Narkomindel that Germany desired a serious improvement in political relations between the two countries. Two days later, the Russians handed the Germans a draft reply calling, first, for the conclusion of a trade and credit agreement, and second, for a nonaggression treaty, including a "special protocol defining the interests of the contracting parties in this or that question of foreign policy."[62] Hitler, with the invasion of Poland set, a Western offensive in the works, and the future invasion of Russia in mind, did not quibble with the wording. The Germans proposed that Foreign Minister Joachim von Ribbentrop fly to Moscow to finalize and sign the treaty. The Russians wired their acceptance on August 21, and Ribbentrop arrived two days later. "The Russians," remembers Bohlen, "had no Nazi flags to greet the German Foreign Minister and had to get them at a studio that had been making anti-Nazi films. . . . A Russian band hastily had to learn the 'Horst Wessel Lied,' which it played at the Moscow airport with the 'Internationale.' "[63]

The Nonaggression Treaty declared that the two signatories, "guided by the desire to strengthen the cause of peace between" them, undertook "to refrain from any act of force, any aggressive act, or any attack against each other, either individually or in conjunction with other powers." The Secret Additional Protocol confirmed the northern border of Lithuania as the frontier separating the spheres of Soviet and German interests in the Baltic, the rivers Narev, Vistula, and San as the frontier of their interests in Poland, and Soviet interest (and German disinterest) in Bessarabia.[64]

Ribbentrop concluded from the negotiations that the Comintern no longer existed and that Stalin had "become the effective champion of Russian nationalism."[65] The German Foreign Minister's intuitions were basically correct. Molotov, in his speech to the Fourth Special Session of the Supreme Soviet on August 31, said that the British and French had left the USSR with only the Nonaggression Treaty as a means of preserving peace and eliminating the danger of war with Germany. He also criticized those "short-sighted people" who became so "carried away by anti-fascist propaganda" they could not see that the enemies of the Soviet Union had been trying to set Germany and the USSR at "loggerheads," and concluded that the German-Soviet Nonaggression Treaty served "the cause of universal peace."[66]

Chapter 6

Popular Front Anti-Fascism in France

During the interwar years, France suffered economic and social divisions nearly as paralyzing as those that undermined democracy in Italy and Germany, witnessed a radical Right efflorescence equal to Austria's, and generated an anti-Fascist response—the Popular Front—matched only in Spain. However, the French radical Right did not mount a concerted offensive against the republic and the traditional Right did not launch a civil war against the Popular Front. But throughout the interwar decades, radical Right groups disrupted order in the streets, while the traditional Right used institutional methods to cripple Left-wing governments. The efforts of the entire Right, when combined with the intramural dilemmas of the French Left, the dislocations between leaders and led in Popular Front ranks, and international events, broke the Popular Front and drove its moderate element, the Radical-Socialist Party, back in to the arms of the Center and Right. But, as events had demonstrated, and would demonstrate again, French conservatives and moderates faced their own intractable problems, which they consistently failed to solve in a manner salutary for France.

Post-World War I France faced an external situation requiring internal changes capable of providing her with the financial and military strength needed to maintain a European peace settlement no other major power supported. However, whether in or out of power, the Right and Center refused to approve the social and economic reforms that might have improved French national security. Indeed, they twice allowed a Left-governed France to approach the brink of economic crisis. Then, in 1926 and 1938, conservative-oriented ministries took command and issued decree laws further dividing Right from Left, workers from employers.

Under the best of circumstances, as Stanley Hoffmann has persuasively argued, the French electoral system of the Third Republic was not intended to produce competent, energetic governments. The product of an undynamic, slowly industrializing economy and a population heavily concentrated in rural areas employed in small proprietary enterprises, "the regime had plenty of brakes and not much of a motor."[1]

No major party emerged to dominate the political process. Instead, a series of blocs and cartels emerged to compete for power—thinly veiled and tenuously united alliances, whose slogans could attract voters but not produce effective governing policies. The French voting system (single-member constituencies decided by two rounds of voting) frequently created a large swing of seats in the Chamber of Deputies by means of a small swing in national voting preference. As a result, the Bloc National of 1919 refused to enact programs desired by a majority of the French people, and the Popular Front of 1936 passed legislation opposed by a substantial minority. In sum, social, economic, and political circumstances created a situation in which governments were forced to become more adept at artful dodging than creative solution of problems.

The unstable, at times dysfunctional, governing coalitions generated by the electoral system frustrated and angered those outside the consensus and trapped in undesirable niches of the unreformed social system. They, in turn, formed groups, parties, and movements primed to engage in disruptive, destabilizing extraparliamentary methods. These direct action groups, on the Right and Left, did not mount a serious threat to the governing status quo, but periodically proved capable of distorting it. Their activity further weakened the French political process by fracturing blocs, fragmenting parties or making them more rigid, and engendering an ongoing crisis atmosphere that was frequently met with repressive legislation.

Even when, as it happened in three of the five general elections, a Left coalition formed a governing ministry, few significant changes occurred. The Left, in power, proved disunited and spiritually feeble when confronted with powerful opponents or demanding allies. Not one of the three major parties of the Left—the Radical-Socialists, Socialists (SFIO), or Communists (PCF)—developed a concrete program of change popular with a majority and realizable within the constraints of the current system, or steadfastly implemented the programs they did develop.

The equilibrium of internal forces and disequilibrium of external forces that ultimately paralyzed France in 1940 began to appear as soon as the Great War ended. Voters alienated from political parties associated with war opposition, the Russian Revolution, and workers' strikes awarded the conservative Bloc National a parliamentary majority disproportionate to its popular support. This Chambre horizon bleu, opposed only by a Left disheartened and weakened by defeats of major strikes and schisms in the Socialist Party and labor federation (CGT), laid the foundations for serious future financial problems. The Right's refusal to enact an income tax and its insistence on borrowing created an inflationary situation that economically harmed many people and made France dependent on British and American goodwill in the realms of repayment of old debts, negotiation of new loans, and strict accountability of reparations.

France's allies and creditors, however, did not approve of the Bloc's foreign policy of arming against, encircling, and punishing Germany. The crisis in international finance caused by French occupation of the Ruhr in 1923 exposed these disjunctions. France's acceptance of the Dawes Plan's regulation of war debt and reparations payments represented her admission that she could not maintain the Versailles settlement alone, but was dependent on British support.[2]

The plan did not, however, force France to cease relying on loans and reparations and to undertake fiscal reform and taxation. Inflationary pressures on income, savings, and pensions, caused by continued borrowing and budget deficits, stimulated the formation of new radical Right leagues (e.g., the Jeunesses Patriotes),* while a weak franc turned traditional conservatives to "authoritarian anti-parliamentarism" in the form of Ernst Mercier's Redressement Français.[3]

The French Left failed to halt or redirect those drifts, mainly because of the wide gap separating SFIO and Radical-Socialist economic policies, the equally wide but far more hostile gap dividing the Socialists and Communists, and the schism in the ranks of organized labor that produced a reformist federation (CGT) and a Communist-controlled federation (CGTU). Though all three parties wanted peace, the Radical-Socialists were a party of national defense, the Socialists wanted to end the possibility of all war through disarmament, and the Communists wanted to prevent "imperialist" war against Germany, Morocco, China, and the Soviet Union. Henri Barbusse, author of the hugely popular antiwar novel Le Feu, tried to create a unified Left antiwar movement by means of

---

*At the end of World War I, the only radical Right group of any significance in France was Action Française, founded in 1898; its militant wing, the Camelots du Roi, was established in 1908.

the Republican Association of War Veterans (ARAC), Clarté, an international association of antiwar intellectuals, and committees to protest the
acts of reactionary regimes and provide aid to their victims and refugees.
Barbusse, however, was too closely associated with the PCF, although he
did not join the party until 1923, and these early front groups did not
become mass-based organizations.

A united Left probably could have won a majority in the elections of May
1924. The PCF wanted to form a Bloc Ouvrier et Paysan, a firm nationwide
proletariat alliance, without the Radical-Socialists, but the SFIO, fearing
the effects of such a close association, would agree only to activity in
selected locales. The PCF refused, and the Socialists and Radical-Socialists
formed the Cartel des Gauches, which won a plurality of votes, but not a
majority of seats. The Cartel government was one of exhausted slogans
(laicization), traditional nationalist acts (wars in Syria and Morocco), symbolic gestures (placing Jean Jaurès' ashes in the Panthéon), and ineffective
leadership. Financial problems remained unsolved.

The PCF separated itself further from the Cartel parties by finally
acceding to the Comintern's united front from below tactic. Albert Treint,
the party's leading figure then, explained that the era of "pacifistic democracy" had ended, Fascists and the bourgeoisie were forming a "class
bloc" against Communists, and social democracy was of the same nature
as Fascism, "a weapon in the bourgeoisie's battle against the proletariat."[4]
The *grande bourgeoisie,* as a result of the economic crisis, was openly
calling on the *petite bourgeoisie* to organize itself into Fascist leagues.
This improvised type of Fascism, Treint argued, would be much easier to
defeat than the spontaneous Italian variety.[5]

Fernand Loriot, the leading spokesman for the PCF's so-called "Right
Tendency," rejected Treint's analysis. Loriot argued that Fascism neither
had appeared in France nor would it in the foreseeable future. Reactionary
groups existed, but they had to be fought as reactionaries, by a united
front of "all the forces of the proletariat," organized from above and
below. Loriot also condemned the concept of "Social-Fascism."[6] Although
pitiless criticism was heaped on Loriot, PCF leaders continued to pursue a
modified united front from above: negotiating with SFIO leaders, with-
drawing weak Communist candidates from second-round election runoffs,
and proposing conditional accords for "determined goals (the fight against
fascism, for example)" when the Socialists were not part of a governing
coalition.[7]

In early 1928, though, the ECCI ordered the PCF to break radically with all Social Democrats and cease second-round withdrawals. This "class-against-class" turn, bitterly resisted by French Communists, cost the party and the Left dearly. The Right won control of the Chamber, and the SFIO Seine Federation declared war on the "cadres of the Communist Party."[8] PCF membership declined as the police began raiding its offices, arresting its leaders, and breaking up its demonstrations.

The efforts of Barbusse and Romain Rolland, however, preserved the shell of interparty anti-Fascism from the worst effects of the Comintern's Third Period. The two had quarreled in 1922 over Rolland's criticism of Bolshevism and his praise of Mohandas Gandhi,[9] but they had reconciled and, in 1926, founded the International Anti-Fascist Committee. Two years later, with the financial assistance of the Comintern, Barbusse began to publish *Monde*, the French organ of the International Union of Revolutionary Writers, promising to make it an "absolutely autonomous" journal, free from interparty polemics, filled with information, and dedicated to struggle.[10] Barbusse ignored the epithets of "deviationism" and "eclecticism" hurled by the ECCI and PCF,[11] and invited writers from all parts of the political and geographical landscape of Europe to provide extensive and intelligent coverage of political, social, economic, and cultural developments. According to Daniel Guérin, no friend of Moscow-backed initiatives, "the intellectuals of the Left were received at *Monde* without discrimination as long as their name and talent could enlarge the range of influence of Stalinism."[12] Barbusse even printed articles by ex-Communists, e.g., Angelo Tasca and Ignazio Silone. The evils of Fascism were exposed and the mistakes of anti-Fascists criticized. When, in 1932, the anti-Nazi tactics of the KPD came under attack, a French Communist called *Monde* a "camouflaged agency of social fascism."[13]

Barbusse intended to use *Monde* to build an international anti-Fascist movement. He wrote in the second issue: "The hour has arrived where we must envisage a grand demonstration, a solemn concentration of the forces opposed to fascism, by calling an international anti-fascist congress."[14] Organized by Münzenberg, the congress met in Berlin in March 1929, but was basically a gathering of Communist Party loyalists, and did not lead to any concrete achievements. French Socialists, at their national congress that year, criticized the Comintern's Third Period tactics, but offered no anti-Fascist strategy of their own. Those Leftists who called for unity lacked the influence to consummate it. Trotskyists demanded a united front of workers' parties based on daily struggles for specific demands,[15] while Albert Vassart, soon to be a member of the PCF Politburo and its Secretariat, suggested that the PCF should unite with the SFIO on concrete proposals for common action.[16]

While party leaders stood rigidly apart, the heightened presence of the French radical Right (enhanced by George Valois' Faisceau and Colonel Pierre de la Rocque's Croix de Feu) and the NSDAP victory in the September 1930 elections in Germany increased the militancy of young Leftists. Jacques Doriot, a rising Communist star, was growing restive with Moscow's directives; numerous *gauchiste* (revolutionary Left) groups and newspapers appeared; and Radical-Socialists such as Pierre Cot, Jean Zay, and Jacques Kayser tried to remake their party into a zealous protector of the French wage-earning class. Even France's greatest writer, André Gide, stirred: "The Spanish revolution [of 1931], the struggle of the Vatican against Fascism, the German financial crisis, and, above all, Russia's extraordinary effort . . . all this distracts me frightfully from literature."[17] Finally, the rank and file began to move on its own. Indications are that Communists broke ranks and voted for the strongest Left candidate in the second round of the 1932 elections,[18] and CGT and CGTU locals began working together against wage cuts and speedups.

Then, when a group of Socialists attended the Amsterdam Antiwar Congress and returned to organize a meeting in September to rally support for SFIO and CGT affiliation to the World Committee, Communist antipathy toward Social Democrats began to weaken.[19] Socialists also attended the anti-Fascist congress held the following year at the Salle Pleyel, and joined the World Committee of Struggle Against War and Fascism that resulted.

The SFIO, CGT, and Trotskyists, however, condemned these Communist fronts, and independent Leftists tried to find a third way, between a dying capitalism and a spent Marxism, to fight Fascism. One group formed around Emmanuel Mounier, the editor of *Esprit*, while another, La Troisième Force, was organized by other writers for that journal. Mounier tried to chart a course between dictatorship and bourgeois liberalism. He opposed all ideologies, believing instead in a personal revolution of the spirit and moral answers to political problems.[20] La Troisième Force tried to "rally the masses" to its "admirable ideal" of a decentralized, classless society "founded on the unique merit and value of human beings."[21] The Communists were not pleased by the competition, and

Commune, the organ of the Association of Revolutionary Writers and Artists, accused *Esprit* of being confusing, counterrevolutionary, and illusionist.[22] Marcel Martinet, a poet and pacifist, responded that the more Bolshevism became defined by the needs of the Soviet Union, the more indistinguishable it became from Fascism. The true anti-Fascist, he concluded, would soon have to defend people from Stalinist as well as Western Fascism.[23]

Still another third way was marked by Gaston Bergery, who had been one of the two French representatives on the International Committee of Jurists and Technical Experts assembled by Münzenberg to conduct the Reichstag fire countertrial. Victor Serge, who met Bergery in 1937, described him as "an elegant, pugnacious character with open but subtle features, and with talents equally appropriate, it seemed, either for mass agitation or a government position. He was also fond of rich living and quite evidently ambitious."[24] (Bergery would become Vichy France's ambassador to Russia and Turkey.)

Disgusted with the unending quarrels among Left parties, Bergery resigned from the Radical-Socialist Party and formed Front Commun, intended as an anti-Fascist movement of workers, cultivators, technicians, and the proletarianized elements of the middle class.[25] The group's first meeting, on May 26, 1933, was attended by representatives of the SFIO, the League of the Rights of Man, the Association of Revolutionary Writers and Artists, the League Against Anti-Semitism, and the PCF. Its manifesto made an appeal to every worker, woman, and young person in France to unify and avoid "the experience of our German comrades, whose fractions were crushed separately while they, continuing to fight among themselves, fell under the blows of a unified assassin."[26]

Concerned about the number of Communists and fellow travelers he had attracted, Bergery quickly and publicly separated his movement from the Amsterdam-Pleyel movement, and urged the PCF and SFIO to affiliate openly with Front Commun.[27] Barbusse responded that Front Commun was schismatic and divisive and that Bergery was blind to the link between anti-Fascism and revolution.[28] PCF leaders adamantly opposed Doriot's call for a united front from above, but individual Communists were allowed to join Front Commun and work with Socialists in factory action committees or local worker self-defense groups.[29] The SFIO refused to allow its members to join Front Commun or to participate with the CGT in a material and moral boycott of Germany.[30]

The Socialists' failure to find common ground with the Communists paralleled the loss of it with the Radical-Socialists. The Cartel des Gauches disintegrated when Socialists and Radical-Socialists could not agree on a fiscal program, and Socialist deputies voted against Prime Minister Edouard Daladier's proposal to cut the salaries of government employees by 6 percent. Two very short-lived ministries followed, and Daladier returned to power on January 29, 1934, just in time to face the shock waves from the Stavisky affair. Serge Stavisky, a third-rate swindler, had been accused of issuing fraudulent bonds secured by a municipal pawnshop in Bayonne. The Radical-Socialist ministry, worried by the number of connections Stavisky had with prominent government officials, did not order a full investigation. Stavisky committed suicide on January 3, and the official from the public prosecutor's office who was investigating the case was found dead under suspicious circumstances.

The Right and the Communists screamed cover-up and corruption. *Action Française* called for the fall of the government ("A Bas les Voleurs!") and street demonstrations against the Chamber of Deputies. *L'Humanité* featured equally clamorous headlines ("A Bas le Regime des Escrocs à la Staviski!"), but the PCF limited its direct action to a mass meeting at the Salle Bullier on January 16, and a demonstration in front of the Hôtel de Ville on January 22. Then, when Daladier removed the Right-inclined head of the Paris prefecture, Chiappe, and made him Governor-General of Morocco, both the radical Right and PCF exploded in anger.

The leagues planned a large anti-Parliament demonstration for February 6. The PCF called on workers to counterdemonstrate at their worksites, while its veterans' group demonstrated at the Rond Point des Champs Elysées (one-half mile from the Place de la Concorde where the National Veterans' Union would be demonstrating with the leagues). Communist-organized demonstators were told to demand dissolution of the Chamber and installation of a workers' and peasants' government.[31]

"On the morning of February 6," wrote Lucie Mazauric, "Paris was a dead city. . . . People awaited the worst, in silence."[32] At dusk, as the Chamber began to debate the Stavisky and Chiappe issues, a large crowd gathered in the Place de la Concorde. Although followers of the Right-wing leagues and Communist veterans were very much in evidence, thousands of the demonstrators were average Parisians angry with Parliament, parliamentarians, and ministers.[33] As the crowd grew in size, it became disorderly and tried to force its way across the Pont de la Concorde to the National Assembly building. The police fired, killing 20 and wounding 300. Hearing the shots, Léon Blum made an impassioned plea for a government of "Republican defense." His words were greeted with acclaim by the Socialists, the "icy silence" of the Communists, the timid approval of the Radical-Socialists, and the "howls" of the Right.[34]

Even though the leagues did not pursue or exploit the situation, Daladier resigned when the Chamber refused to vote him decree powers. Blum called for public demonstrations against the leagues, but SFIO secretary Paul Faure argued that the Socialists should examine events first. CGT leaders debated the wisdom of a counterdemonstration; they feared leaving the Right's challenge unanswered, feared stimulating united front talk by inviting the Communists, and feared what the Communists might do, on their own, if not invited.[35] Finally, the Confederal leaders' greatest fear, that the increasingly anxious and militant rank and file would act spontaneously and march without orders, pushed them to announce a general strike in the form of a march across Paris on February 12. The SFIO decided to join.

PCF leaders also floundered in indecision. During January, Doriot had argued for an anti-Fascist campaign based on occasional joint actions with Socialists. Thorez had repeatedly denounced him as a "Right Opportunist" who did not understand that the SFIO was part of the "fascization" process.[36] On February 1, Thorez had written that negotiating a united front of action with the SFIO "would represent the height of a pessimistic appreciation of the situation and scarcely conform to the reality of our revolutionary movement."[37] Finally, the Politburo decided that the Communists should organize their own demonstration on the night of February 9, but the leaders, to avoid arrest, should stay away from Paris that day. Doriot protested the decision and refused to leave; he marched at the head of the demonstrators from his commune, St.-Denis. The police responded brutally to the PCF protest, killing 4 demonstrators, injuring 250, and arresting 1,200.

Two days before, on February 7, Doriot and Henri Barbé had met with SFIO Leftists Marceau Pivert and Jean Zyromski and some Trotskyists, and they had agreed to establish local committees of vigilance and heighten their demands for working class unity.[38] When the Politburo decided to organize a second Communist demonstration for February 12, Doriot organized the St.-Denis Unity of Action Committee with Socialists, and refused direct PCF orders to dissolve it.[39]

The February 12 working-class demonstration affected French politics far more momentously than the leagues' demonstration of February 6 had. Two massive columns of people formed, one organized by the SFIO and CGT, the other by the PCF and CGTU. They converged from two directions on the Place de la Nation. When they met, remembered Mazauric, "there was a silence, a brief moment of anguish; then, to the astonishment of the party and trade union leaders, a delirious enthusiasm and an explosion of cries and joys reverberated along the entire line of both marches." Everyone began to chant: "Unity! Unity!"[40]

Major demonstrations occurred in all parts of France that day, but they were most spectacular in the cities where organized labor had a strong foothold: Bordeaux, Nantes, Toulouse, Marseille, Grenoble, Lille, and Mulhouse. Antoine Prost has demonstrated that there existed, in those cities, "a very close correspondence between the number of union members and the number of demonstrators." His conclusion is logical: in early 1934, it was not Left-wing unity but trade unionism that "constituted the nucleus of republican defense."[41]

On the surface of French politics, nothing seemed to have changed. The PCF and SFIO did not unite, Socialist ministers did not participate in the new government, and the new government failed to tackle the country's economic and social problems. On the Left, however, everything had changed. Workers had entered the political arena and intellectuals were prepared to unite with them. Barbusse responded first to the palpable sense that a new political era had dawned for France by announcing, on February 15, a *grand rassemblement national*—of workers, peasants, small businessmen, artisans, intellectuals, and veterans against the common enemy— Fascism—to be held in Paris in May.

On February 17, the Vigilance Committee of Anti-Fascist Intellectuals was formed, led by Alain (né Emile-Auguste Chartier, a philosopher close to the Radical-Socialists), Paul Rivet (an ethnologist and member of the SFIO), and Paul Langevin (a physicist on intimate terms with the PCF). Hundreds of writers and artists signed the manifesto, telling "all workers, our comrades, our resolution to fight with them to save from a fascist dictatorship the civil liberties and rights which the people have won."[42] The majority of the Vigilance Committee's members were teachers and professors. It drew together representatives of all the currents and tendencies on the French Left, based itself on provincial committees (to place intellectuals closer to the masses), and published a monthly newspaper, *Vigilance*, and many pamphlets (e.g., "The Monied Powers and the Riot of February 6," "The Social Pretensions of Fascism," and "Youth Confronts Fascism").

Not all Left-leaning French intellectuals were swept up by the enthusiasm. Simone de Beauvoir felt "such a stranger to all practical political activities that it never occurred to me that I might join them."[43] Emmanuel Mounier felt repelled by the era he saw dawning, one which would, he feared, be dominated by dangerous political myths. He wrote: "The grave event of this month of agitation is not the visible disorder, but the massive proliferation of the lie and the spiritual perils with which that lie will burden revolutionaries."[44]

Although PCF leaders echoed Barbusse's call for a *rassemblement national* and Léon Blum demanded his party issue an appeal to the "popular will" of the French people, neither party made an official move toward the other. Thorez was the main obstacle. He did not know what the ECCI wanted and he feared that Doriot, with his progress toward a united front from above, might replace him as party leader. In fact, the Comintern was unhappy with both men: Doriot was moving too independently and too fast; Thorez was not moving at all. They were summoned to Moscow on April 23, but Doriot, justifiably fearing he would be kept there, refused to leave Paris. Instead, he resigned as mayor of St.-Denis (to run for reelection on a platform critical of the PCF), and organized a unity of action meeting for April 26. It attracted many Socialists and, in the words of Guérin, "overflowed the borders of the 'red city' "—"for the first time, a voice of the Comintern spoke out for a united front, for *truth*."[45]

The Grand Rassemblement or National Anti-Fascist Assembly, as it was officially titled, met on May 20, attracting over 3,000 delegates, 90 percent of whom were Communists or fellow travelers. Thorez and Doriot clashed publicly. Thorez announced that the PCF was prepared to unite with the SFIO on "precise demands, precise modes, and precise action," but would not "allow to develop in our own ranks . . . a politics which, under the dissembling mask of the united front, begins by sowing disorganization and schism in the ranks of the Communist Party." Doriot, in turn, criticized party leaders for allowing so much time to elapse between February 6 and this meeting and taking control of it from local activists.

The delegates ignored the strafing, and voted a Charter of Unity, undoubtedly written by Barbusse, calling on all workers, veterans, artisans, small business people, farmers, students, women, intellectuals, immigrants, and colonials to form anti-Fascist committees in all parts of France, confront all Fascist activity, build a workers' self-defense force, and struggle against imperialist war.[46]

The Charter of Unity did not satisfy the Russians or meet their diplomatic needs. Litvinov and Barthou had met in Geneva on May 19 to negotiate a mutual assistance pact, and the PCF had still not laid the political foundation on which a stable and solid ally of the Soviet Union could be built. Instead, Thorez continued to drag his feet and criticize the Socialists, while Doriot criticized PCF leaders for dragging their feet. Once again, the ECCI "invited" Doriot to Moscow; once again he declined. Finally, on May 23, a *Pravda* article called on the world's Communist parties to make united front offers to their Social Democratic counterparts, and the ECCI ordered the PCF to approach the SFIO about a joint campaign on behalf of the imprisoned KPD leader Ernst Thälmann.

By coincidence, the SFIO Congress held its last session on May 23, and voted by a 2–1 margin against an anti-Fascist union based on Amsterdam-Pleyel, but to consider forming action committees with the Communists on the condition that both sides were equally represented.[47] The Socialists agreed to hold talks on the Thälmann campaign, but walked out when the Communists continued to attack them publicly. A furious and disgusted Dmitri Manuilsky then wrote a unity plan and sent it to Paris with orders for Thorez to announce it at the PCF national congress, scheduled for June 23.[48]

Thorez's opening speech at the Ivry Congress did not contain any conciliatory or inviting language, but the subsequent expulsion of Doriot and the arrival of a second strong telegram from Manuilsky instigated a very different closing speech. The Communists, Thorez said on the last day of the conference, wanted unity of action with the Socialists "at any price," unity between the CGT and CGTU, and, an unexpected twist added on his own initiative, inclusion of the middle classes in the fight against Fascism.[49] Blum expressed suspicion at this sudden turn, and the Trotskyists feared it presaged a party-controlled, nonrevolutionary anti-Fascist front.[50]

Impatient with the slow pace of the parties, the Vigilance Committee decided to organize, on July 14, "a popular Republican festival and assembly of all citizens on behalf of defense of democratic liberties, bread for workers, and peace."[51] Four days before the event, Blum wrote that the SFIO should initiate common actions against Fascism and war, and on Bastille Day, Thorez renounced all impediments to unity: "Everything is a matter of indifference to us as long as we are able to organize common action."[52]

The assembly attracted and excited hundreds of thousands of people, and on July 24, *Le Populaire* announced that the SFIO had accepted the PCF's proposal for a unified campaign against Fascism and war. The parties signed a Unity of Action Pact, which established a coordinating committee of fourteen, outlined an anti-Fascist campaign of meetings and counterdemonstrations, and called a halt to interparty polemics.[53] As the Trotskyists had feared, a party-based anti-Fascism had emerged, and they were not part of it.[54] They decided to join the SFIO—in what has been called the "French turn"—and work from within to create a unified, mass revolutionary party in France.*

Behaving as though a giant switch had been thrown, PCF spokespeople instantly jettisoned Third Period rhetoric, and stretched their new tactics of moderation and pragmatism to previously unthinkable limits. In August, Jacques Duclos spoke about bringing Radical-Socialist workers into the anti-Fascist front; Thorez proposed, on October 10, a vast *rassemblement populaire;* and two weeks later, Marcel Cachin urged the formation of a *front populaire.* When Prime Minister Doumergue responded with a series of radio addresses asking for increased powers and accusing the Communists and Socialists of fomenting civil war, the three Left parties accused him of attempting to alter the constitution and introduce a Fascistic government. They combined to topple his government, by a no-confidence vote, on November 8—the first political victory of a united French Left.[55]

One of the catalysts for this unity, however, fear of an impending war, also opened a divide among Leftists on the meaning of peace: to some, it meant no war, unless and except if certain conditions were met; to others, it meant no war ever. The Socialists were officially committed to disarmament and nationalization of the armaments industries and opposed to extension of the army term of service, while the Communists were mov-

---

*They proved to be a disruptive influence, and were expelled from the Young Socialists in June 1935 and from the SFIO in November of that year. They then split, those disowned by Trotsky forming the International Communist Party, those remaining loyal forming the Revolutionary Workers Party.

ing toward a national defense posture. But within the SFIO a gap was opening between Right and Left pacifist fractions on the one hand, and the "bellicistes" associated with Blum's traditional posture of republican defense and Jean Zyromski's class-oriented national defense. At the same time, a divide had opened between the PCF and the various anti-Fascist groups. In November, Front Commun merged with Troisième Force to form Front Social, which proclaimed itself utterly opposed to foreign alliances and national defense fronts.[56] The Vigilance Committee announced that "anti-fascism can never be the justification for any war."[57] And in December, the Russians did not send a representative to the Youth Congress organized by Amsterdam-Pleyel.[58]

This simmering issue reached a boiling point the following May, when Prime Minister Pierre Laval and Josef Stalin signed the Mutual Assistance Pact, and then issued a communiqué that made it sound like an updated version of the Franco-Russian Alliance of 1892: "The first duty which falls upon them is to permit no weakening of their respective national defenses. In this respect, Stalin understands and fully approves the policy of national defense pursued by France in order to maintain its armed forces at a level consistent with its security."[59]

This unambiguous Communist turn toward a national defense posture, coming directly after the PCF had joined with the SFIO to oppose an extension of the term of military service, raised a storm of protest on the Left. Blum claimed he was in a daze, that he could not understand how it was possible for the Soviet leaders to approve such a message.[60] Bergery called the communiqué "inadmissible" and the pact, with its threat of encircling Germany, a war danger.[61] The Trotskyists labeled it the death warrant of the Third International and accused Stalin of becoming a "socialist-patriot."[62] A gathering of gauchistes warned that only national revolutionary struggles, not imperialist wars, could defeat Fascism.[63] Only the Vigilance Committee refrained from polemics, and simply expressed its hope that the pact would serve as a preface to general European negotiations.[64] Finally, a small group within the PCF, Que Faire? called the pact "the clear and brutal disavowal of all politics followed by the Comintern and the French Communist Party since their origins."[65]

Momentum, however, fueled by the PCF's unprecedented successes in the October 1934 cantonal elections and the March 1935 municipal elections, and a direct order from Moscow in May, rushed the PCF past these outcries and to the door of the Radical-Socialists. Thorez told them on

May 31 that if they formed a government based on their traditional principles, which included national defense, the Communists would support it. Radical-Socialist leaders were in a mood to accept. The party had lost ground to the PCF and SFIO in the cantonal and municipal elections, and the rural sections were demanding action against the Right leagues and their armed combat groups.[66] SFIO leaders, however, still distrusted the Communists and did not appear eager to repeat their Cartel des Gauches experience. Even though a unity of action agreement had been reached by the Socialist and Communist youth organizations in March, Socialist party members were warned, at the Mulhouse Congress (June 9–12), that they could not "affiliate to any political formation whatsoever" without the consent of the Permanent Administrative Commission.[67]

When, however, Amsterdam-Pleyel suggested a *rassemblement populaire* for July 14, and Vigilance and the League of the Rights of Man approved, a Committee for a Rassemblement Populaire was quickly formed on June 17. Eighty-nine organizations, including all the major Left parties and trade unions, adhered and helped organize a massive demonstration for "bread, peace, and liberty."[68] The excitement generated by the hundreds of thousands of demonstrators on Bastille Day, and the news of the Seventh Comintern Congress' approval of a people's front, swept away the last impediments blocking a meaningful PCF-SFIO alliance.

On September 17, the CGT and CGTU announced their merger, and six days later, the PCF and SFIO signed a Platform of Common Action. The platform was not simply a codicil to the 1934 Unity Pact, but the embryo of a future electoral program. It accused the Laval government of failing "to defend the daily bread of workers," "alleviate unemployment," "defend peace," or "safeguard liberty." The two parties pledged to build "a large popular movement" which would alter the political situation and government policy.[69] Almost simultaneously, the organizers of the July 14 demonstration, the Committee for a Rassemblement Populaire announced it would continue to function, as a builder of popular support for the party alliance (Front Populaire) that was taking shape.

The spirit of unity infected the entire Left during the summer of 1935. Left-wing students from the Latin Quarter, exhilarated by their work in the municipal elections and their counterdemonstrations against Action Française, formed the University Anti-Fascist Front in May.[70] A Congress for the Defense of Culture attracted thousands of intellectuals to Paris in June, and led to the formation of an International Association of Writers for the Defense of Culture. And immigrant Jews organized, that autumn, the Popular Jewish Movement to fight Nazism and defend the interests of Jews in all countries.[71]

A few voices tried to make themselves heard above the roar of the flood, warning of Russian and Communist perfidiousness. At the Defense of Culture Congress, Magdeleine Paz and Gaetano Salvemini tried to raise the issue of Victor Serge, a writer and former Comintern employee, imprisoned in Moscow because of his criticism of Stalin.* Jean Guéhenno resigned from the editorial board of *Europe* because, he charged, the PCF had taken control and was trying "to establish its power and force intellectuals to submit to party discipline."[72] And Emmanuel Mounier wrote: "The fact that it is possible for people who cannot possibly be categorized as dupes . . . to perform, in the space of a few weeks, such an about face, provides us with firm ground for being suspicious of them."[73]

The large number of Left intellectuals who were partisans of the budding Front Populaire gathered around *Vendredi*, which appeared in November 1935. For them, it "signified the intelligentsia in action; literature engaged; journalism brought to a work of art and struggle."[74] André Chamson, with financing from an anonymous Radical-Socialist, started it; he coedited it with Guéhenno, an ardent supporter of Léon Blum, and Andrée Viollis, who was on friendly terms with the Communists.[75] It announced itself as a medium through which writers of all views could communicate with other writers and thereby build a "broad literary front" to save France from the fate of Italy and Germany.[76] It became a passionate supporter of the Popular Front, indeed its main one, since *Monde* and *Front Mondial* did not long survive the death of Barbusse (in September 1935).

The Front Populaire, to which *Vendredi* pledged its loyalty, had come into existence only a month before the journal. Thorez, for once moving well ahead of the ECCI, decided to travel to Nantes, the site of the Radical-Socialist Congress, and invite the party to join an electoral alliance with the PCF and SFIO. Togliatti and Gottwald were sent to dissuade him, but Thorez refused to listen, and the Radical-Socialists assented to his proposal.[77]

*Gide tried to smooth over matters at the congress, but afterwards he warned the Soviet ambassador to France that the Serge affair was creating a terrible impression among non-Communist Leftists and intellectuals. Rolland personally intervened with Stalin to secure Serge's release.

As a result of that agreement, anti-Fascism in France now focused almost completely on the national elections, scheduled for April and May. On January 11, the Committee for a Rassemblement Populaire published the Left's platform—a farrago of vague promises and vast undertakings, promising "to defend democratic liberties, to give bread to workers, employment to the young, and human peace to the world." The "defense of liberty" section presented the most coherent, realistic, and attainable set of goals: amnesty for political prisoners, disarming and dissolving the leagues, ending political corruption, increasing freedom of the press, defending labor union rights, reforming public education, and investigating conditions in the colonies. The economic sections contained a French version of the American New Deal, but no plans for restructuring the economy and neutralizing the Senate, and no details of tax reform and capital export controls. Clearly, the SFIO had surrendered the most—its traditional demands for central planning and nationalization of industry. In compensation, the "defense of peace" section was dominated by Socialist themes: mobilization of the people against war, reliance on the League of Nations, disarmament, nationalization of armaments industries, and regional security networks.[78]

The platform could not and did not please everyone, but its very existence symbolized the culmination of the wave of Left popular sentiment that had burst forth in February 1934. Claude Jamet called it "a movement without precedent in our history"—one that would prevent Fascism from coming to power.[79] Simone de Beauvoir, Jean-Paul Sartre, and their friends relied on it "to save the peace abroad and to lend cohesion at home to a movement which would one day lead to true socialism."[80] All its supporters spoke of "hope": Rivet of an "immense espoir" and Bergery of a "grand espoir."[81]

The gauchistes, however, called the Popular Front a delusion. They placed their faith not on elections but on the revolutionary possibilities generated by a two-year wave of worker militancy: the February 12, 1934, antileague demonstration; the march of February 10, 1935, to commemorate those who had fallen the year before; the rassemblement populaire of July 14, 1935; the strikes of the Brest and Toulon munitions workers in August 1935; and the massive outpouring for Barbusse's funeral on September 7. This loose collection of Pivertists (the gauche révolutionnaire faction in the SFIO), anarchists, Trotskyists, revolutionary syndicalists (represented by La Révolution Prolétarienne), and the schoolteachers grouped around *L'Ecole Emancipée* failed to convince French workers that the Popular Front was not the answer, that only the overthrow of capitalism could defeat Fascism, and that only a mass general strike could prevent war.

The radical Right responded to the new Left alliance with intensified vituperation. A torrent of anti-Semitic abuse poured from the Right's presses, Camelots du Roi and Croix de Feu gangs increased their violence, and on February 13, a mob of leaguers severely beat Léon Blum.

Each Front Populaire party campaigned on its own platform for the first round of voting (April 26), attacking only the "candidates of reaction," not each other. The PCF's campaign was the most colorful; the Communists made lavish use of posters bearing patriotic slogans ("For a France free, strong, and prosperous") and patriotic symbols (Joan of Arc). "Moscow themes and Moscow terminology were carefully excluded from them; they breathed, if anything, the romantic revolutionary spirit of Paris, with reminiscences of the Great French Revolution, 1848, and all that. (Even the Commune was put aside as something suspect in the eyes of the bourgeoisie.)"[82]

Eighty-five percent of the electorate voted; they cast 5,628,921 votes for candidates endorsing the Front Populaire, and provided the most precise measure of anti-Fascist sentiment that the interwar period witnessed. The Popular Front parties won 378 of the 598 electoral districts in metropolitan France, although the actual shift in voting percentage from Right to Left was small—about 3 percent. The actual closeness of the individual contests, and the decisive impact of the Popular Front's agreement to withdraw weak candidates on the second round, was indicated by the large number of runoff elections—424. The PCF enjoyed the largest percentage gain, jumping from 10 to 72 seats, while the SFIO, with 146 seats (up from 97), became the largest party in the Chamber. Radical-Socialists lost 43 of the 159 seats they had won in 1932, the moderate Right lost 44, and the Right maintained its 138 seats.[83] "We laughed, we were happy, we dreamed, we hoped," Lucie Mazauric remembered; it was "the last happy spring of my life," wrote Ehrenburg; and it opened, for Jean-Louis Barrault, the "years of light" and made Paris the "spiritual capital of the world."[84]

The *gauchistes*, however, saw only a set of numbers and a future of class collaboration.[85] To offset what he viewed as the Popular Front's stifling legalistic posture, Marceau Pivert tried to mobilize worker demonstrations demanding that the new Popular Front government take office immediately (May 4), and not wait the customary one month. Blum, the designated Prime Minister, ignored Pivert. Blum also seemed relieved when the PCF Politburo, fearing to become the prisoner of a ministry it did not control, voted against participating in the new cabinet. All of Blum's careful preparations for a peaceful transition of power, however, were swept aside by a massive burst of worker discontent that erupted two days after he assumed power.

Nearly two million workers struck. "Paris was unrecognizable," wrote Ehrenburg. "Red flags fluttered over the grey houses. Everywhere floated the sound of the Internationale or the Carmagnole."[86] The strikes were largely the spontaneous response of workers to the election results, which provided them with the most favorable set of political conditions they had enjoyed since the end of the war.[87] The strikes were not directed against the Blum government and their intent was not revolutionary; the workers wanted immediate wage raises, a forty-hour week, paid vacations, and collective bargaining rights.

Only the *gauchistes* welcomed the outburst. Popular Front leaders saw in the form of the movement (occupation of factories), its extent (aviation, auto, machine shops, chemical works, textile factories, and department stores), and the strikers' determination the beginning of a social revolution. Pivert, with the slogan "Les Soviets partout," and the revolutionary syndicalists, with their calls for a workers' front, failed, however, to transform this mass movement into a massive revolution.

The CGT, Blum, and the PCF, all of whom wanted the strikes to end quickly, had far more leverage. CGT leaders refused to coordinate, direct, or expand the strikes. Blum immediately summoned labor leaders and employers to his official residence, the Hôtel Matignon, and extracted an agreement from them in three days. On June 9, it was announced that workers would receive a pay raise averaging 12 percent, paid vacations, a forty-hour week, and recognition of their collective bargaining rights. In addition, Blum announced, the armaments industries would be nationalized and the government would gain control of the Bank of France. The accord did not satisfy most of the workers, and the return to work proceeded slowly. It required a speech by Thorez to the most militant strikers, the Paris metalworkers, to blunt the strike's edge. Worried that the work stoppage and threat of disorder would alienate the Radical-Socialists, Thorez said on June 11: "Though it is important to lead a movement of change well, it is also necessary to know how to terminate it." All was not yet possible, he concluded, and the *gauchiste* tendencies inside and outside the party had to be combatted.[88] Marcel Gitton, several weeks later, cautioned those strikers slow to return to work that they must allow the Popular Front to pursue its goals in an "orderly, calm, and disciplined way."[89]

The Matignon Accord did not please employers either. They launched an immediate counteroffensive against its provisions. Although the massive strike wave receded in July, strikes continued throughout the summer, averaging twice as many strikers as the previous year. Not only did the nature of the strike settlement weaken popular support for the Popular Front government, the entire strike situation displeased its member parties. The Radical-Socialists disliked the continuing instability, the PCF its lack of control over the workers, and the SFIO ministers the sizable pledges it prematurely had to make.

Blum's foreign policy further eroded popular support and the links between the parties of the Left. The "exercise of power" made Blum exceedingly cautious and transformed him from an idealist to a pragmatist, one who readily understood that France could not afford to act counter to British desires and that a Popular Front government could not, without provoking potentially serious domestic political repurcussions, become the moral leader of European anti-Fascism. His first major diplomatic decision, terminating sanctions against Italy, did not arouse hostility from the Right, Center, or Left; Abyssinia was conquered, and both Britain and the Soviet Union saw no need to maintain an empty gesture. The Spanish Civil War, however, which began on July 18, divided French public opinion and France's two main allies. At first, Blum chose to provide matériel aid to the Spanish Popular Front government, and the Committee for a Rassemblement Populaire created a Commission of Solidarity to Aid the Spanish People. But in August, Blum reversed himself and opted for nonintervention because he did not want to distance France from Great Britain, alienate powerful Radical-Socialists from the Popular Front, or goad the radical Right into violence.

These compelling reasons of state and realpolitik did not impress those who had worked and voted for the Popular Front. They were strongly anti-Fascist and pro-Loyalist. And, as two huge public meetings in September proved, they were torn between their desire to supply arms to Spain and the fear that such provision might mean war. On September 3,

Dolores Ibarruri ("La Pasionaria"), a Spanish Communist Party leader and a deputy in the Cortes, addressed a fervent pro-Loyalist meeting at the Vélodrome d'Hiver, which ended with the audience shouting "Airplanes for Spain! Airplanes for Spain!"[90] Three days later, Blum told another vociferous audience: "It is impossible for me to act other than I did without opening in Europe a crisis whose consequences would be difficult or, unfortunately, all too easy to predict."[91] His listeners knew he meant war, and "the clamor for 'airplanes for Spain' subsided very noticeably."[92]

Blum's support of nonintervention divided Popular Front groups as well. The League of the Rights of Man, Front Social, and Vigilance supported him. Chamson and Guéhenno of *Vendredi* hoped for a peaceful solution to the Spanish war, while Jean-Richard Bloch wrote that "neutrality in the face of this drama is inconceivable."[93] The *gauchistes* in the SFIO also split, with Pivert supporting Blum and Jean Zyromski forming a Committee of Socialist Action for Spain. Finally, CGT secretary Léon Jouhaux spoke against neutrality, but most of the Confederal Committee preferred to tighten the nonintervention mechanism.[94] The following year, Pivert and Vigilance reversed their positions.

The question of arms for Spain also widened a growing gap between the PCF and the government. Communist grass-roots activity had been especially energetic that summer. Communist membership had crept ahead of Socialist enrollment in May (131,000 to 127,000),[95] the PCF had renewed its open campaign to control French workers, and party members had begun building local action committees. Communists joined the many new front groups in support of the Spanish Loyalists, Amsterdam-Pleyel once again became a party favorite,[96] and Thorez demanded, at a public meeting on August 25, that the Spanish government "be free to purchase unlimited quantities of airplanes, cannons, and munitions."[97] "Patiently, quarter by quarter, we created defense committees for the control of municipal activity," wrote Charles Tillon, and after October 1936, "the recruitment of volunteers for the International Brigades solidified the Party's grip on the neighborhoods, worksites, and labor unions."[98] Duclos appealed to the workers to block attempts to aid the Spanish rebels, and Thorez made his most extreme pitch for national defense—a French Front composed of patriots of the Left and Right.

This independent Communist activity, news of the Moscow trials, and reports of Communist activity in Spain awakened strong doubts about

PCF fidelity to the Popular Front. Jamet called the French Front proposal a sacred union against Hitler for the benefit of the Soviet Union, resigned from the PCF, and joined the SFIO, "the party of Blum and peace."[99] Paul Faure accused the Communists of weakening the Blum government and strengthening Fascism.[100] A *gauchiste* accused the PCF of playing its old trick, using front groups "to maneuver, to use, to break obligations, and to disguise its intentions."[101] CGT Communists were accused by their non-Communist counterparts of fomenting disorder.[102] The Radical-Socialists feared that the PCF was trying to precipitate a confrontation between France and Germany.[103]

More latent fissures within the Popular Front were exposed when André Gide broke with the Communists. His support of the Russian Revolution had made him, since the early thirties, a much sought after figurehead for Communist fronts. He responded to many of the invitations, presiding over meetings of the Association of Revolutionary Artists and Writers, codirecting (with Barbusse and Rolland) *Commune*, joining the editorial board of *Regards*, going to Berlin with Malraux to protest the Dimitrov trial, speaking at writers' congresses, and supporting the campaign to free Ernst Thälmann from a Nazi prison. But he refused to become a member of any organization, because, as he wrote in December 1932: "I believe that my assistance . . . can be much more profitable to your (our) cause if I bring it freely and from a *non*-enrolled position."[104]

Hoping to associate him even more closely with their cause, the Russians invited him to visit the USSR. He left France on June 17, 1936, with five other writers. Following his return on August 22, he wrote his English friend Dorothy Bussy: "What an extraordinary trip! And what an extraordinary lesson. I need some time to let the experience ferment and to consider what I should say about it."[105] Before he began to write, however, he read transcripts of the Moscow trials (prepared by Trotskyists) "with an inexpressible discomfort. What is one to make of these 16 defendants accusing themselves, in almost the exact same terms, and celebrating a regime and a man they had risked their lives to overthrow?"[106]

The manuscript Gide wrote reflected his hopes for and doubts about the Soviet Union. Few who read it disagreed with the balanced critique Gide presented; almost all, however, argued that it would be wrong to publish it at this time, when the Soviet Union was the sole supporter of the Spanish Republic. Gide, who believed that truth could not harm the revolutionary enterprise, offered the foreword to *Vendredi*, which printed it on November 6. Accusations of poor timing rained on him, but he did not bow before the storm. In fact, as his letters indicate, his attitude toward Soviet Communism was becoming increasingly negative.

When Gallimard published *Retour de l'URSS* in January, the small book (ninety-two pages) provoked a large commotion. *Retour* was by no means a devastating assault; it simply indicated that Russia was not a workers' paradise, but that it was trying to become one. His toughest words concerned the atmosphere of conformity he perceived wherever he traveled: "I doubt that in any country today, even Hitler's Germany, is there a spirit less free, more curbed, more fearful (terrorized), or more vassal-like."[107] Though he paid homage to Soviet aid for Spain and the prodigious accomplishments of the Soviet Union, and acknowledged the political capital opponents of Communism would reap from the book, he forthrightly stated his concern that Russian errors were having a harmful effect on the causes of humanity and international Socialism.[108]

Communist response was critical, but not polemical. A non-Communist, Romain Rolland, wrote the harshest words, calling the book bad, superficial, childish, and contradictory.[109] No one read Gide out of the movement, and his name remained on the masthead of *Commune*. (Though Arosev, the Narkomindel official who had arranged Gide's visit—and committed who knows how many other errors—was not as fortunate. He was arrested later that year and shot.)[110]

Gide, however, was angry with the efforts to silence his criticism, and furious with the editors of *Vendredi* for trying too hard to placate Communist opinion, tying the revolutionary cause too tightly to the Soviet Union, and straddling the issue of the purge trials.[111] He expressed his anger in a second small book, *Retouches à Mon Retour de l'URSS*, which was, he told friends, "much better documented" and "better motivated" than the first.[112] In *Retouches* Gide accused the Soviet Union of betraying the ideals of the revolution, turning its back on Socialism, exploiting its workers, and eliminating freedom of thought. He condemned the Russians for betraying the hopes of their supporters, non-Russian Communists for deceiving the workers they pretended to serve, and intellectuals who hid their doubts behind a screen of dialectical reasoning. Communists and fellow travelers denounced Gide in their publications and publicly attacked him at the Congress for the Defense of Culture, which met in Spain and France during the summer of 1937. *Vendredi* never recovered. "It was," wrote Chamson, "the beginning of the troubles that killed our journal"; circulation dropped 33 percent at once, and declined steadily thereafter.[113]

Gide's critique and *Vendredi's* demise reflected the failure of the Popular Front to live up to expectations. The Radical-Socialists, at their October 1936 congress, expressed displeasure with the ongoing strikes and demonstrations. PCF deputies, in December, abstained from a vote of confidence on Blum's foreign policy, and, in February, attacked Blum for declaring a "pause" in the enactment of further economic and social reforms.[114] The Popular Front's non-Communist supporters were alienated by the Moscow trials and the news of Communist behavior in Spain.

A radical Right demonstration in March 1937 nearly destroyed the increasingly fragile Left coalition. Although the leagues had been dissolved by law, on June 19, 1936, the two largest had transformed themselves into "political parties"—the Croix de Feu had become the Parti Socialiste Français, and Doriot's increasingly Fascist-inclined followers the Parti Populaire Français. The Parti Socialiste, with the backing of the Right-wing press, started to hold meetings in working-class neighborhoods, provoking counterdemonstrations and strikes from workers angry with employers and government ministers. Serious Right-Left clashes occurred throughout the autumn and winter.

When Colonel de la Rocque announced he would appear at a Parti Socialiste meeting in Clichy on March 16, the Socialist mayor and Communist deputy mayor of that commune appealed to Blum and Marx Dormoy, the Minister of the Interior, to prohibit the gathering. The government refused, because the Parti Socialiste had not broken any laws, but it did mobilize the arrondissement's emergency police force to prevent a clash between the demonstrators and the counterdemonstrators organized by Clichy's Popular Front committees. The demonstrators departed quickly in the face of the massed workers, but the poorly prepared and led police panicked and fired, killing 5 counterdemonstrators and wounding over 200.

L'Humanité called it "A Conspiracy Against the People" by the very government they had elected to protect them; *Le Populaire* blamed the leagues and urged calm; and *L'Oeuvre*, a Radical-Socialist newspaper, seemed more concerned with the leagues' continued freedom of assembly than the dead and wounded Popular Front supporters. The Committee for a Rassemblement Populaire, anxious to maintain unity, issued a resolution on March 18, placing its "entire confidence in the Popular Front government's ability to establish responsibility and impose the necessary sanctions," and affirming "the indisoluble solidarity of the Popular Front and its will to fight Fascism."[115]

The PCF organized a half-day general strike–funeral procession on March 18. Over 200,000 people marched. Although Blum ordered an investigation, proclaimed the firmness of the Popular Front, and easily survived the Right's interpellations in the Chamber, observers recognized that Clichy had been a watershed event. Juliusz Łukasiewicz, the Polish ambassador to France, reported to Warsaw that the "events of March 16 constitute a new stage in the Socialists' evolution toward resisting the Communist Party. . . . The quiet showdown between the Socialists and the Communists, which has been in the making for several months, thus is gaining in intensity."[116] And Henri Noguères, a leader of the student Left, wrote later: "Something had definitely been broken. Militants never again recaptured, for any march in the streets of Paris, the spirit which, on numerous occasions over a long period of time, had animated them."[117]

In fact, there was one more huge demonstration three months later, but it symbolized ends rather than continuations or beginnings. Two hundred thousand mourners followed the caskets of the founder of Justice and Liberty, Carlo Rosselli, and his brother Nello, to Père Lachaise Cemetery in mid-June. The two had been assassinated outside the Normandy town of Bagnoles-de-l'Orne. Most newspapers treated it simply as a police matter and hinted that anarchists might have committed the crime, but the newspapers of the Popular Front parties all gave the story front-page treatment for a full week. L'Humanité accused "Mussolini's Fascist police" of the deed. Le Populaire called it a "Fascist Crime"; and L'Oeuvre termed it a "Fascist Attack." Only the fiercely independent, but tiny, Nouvel âge outrightly charged Mussolini with complicity and the Blum government with a cover-up.[118*]

In actuality, the Blum government did not pay much attention to the assassinations, and the Popular Front newspapers soon lost interest in the investigation. Their attention was focused on Parliament, where Blum's

---

*Eventually the truth emerged. The Mussolini regime was angry with Carlo Rosselli's constant attacks against the Fascist regime, and Foreign Minister Ciano ordered the Military Intelligence Service to eliminate the brothers. The service approached a new French radical Right terrorist group—the Secret Committee for Revolutionary Action or Cagoule—and paid it 100 carbines to commit the crime. Charles F. Delzell, *Mussolini's Enemies: The Italian Anti-Fascist Resistance*, (New York: Fertig, 1974), pp. 158–160; J.-R. Tournoux, *L'Histoire Secrète . . .* (Paris: Plon, 1962), p. 60.

effort to secure plenary powers to halt the flight of capital from France was approved twice by the Chamber of Deputies and rejected twice by the Senate (led by conservative Radical-Socialists). Even though the Communists had offered in early June "to take all necessary responsibilities in a government strengthened and reshaped in the image of the Popular Front,"[119] Blum decided to resign. When he told the SFIO of his decision on June 22, Pivert pleaded with him to remain in power and force a Senate reversal by means of street demonstrations. Fearing a second Clichy, Blum rejected the idea, but Pivert proceeded on his own.[120] The pitched battle between the SFIO's Seine Federation and the gardes mobiles did not affect Blum's decision, nor prevent him from joining the new government organized by Camille Chautemps. The Communists also supported the Radical-Socialist Prime Minister. But, wrote Lucie Mazauric, "no one was deceived. The Front was broken."[121]

Groups supporting the Popular Front also began to crumble. Jewish anti-Fascist and self-protection groups died quietly in June, marking the end of active Jewish protests in Paris.[122] Seven members of the Executive Committee of the League of the Rights of Man resigned when its journal refused to print an article criticizing the Moscow trials.[123] And within Socialist ranks, Pivert was threatened with expulsion unless he dissolved his faction. He complied, but simply founded a new journal, Les Cahiers Rouge, and cosponsored with Zyromski a motion opposing Socialist participation in the Chautemps government that almost succeeded at the July congress. During the last three months of the year, Gide and the editors of Vendredi quarreled publicly over Vendredi's refusal to publish a letter from Gide and four other writers demanding a fair trial for the Spanish Popular Front's political prisoners. The exchange of recriminations culminated with Gide accusing the newspaper of no longer acting as a free agent and Guéhenno telling Gide: "You are not the Popular Front, André Gide! Why should we have to take up all your quarrels?"[124]

As the Left faltered, Right-wing anti-Semitism and terrorism increased. Several new propaganda organizations, funded by the German-based World Center for the Struggle Against Jewry in Europe, flooded France with copies of the Protocols of the Elders of Zion and Nazi pamphlets. Gringoire and Candide heightened the pitch of their racial abuse,[125] and the Cagoulards broadened the scope of their terrorist activity. Right-wing racial invective increased in November, as German Jews flowed into France to escape the horrors of Kristallnacht. The Popular Front and Popular Front groups did not directly confront this tide of anti-Semitism, partly because it was considered a small symptom of the larger anti-Fascist illness and partly because French workers disliked the competition from immigrant Jewish workers.

In fact, by the end of 1937, there was little in France that pleased French workers. Employers were refusing to bargain, compromise, or arbitrate, the Chautemps government was not enforcing the forty-hour week, and when strikers in Colombes occupied a factory during a strike, the gardes mobiles was sent in to evict them. The *gauchistes* and Communists increased their agitation among the workers, and the strikers' index began to climb: from an average of 10,000 a month between June 1937 and February 1938, to 65,000 in March and 150,000 in April.[126]

No formula could be found to hold together the Popular Front. The editors of *Vendredi* wrote in January 1938: "We no longer recognize our face in any of the fragments of the broken mirror."[127] Chautemps wanted to govern without PCF support, but found that the Socialists would not participate in such a ministry. Blum tried to form a broad-based government of national union, but the conservative Radical-Socialists refused in December, and the Right rejected the idea in March. Finally, when the SFIO National Council rejected Socialist participation in another Radical-Socialist cabinet, Blum established, in April 1938, his second ministry. It lasted less than a month, once again falling before the refusal of the Senate to approve extraordinary financial powers.

The story of anti-Fascism in France, from the fall of the second Blum government in early April to the start of World War II, is one of entropy. PCF policy fluctuated wildly, as party leaders tried to maintain the mass base accumulated in 1936 and 1937. But membership numbers, sales of *L'Humanité*, and election vote totals were declining, serious cracks had appeared in the CGT, the local action committees had no impact on the Daladier government, and relations with the SFIO remained tenuous.[128] Communist leaders supported the Radical-Socialist government of Daladier in April and opposed it in September; criticized Blum's governing policies but campaigned for closer links with the SFIO; curbed the April strikes, then promoted a general strike in November. Thorez, however, was constant on one point—he consistently spoke of the need to maintain the Popular Front. The Communists were caught in a bind: they could not find a way to work within the Popular Front, and feared having to find their way outside it.

The SFIO, for its part, began to dismember itself. Pivert was suspended and the Pivertist-dominated Seine Federation was dissolved in the spring of 1938. They formed the Workers' and Peasants' Socialist Party, rejected proposals to help rebuild the Popular Front, and attracted many members from the divided Trotskyist movement.

Disagreement and dispute over Czechoslovakia and the Munich Conference completed the wreckage of anti-Fascism in France. Even though an international, multiparty assemblage of over 1,000 delegates had gathered in Paris on July 23 for a World Conference Against the Bombardment of Open Towns and for Action on Behalf of Peace, only the Communists spoke strongly on behalf of military defense of Czechoslovakia. Workers failed to respond, a bitterly divided CGT remained inactive, the SFIO rejected a PCF proposal for common action, and Blum gave a delegation from the British Labour Party a dispiriting account of the defeatism within SFIO ranks.[129]

With the specter of the German military buildup and Hitler's aggressive words and deeds looming over them, their society divided, and their economy stagnating, the vast majority of French people received the news of the Munich settlement with joy and relief. On the Left side of the Chamber of Deputies, only the Communists voted against it, but Earl Browder, the general secretary of the American Communist Party, who was in Paris that September, claims that French Communists actually shared the national rejoicing over Munich, and that the negative vote was in response to a direct order from Moscow.[130]

Reactions and responses were mixed in most segments of the anti-Fascist movement. The League of the Rights of Man issued a manifesto cheering the result "insofar as it brings deliverance to an anguished humanity," but refused "to see in it a victory and a promise of peace for the future."[131] The CGT Confederal Committee voted "a white and black resolution, a true hodge-podge of general formulas, of hopeless banalities . . . the most complete confusion."[132] Since *Vigilance*, now entitled *Informations*, had renounced politics and *Vendredi* was nearly moribund, Langevin, Victor Basch, and Albert Bayet tried, and failed, to rally anti-Munich intellectuals to a new organization, Peace and Democracy.[133]

At their national congress in October, the Radical-Socialists delivered more bad news: they formally severed their ties with the PCF and resigned from the Committee for a Rassemblement Populaire. Then in November, Prime Minister Daladier used the decree powers that had been voted in early October to increase taxes, devalue the franc, scrap the public works program, abolish the five-day week, mandate compulsory overtime, and terminate one million public employees. He was determined to strengthen France by increasing production and was convinced that he could easily break the strike he knew his measures would provoke.[134]

A divided CGT hesitated to call a strike, but thousands of workers in the Nord and Seine departments launched wildcat actions. The Confederal Committee decided to organize a twenty-four-hour general work stoppage on November 30, 1938, but took steps to insure that it would not be seen as a direct challenge to the government. No factories would be occupied, no essential services would be interrupted, and work would be promptly resumed on December 1. Most Confederal leaders and many members of the Committee for a Rassemblement Populaire hoped that a compromise could be negotiated.[135] Daladier, instead, took full advantage of the delay, drafted railroad and public service workers, stationed army troops at key places in Paris, and threatened to dismiss any government worker who struck. Less than two million workers (or one-half the CGT's members) heeded the call on November 30, with the Communist-dominated federations displaying the best turnouts.[136] Many strikers were arrested. In the weeks that followed, a "deliberate, systematic, and pitiless repression hit all the workers who had struck, and permanently decapitated the trade union movement. . . . For the government and the employers, henceforth, there was no social problem."[137] Workers resigned from the CGT in droves. Sherry Mangan, a visiting American poet, noted that the effects of the defeat remained clearly visible five months later: "The too often betrayed French workers . . . cannot yet regain their courage or their faith."[138] Daladier applied the coup de grâce in December—he reconstituted the Bloc National.

Only Thorez seemed to think that a Front Populaire still existed. Despite its stumblings, despite the blows inflicted on it, he told Algerians in February 1939, "It lives and it will triumph."[139] The party continued to organize meetings to enlarge the Popular Front's scope, but only a few non-Communists could be enticed to speak at them.[140]

The fall of Barcelona in January 1939, Germany's seizure of the remainder of Czechoslovakia in March, and Italy's invasion of Albania in April brought the threat of war closer and further divided the Left over the question of peace. The PCF and Blum advocated a peace front with the

Soviet Union, the Pivertists and Trotskyists called for a general strike to prevent war, and Paul Faure and the schoolteachers' union urged the French to be pacifistic. By August, the French in general and French anti-Fascists in particular had become observers rather than participants. At what would be the final meeting of the Committee for a Rassemblement Populaire on August 18, the participants overwhelmingly defeated a Communist proposal to organize actions against Daladier's decree laws.[141]

Most eyes were turned toward Moscow, the site of alliance talks between Britain, France, and the Soviet Union. When, instead, the news broke that German Foreign Minister Ribbentrop was en route to Moscow to sign a Nonaggression Treaty, *L'Humanité* proclaimed it the cornerstone of collective security for peace in Europe and called on Paris and London "to complete and reinforce the framework of security by concluding, without further delay, an Anglo-French-Soviet alliance."[142]

Few other Leftists found comfort in the newly signed treaty. Blum called it "an extraordinary event, almost unbelievable, and one staggers from the impact of it."[143] The Union of French Intellectuals, which included many Communists, condemned the pact.[144] The Pivertists called Stalin a warmonger who had opened the door to Hitlerian aggression and paved the way for "a bloodbath of all the peoples of Europe."[145] Simone de Beauvoir probably spoke for the majority of unaligned anti-Fascists when she wrote, "Night was falling over the earth and entering our very bones."[146]

Many Communists were equally stunned by the news but felt reassured when the party Central Committee stated on August 25:

The group of Communist deputies has proclaimed unanimously the unshaken resolution of all Communists to place themselves in the first rank of resistance to the aggression of Hitlerian fascism, and for the defense of freedom. In the face of the insolent aggression of Hitlerian fascism, against which they were and remain far-seeing and resolute adversaries, the Communists will stand as the best defenders of democracy and independence.[147]

One week later, PCF deputies voted for the war credits requested by Daladier.

On September 20, however, three days after news arrived of the Soviet invasion of Poland and the existence of an Added Secret Protocol to the German-Soviet pact, *L'Humanité* announced that Communists would not be part of a national defense effort on behalf of what was now an imperialist war. The PCF paid dearly for its fealty to Moscow. The CGT excluded

Communists from all Confereral offices, and the Daladier government dissolved the PCF and all organizations linked to it or led by Communists (including trade unions), proscribed its publications, arrested some leaders and drafted others. Thorez deserted his army unit and made his way to Moscow, where he would spend the war; Duclos fled to Brussels; hundreds left the party. Those who remained hastily reformed themselves into the French Peasant and Worker Group.

The choices facing anti-Fascists were grim. The isolated but sincere Communist anti-Fascist had, according to Tillon, "a choice between two forms of defeatism, both of which were base: that which Stalin imposed on the PCF and that of the realpolitik of Munich, defeatism in the guise of a phony war."[148] Non-Communist anti-Fascist alternatives were equally bleak, but not nearly as base. They could pray for peace or prepare to defend a badly divided, poorly led, militarily unprepared, and spiritually depressed country from the inevitable German onslaught.

Chapter 7

The Books and Bricks of British Anti-Fascism

Neither British citizens nor the British government thought that Fascism represented an internal threat during the interwar years. In fact, however, between 1934 and 1937, British Fascists became a direct menace to the Jewish residents of several British cities, notably London's East End. Oswald Mosley's black-shirted thugs chalked anti-Jewish slogans on buildings, screamed anti-Jewish threats on street corners, and assaulted all who dared challenge them. Yet the Metropolitan Police seemed more antagonistic toward these challengers than toward the British Union of Fascists (BUF). Between July 1936 and February 1937, for example, even though the average Fascist demonstration outnumbered the average anti-Fascist counterdemonstration 225–190, the ratio of arrests was 89–226.[1] Similarly, on the international plane, the National Government coalition successively headed by Labour's Ramsay MacDonald and the Conservatives' Stanley Baldwin and Neville Chamberlain, appeared more hostile to Russia and Spain, the two countries actually fighting Fascist aggression, than to Fascist Italy and Nazi Germany, the aggressors.

Thousands of British people organized or demonstrated against government policy, but failed to alter it or convince the majority of British citizens to alter the government. Anti-Fascists could not overcome the divisions within their ranks or the deep and widespread revulsion people harbored against the war that had ended in 1918.

The Great War stimulated a vast number of very popular memoirs, novels, poems, paintings, plays, and movies. In one of the most widely read books, *Memoirs of a Fox-Hunting Man*, Siegfried Sassoon precisely captured the attitude that still existed in 1928: "The war was justifiable and inevitable. Courage remained a virtue. And that exploitation of courage . . . was the essential tragedy of the war, which, as everyone now agrees, was a crime against humanity."² Even those who had not directly suffered could still feel, some fifteen years after the armistice, what Sarah Burton, the heroine of Winifred Holtby's *South Riding*, felt when she attended a musicale that concluded with a "Grand Patriotic Finale": "With increasing awareness every year she realised what it had meant of horror, desperation, anxiety, and loss to her generation. . . . She was haunted by the menace of another war. Constantly, when she least expected it, that spectre threatened her, undermining her confidence in her work, her faith, her future. A joke, a picture, a tune, could trap her into a blinding waste of misery and helplessness."³

These feelings made people wary of war but did not turn most of them into pacifists. Pacifism did enjoy a certain high tide of influence, though, principally between 1929 and 1934, when the collective memory of the Great War began to shade, barely perceptibly, into a collective fear of the coming one, but it never became a significant factor in British politics. For one electrifying moment, though—on February 9, 1933—it seemed as if pacifism had triumphed. On that day, the Oxford Union Society voted 275–153 to affirm the motion "that this house will in no circumstances fight for its King and Country." That vote, and the subsequent one defeating a motion to expunge (750–138), had little to do with pacifism. It was influenced by "sensational outside interference" and the urge "to protest against jingoism and the cynical exploitation of patriotic idealism at a time of international jitteriness when the government's half-heartedness over disarmament was causing it to be branded as itself a major threat to peace."⁴ The debate and vote received enormous publicity. "Seldom," wrote Robert Vansittart, then Permanent Under Secretary of State, "has a pebble made such a splash."⁵

Several future anti-Fascists passed through pacifism on their way to militant belief in armed resistance to aggression. Jessica Mitford, for example, read, when she was fourteen, Beverley Nichols' hugely successful indictment of war, *Cry Havoc*. "I was," Mitford remembered, "enormously impressed with the originality and force of its arguments. A whole new world had opened for me. Pacifist literature led directly to the left-wing press, of which I became an avid reader."⁶ Her second cousin (and future husband) Esmond Romilly followed a somewhat similar path to the same destination. His hatred of the militarism embodied in the Officers' Training Corps requirement of his public school led him to "read a good deal of pacifist literature. Like many people, I mixed up pacifism with Communism." He, too, began to read the *Daily Worker*. He did not learn much about Communism from it, but did discover "that there was another world as well as the one in which I lived."[7]

The "Peace Ballot" of 1935 provided further proof that pacifism did not dominate British popular thinking about international events. Over 11 million people voted in favor of the League of Nations, international reduction of armaments, control of arms profits, and economic sanctions against aggression, and nearly 7 million (6,827,699) voted "yes" on question 5(b): "Do you consider that if a nation insists upon attacking another the other nations should combine to compel it to stop by, if necessary, military measures?" Slightly over 2 million voted no, while another 2.4 million abstained or did not know.[8]

This vote, like so many other events that occurred in Great Britain during the interwar period, reflected an instance of assembled individual witnesses, rather than a mass movement. The roots of broad support for extraparliamentary political activity did not exist in the twenties and were not skillfully tended when they appeared in the thirties. Inflation was severe and unemployment nagging, but the economy of the twenties did not seem on the verge of collapse. People questioned the sacrifices the war had required, but no deep pool of resentment against the British form of government gathered. Postwar governments did not move quickly or decisively to improve social conditions, but there was no serious disaffection from the parliamentary tradition nor widespread loss of faith in democratic institutions. Political leaders quarreled among themselves, unstable coalitions formed and dissolved, parties divided, but party and government leaders maintained firm control. The British Left not only had a spotty record of sustained, spontaneous, and direct action to achieve its goals, but had erected, by the twenties, two bulwarks against extremism and serious polarization. The Labour Party and the Trades Union Congress (TUC) were deeply entrenched and unshakably moderate; they easily withstood the tremors of discontent the events of the twenties and thirties sent through their monopoly over worker activity, and the challenges of rivals.

The League of Nations Union tried to push the British political system toward a more pronounced antiwar stance, gained a wide following (3,000 branches and nearly 500,000 members by 1928),[9] and supported the same principles as Labour. The party's leaders, however, kept their distance from a movement they could not control, thereby limiting the union's influence. The other would-be mass movement, the Communist Party of Great Britain, branded the League of Nations Union a convocation of anti-Russian powers plotting to launch an imperalist war against Soviet Russia. The Communist counterpart, the British Section of the League Against Imperialism and for National Independence, attracted some Labour MPs to its Executive Committee, but Labour refused to affiliate, and the great majority of workers did not join.

British workers could be militant. In 1921, for example, nearly eighty-six million working days were lost to labor strikes. But their demands were of the basic, bread-and-butter type, and their leaders preferred not to challenge domestic tranquillity with extended work stoppages. The spontaneous bursts of political militancy that occurred were short and isolated. In 1919, 3,000 soldiers occupied the Horse Guards Parade to protest the plans for demobilization, and Glasgow dockworkers called a "general strike" to secure a forty-hour week. In May 1920, London dockworkers refused to load the *Jolly George* with munitions consigned for the Polish war against revolutionary Russia.

Three instances of mass worker activity did occur during the twenties, but Labour leaders maintained full control over them all. In July and August 1920, the National Council of Labour (representing the General Council of the TUC, the National Executive of the Labour Party, and Labour's Parliament group) voted to launch a general strike if the British government actively backed Poland against the Soviet Union. The government did not, but it did begin to alter the country's welfare framework and precipitated a revolt by the Labour Party borough councillors and Poor Law Guardians in Poplar (East London). Led by George Lansbury, the Poplarists fought for a national poor rate, full maintenance for the unemployed, adequate living allowances for children of the unemployed, and equal pay for women. They broke the law, resisted the government, and went to prison. Although the Poplarists organized mass meetings to explain and inform, and mass demonstrations, they did not create a mass movement of protest. Poplarism remained securely in the hands of a small group of organizers. That control did not impress Labour Party leaders, who disapproved of this example of mass civil disobedience and succeeded in keeping it tightly circumscribed. By 1925, when Poplarism had lost its momentum, it had raised the living standards of its supporters, but it had not convinced the rest of the Labour movement to follow suit.[10]

Labour and TUC leaders also limited the great strike of 1926, a potentially powerful symbol of working-class solidarity. This extensive workers' support of a miners' strike cost the country over 160 million workdays, but the TUC suddenly truncated the movement and left the miners at the mercy of the mine owners and government. That decision cost the TUC members (nearly four million) and strike potential (2 million workdays lost in 1927 and 1928), but, ironically, gained votes for British Labour. In the 1929 elections, the party won 37 percent of the vote, 287 seats, and the right to form a government, its first.

The Labour government, however, seriously weakened the Labour Party without helping the country solve the problems of the depression. Prime Minister Ramsay MacDonald, faced with party and trade union opposition to his emergency budget, dissolved his Labour cabinet in September 1931, and replaced it with a "National Government" of four Labour ministers, four conservatives, and two Liberals. The Independent Labour group resigned from the Labour Party and formed a new party (ILP); Oswald Mosley and some of his followers also left the Labour movement and formed the New Party; the Leftists who remained formed the Socialist League. In the general election of October, the LP and ILP combined suffered a loss of 236 seats.

The emergency budget, which cut unemployment benefits and the salaries of government employees, angered workers, but did not, so great was the gap separating British workers from Communism, improve Communist Party (CPGB) prospects. Party membership did not exceed 17,000 during the interwar years, mainly because British Communists never learned how to exploit workers' anger or transform it into political terms. Spontaneous demonstrations by 12,000 sailors at Invergordon and 10,000 teachers in London convinced the government to lessen the planned pay cuts for both, but the demonstrations of the unemployed, in the form of Communist-organized national hunger marches, had no impact on government policy.[11]

The 1931 debacle did not alter Labour's basic political strategy, but it did increase its hostility to the rest of the Left. Walter Citrine and Ernest Bevin, Labour's dominant influences, adamantly refused any form of cooperation with the CPGB. Citrine called Communism a "cancer" on the working class, and the party a vehicle designed "to use every available means to undermine the faith of trade unionists in their elected officers."[12] They heaped equal scorn on the Socialist League, for its unrealistic appraisal of union militancy, and blocked the league's initiatives and resolutions.[13] Arthur Henderson, Labour's new leader, directed the party's offensive against the New Party. Labour hecklers were sent to New Party meetings to accuse the speakers of being upper-class traitors to the working class.[14]

The ILP divided and disintegrated without Labour's assistance. The Revolutionary Policy Committee, the ILP's Leftwing, wanted the ILP to affiliate to the Comintern, if the party could retain its autonomy; the majority, however, had reservations about close ties with the CPGB and did not want to belong to a dictatorial international. Several years of tedious debate within the ILP and hostile exchanges between it and the CPGB ended in 1935, when the Revolutionary Policy Committee merged with the Communists. By that time, ILP membership had declined from 17,000 to 4,400.[15]

The New Party, based on a plan of government activism that Mosley and John Strachey had originally, and unsuccessfully, submitted to the Labour Party, failed to attract workers. Several intellectuals, including Harold Nicolson, Peter Quennell, and G. E. Catlin, found Mosley personally winning and his ideas for an activist party compelling, but they were soon alienated by Mosely's tropism toward the New Party's Youth Movement. Catlin wrote his wife, Vera Brittain, in April 1931 that the New Party was "fascist-militant" and "believes not in science but in miracles by strong men."[16] Strachey, who remained dedicated to improving the lot of workers, left the New Party when it became clear that Mosley disapproved of class struggle and wanted to pursue a course of "corporate identity, the doctrine of the Organic State."[17]

Outside the Labour Party, then, the only "mass" organization on the Left during the early thirties was the Communist-organized National Unemployed Workers Movement, which enrolled, at its peak, perhaps 50,000 people (or less that 2 percent of the unemployed). It would not, however, organize its first national hunger march until October 1932.

But during the spring of 1932, there appeared the first signs of a politicized student movement. Worried about the consequences of the Japanese attack on Manchuria, the editors of *The Outpost* and *The Student Vanguard* devoted substantial space to antiwar matters. An *Outpost* article entitled "The Danger of World War" urged all students "of whatever moral, religious or political opinions, who are honestly opposed to war" to form committees on every university campus "and endeavor to spread awareness of the danger throughout as wide a circle as possible."[18]

That same year, in August, the World Antiwar Congress in Amsterdam spurred the creation of a network of Communist-dominated antiwar committees and, inadvertently, organized Trotskyism in Britain. Twelve London Communists, the Balham Group, criticized the Amsterdam Congress for failing to spotlight National Socialism in Germany, giving leadership roles to "petty-bourgeois pacifists," and substituting a united front from above "for the mobilization of the workers around the Leninist line against war." They formed an antiwar committee with the Clapham ILP group, and promoted a united front of German Social Democrats and Communists to fight Nazism. When the group's members disobeyed direct Party orders to follow the Amsterdam line, two were expelled and one suspended. The Balham Group dissolved and its members turned toward Trotsky.[19] British Trotskyists, however, made little impact on events.

The CPGB tried to build a united front against Hitler from above and below. On the one hand, Communist and ILP leaders agreed on building a revolutionary united front from workers' councils, factory committees, and trade union nuclei.[20] But on the other, the CPGB had issued an invitation to Labour, the TUC, the ILP, and the Cooperative Party to unite in a campaign against Fascism in Germany and Austria and capitalist reaction at home.[21] Labour ignored the invitation and organized its own anti-Nazi campaign (a public demonstration, a refugee fund, and a boycott), and the Socialist League voted overwhelmingly against an LP-CPGB connection.[22] A report entitled "Democracy Versus Dictatorship," prepared by the LP's National Executive for the party's 1933 National Conference, utterly rejected the Communist type of united front in favor of one based on democratic principles and a peaceful path to Socialism. It called on "workers everywhere" to "strengthen the trade unions—the bulwark against capitalist tyranny in Industry . . . the Cooperative societies—the movement created by the workers to counteract private profiteering . . . [and] the Labour Party—the spearhead of political power against Dictatorship—Fascist or Communist."[23] The Communists responded with a torrent of invective against Social Democracy.

The ILP alone seemed genuinely interested in a united front of all working-class organizations to combat Fascism and reaction. James Maxton complained in January 1933 that both Labour and the CPGB wanted to dictate to the working class and control "every step on its road to freedom."[24] The party's newspaper criticized both the CPGB for its domination of the unemployed movement and the Labour movement for its use of the Communist bogey as an excuse not to participate in mass demonstrations planned by other Left groups.[25] The ILP also tried to use the offices of its informal international—the International Committee of Independent Revolutionary Socialist Parties—to bring the LSI and Comintern together to discuss means "to assist the workers who are now oppressed by Fascism in its various forms."[26]

By May 1933, relations between the ILP and CPGB seemed strong. The former had narrowly voted (83–79) to leave the LSI and "approach" the Comintern, and both parties had agreed on the objectives of a united front: to fight Fascism, war, a diplomatic break between Britain and the USSR, and government blows against workers. When the "approach" to the Comintern proved rocky, the relationship began to unravel. The ECCI refused to allow the ILP to act as the intermediary of an LSI-Comintern rapprochement, and the ILP labeled the Third International an instrument of the Russians. Finally, casting a pox on both internationals, the ILP decided to remain with the International Committee, using it as a vehicle to mold international unity on a case-by-case basis, but not as a matrix for a new workers' international.

By this time, though, a significant number of ILP local branches had become restive with the party's coalition policy. In March 1934, they attacked the National Administrative Council for its united front policy. A detailed census of membership opinion followed and revealed

that two-thirds of the Party were participating in the united front uneasily if not unwillingly. The criticism was on two grounds—first, that cooperation with the Communist Party was prejudicing the hopes of a wider working class front, because the Labour Party, trade unions and Cooperative representatives would not touch the Communist Party; second, that the Communist Party was proving untrustworthy by exploiting the united activities for its own sectarian advantages.[27]

The National Conference then voted to limit united front activity with the CPGB to specific issues, but by that time a large number of members had resigned.

As a result of these inter- and intraparty conflicts, anti-Fascism had not assumed a life of its own. Not even the news from Germany of Hitler's activity and the Dimitrov countertrial, which opened in London on September 14, galvanized significant activity. The National Government, however, made three efforts to frustrate the trial[28] and press coverage, although full and objective, did not disclose that it was an anti-Fascist event. The *Times* and Labour's *Daily Herald* buried their small stories on the "verdict" in their back pages.[29]

The only conspicious example of unified anti-Fascist sentiment was the British branch of Willi Münzenberg's Committee for the Relief of Victims of German Fascism, which included liberals, Labourites, and Communists. The British people remained unconvinced that an internal Fascist menace existed or that laws such as the Unemployment Bill (centralizing relief administration) or the Incitement to Disaffection Bill (blocking political propaganda among the armed forces) presaged a Fascist state. No one paid any attention to the rantings of Britain's tiny hate underground (Britons, British Fascists, British National Fascists, and the Imperial Fascist League).

In June 1934, however, the situation changed. Oswald Mosley's eighteen-month-old British Union of Fascists announced a large rally at London's Olympia. By that point, the organization's black-shirted Fascist Defense Force, its black transport vans, its Black House of meeting, and its brutality had made the BUF appear as a reasonable facsimile of German Nazism. About 10,000 middle-class youths, tradesmen, shopkeepers, and anti-Jewish workers from London's East End had been attracted to it.[30] Mosley received some financial support from the upper class and much editorial approval and publicity from some established newspapers, such as the *Daily Mail*.

The CPGB and the London Divisional Council of the ILP organized a counterdemonstration. The *Daily Worker* urged all anti-Fascists to appear and demonstrate their opposition, and CPGB branches organized their members into infiltrating and heckling groups,[31] but the LP's *Daily Herald* refused to advertise the counterdemonstration.

Those who appeared had a memorable time. Vera Brittain and G. E. Catlin "struggled into the one available entrance through an undisciplined crowd of several thousands seething round the stadium; among them were men and women wearing evening dress, workers in overalls, and family parties with young children."[32] The rally quickly degenerated: "A few minutes of speech and then a fight. A few more minutes of speech and then another fight. Scores of men were taken away with blood streaming down their faces."[33] The *Daily Worker* called it a "Great Anti-Fascist Victory," and the *Times* said it displayed Fascism's "uglier colours."[34] The violence cost Mosley much of the popularity he had enjoyed with a segment of the wealthy, and the BUF became increasingly anti-Semitic in its effort to broaden its mass base.

Olympia gave a powerful boost to British anti-Fascism. Those who had participated in the counterdemonstration came away convinced of the value of direct action. A Committee for Coordinating Anti-Fascist Activities, formed under the auspices of the World Committee Against War and Fascism (Amsterdam-Pleyel), with John Strachey as secretary, organized a second counterdemonstration at Hyde Park on September 9. Joe Jacobs, a Communist organizer in the East End, called it "one of the best organized efforts I can remember."[35] The CPGB even issued pamphlets written in Yiddish. Labour's National Executive urged workers to stay away, and the *Daily Herald* stated that Fascism could not be defeated by counterdemonstrators who emulated Fascist methods, but only "before the high court of cool reason."[36] No violence occurred, mainly because 7,000 police separated the 3,000 BUF demonstrators from the 20,000 anti-Fascist counterdemonstrators.[37]

The Hyde Park counterdemonstrators had shouted for unity "to fight the fascist terror,"[38] and popular support for a national congress of anti-Fascists grew. The CPGB Politburo, however, did not approve of the direction anti-Fascism was taking, and issued warnings against attempting to build a united front of direct action against Fascism. John Strachey stated that a united front without the cooperation of "key individuals in the Labour movement" would not succeed. "If we attempt to hold a national Anti-Fascist Congress and to set up a National Anti-Fascist organization before we have [won their cooperation], we run the gravest risk of setting a barrier between ourselves and decisive sections of the working class."[39] Joe Jacobs was told he was paying "too much attention to street meetings and demonstrations, etc., and not enough to work in the trade unions."[40]

Communist leaders wanted to use anti-Fascism to build the party's mass base, not by creating new mass organizations, but by opening other mass organizations of the Left to Communists. Therefore, party members were ordered to focus their efforts on Labour's National Conference and the trade union meetings preparing for it, not on confrontations with the BUF and anti-Fascist congresses. Rank and file organizers, like Jacobs, believed that the Politburo harbored naive illusions about Communist chances to gain acceptance by the LP, and the Southport Labour Party conference proved him correct. Labour delegates overwhelmingly voted against a united front with the CPGB and ILP, and for full disciplinary powers to the National Executive in cases where LP members or groups become involved in "united action with the Communist Party or organizations ancillary or subsidiary thereto without the sanction of the National Executive Committee." Involvement with organizations such as the Relief Committee for the Victims of German and Austrian Fascism, the British antiwar movement, and the European Workers Anti-Fascist Congress were ruled "incompatible with membership in the Labour Party."[41]

There was, however, a division on the issue of Labour's foreign policy. The National Executive's resolution, "War and Peace," restated the party's commitment to the League of Nations, but declared "that there might be circumstances under which the Government of Great Britain might have to use its military and naval forces in support of the League in restraining an aggressor nation." Socialist League members reacted strongly to what they perceived as a national defense posture, and demanded instead withdrawal from the League, constructive relationships with the Soviet Union and other countries with Socialist governments, and a general strike if the National Government should lead Britain to war. "War and Peace" won, 1,519,000 to 673,000.[42]

Students and intellectuals provided the energy and clarity missing in LP and CPGB policy statements and tactics. Five people in particular, though themselves inconsistent and conflicted, symbolized the popular approach to anti-Fascism in Great Britain: John Strachey, who did more than anyone to popularize the Marxist solution to Fascism; Victor Gollancz, who built the most successful anti-Fascist group, the Left Book Club; Harold Laski, Labour's most impassioned spokesperson for unity with the Communists; Stephen Spender, who dramatized the intellectual torn between art and politics, and caught between his inner demands for autonomy and the constraints required by party membership; and Esmond Romilly, who symbolized youth's awakening.

Evelyn John St. Loe Strachey, the son of the owner and editor of the conservative *Spectator*, became the most widely read Left-wing author in Britain during the thirties. He had turned to politics as a means of breaking with the "well-intentioned and public-spirited conservatism" of his father,[43] joined the Labour Party, associated with the Independents, and edited a trade union newspaper, *The Miner*. He was elected to Parliament in 1929, and there worked with Mosley on a plan of economic reform. Labour's rejection of this plan and MacDonald's "betrayal" of Labour convinced Strachey "that the British Social Democracy was not the friend, but the deadliest enemy, of the interests of British workers."[44] He helped Mosley found the New Party, but soon realized that this move was "at bottom, one last desperate attempt to avoid becoming a Communist."[45] He never joined the CPGB, but he spoke and wrote eloquently on its behalf for nearly a decade. Jessica Mitford confessed she "got John and Lytton Strachey mixed up and ploughed gamely through several of Lytton's biographies before discovering my mistake."[46] Nan Green, a nurse who would volunteer for Spain, said that she and her husband decided to join the Communist Party after reading two of Strachey's books.[47]

Spender, one of the young Cambridge poets, was a ubiquitous (Hamburg and Berlin, 1929–1932; Vienna, February 1923; Spain, 1937) presence in the arenas of Fascist and anti-Fascist confrontations. Although he joined the CPGB in the winter of 1936–37, because he considered it the one effective anti-Fascist organization, he sounded relieved he was not invited to join his neighborhood branch and could become, within a few weeks, an ex-Communist.[48] He feared the CPGB would deprive him of his creative and critical individuality, so he tried to carve a niche for what he called the dedicated, nonparty, anti-Fascist intellectual. "If one," he wrote, "is on the side of the greatest possible degree of freedom, if one insists that one should write as one chooses and about what one wishes, one is not a traitor to the cause of world socialism."[49] He struggled more publicly than most artists to merge his literary vocation with his "urge to save the world from fascism," and found his *modus vivendi* in a combination of making appearances at anti-Fascist congresses and writing "out of a sense of public duty."[50] Other artists, like Jason Gurney, a sculptor who would fight in Spain, resisted the CPGB with far less agonizing. He and his friends simply saw no place for themselves in their local party branch: "They were tremendously bureaucratic and earnest to the point of absurdity. . . . In addition, they were always right."[51]

Most newly politically conscious students and intellectuals found it difficult to avoid the Communists. The party may have been small, but it was exceedingly vocal about its causes, and Communists seemed to make things happen. Labour, though large and bearing all the trappings of power, appeared impotent and corrupt. In 1931, a group of Cambridge Communists took control of the Socialist Society there, an October Club was started at Oxford, and a Marxist Society at the London School of Economics. Their appeal as Communists was limited—it is doubtful if their numbers ever exceeded 1,000 at any given time[52]—but their causes, especially the antiwar movement, attracted an increasing number of students.

By the spring of 1933, Communists and fellow travelers at Oxford, Cambridge, and the London School of Economics had disaffiliated from the University Labour Federation, formed the Federation of Student Societies, and begun filling the pages of *The Student Vanguard* with articles on Fascism and the necessity of a united front of students and workers to fight Fascism, war, and reaction in the universities. Thirty British students attended the Salle Pleyel Anti-Fascist Congress in July 1933, two new university-based, politically oriented literary periodicals—*New Oxford Outlook* and *Cambridge Left*—appeared, and dozens of students joined the hunger march of February 1934. The same political, economic, and social factors affected students in secondary schools, and from their ranks emerged the most interesting student publication of the era, *Out of Bounds*.

The force behind it, Esmond Romilly, lived a life compounded of equal parts rebellion and flimflammery. He hated his family's conservatism, his school's Officers' Training Corps, and war. Through a strange process of development, he evolved, before his mid-teens, from a Jacobite to a New Party enthusiast to a Communist sympathizer. Although he claimed to despise Communist theory, Communist fronts offered him the substantive escape from his surroundings he obviously craved. He progressed from reading the *Daily Worker* to visiting the hive of Young Communist activity in London, the Parton Bookshop, to working with the Friends of the Soviet Union and antiwar students from Reading University to combat militarist propaganda in the schools. On Armistice Day, 1933, Romilly and some classmates at Wellington, his public school, pinned antiwar buttons alongside their poppies and placed antiwar leaflets in the school's hymnals. He felt, however, torn in two directions, between "the conventional Conservative world" in which he lived and the world that centered around his "Communist friends," and he feared he moved too easily from Communist Party demonstrations to Devonshire house parties.[53]

Only the Parton Bookshop in Bloomsbury, which seemed to be "a very centre of the English Revolution,"[54] offered him a temporary exit from the contradiction. Philip Toynbee, who would discover the shop in the summer of 1934, was equally enthralled: "That shop! the archetype of all the 'People's Books,' 'Workers' Bookshops,' 'Popular Books' that I was to know so intimately in the next five years. The solemn red-backed classics of the Marx-Engels-Lenin Institute, the mauve and bright yellow pamphlets by Pollitt and Palme Dutt, the Soviet posters of moonlit Yalta and sunlit tractors—the whole marvelous atmosphere of conspiracy and purpose."[55]

University students from the Federation of Student Societies invited Romilly and the other public school boys that congregated at Parton to a conference on January 13, 1934, to organize and coordinate opposition in the public schools and connect it to "the work of progressive students in the universities and with the organized working class." Romilly disagreed. He argued that an organization was premature; the first order of business should be, he said, an "anti-reactionary" magazine for the public schools.[56] The students accepted Romilly's proposal and resolved to oppose "reaction of all kinds, both political and cultural, and particularly Fascism and Militarism in public schools," by means of a magazine, *Out of Bounds*. When a spate of sensational newspaper stories exposed the project, and the Wellington authorities demanded the right of censorship, Romilly abruptly left the school. In February 1934, he moved to London, worked at the bookshop, published the first issue of *Out of Bounds*, and participated in various Communist campaigns and demonstrations, including Olympia.[57]

Four issues of *Out of Bounds* appeared between March 1934 and June 1935. Their successive subtitles clearly marked the editors' progress from united to people's front rhetoric: "Against Reaction in the Public Schools"; "Public Schools' Journal Against Fascism, Militarism, and Reaction"; "The Progressive Journal of the Public Schools." The first editorial declared war against the "sterile and reactionary impulses which permeate the Public Schools," and promised to teach students to undermine the position "the Public Schools hold within the framework of the capitalist state" and oppose the "more vigorous offensive of capitalism, under the emblem of the Fasces."[58] The editors' dependence on Communist analysis and rhetoric was unmistakable, but the journal was much more lively and varied than other party-run or -influenced publications. It spoke to the spectrum of concerns, including sexual, of its student readers: the first issue criticized separate schools for boys and girls; the second issue contained the periodical's most notorious article—Giles Romilly's "Morning Glory (Sex in Public Schools)."

Esmond Romilly had become a confirmed anti-Fascist, but his association with London Communists left him feeling that "politics were unreal. How could they be anything else, when the people themselves were unreal?" He also felt isolated at the Parton Bookshop, where "the sum value of our opinions, and the sum value of our actions remains the same: just nil."[59] In June 1934, he rejoined traditional student ranks, enrolling at Bedales, a progressive institution. The following year, 1936, the brothers published an autobiography, *Out of Bounds.*

Students, university graduates, writers, and artists moved in and out of thirties' political activity as if were a revolving door. Magazines, organizations, and projects appeared, as if by magic, to mobilize them. A teachers' antiwar movement was organized in May 1932, "as the spontaneous manifestation of a movement among teachers to resist war preparations which, apart from their evilness per se, are even more foul when made at the expense of education."[60] A small Left theater movement produced plays with a social content, artists organized antiwar and anti-Fascist exhibitions that traveled around Europe, and Moscow developed Artists' and Writers' internationals.

A survey printed in *New Verse* (a nonpolitical journal), however, indicated that many writers remained nonpolitical. Forty questionnaires were sent to American and British poets; twenty-two were returned. Question five asked: "Do you take your stand with any political or politico-economic party or creed?" Fourteen either avoided the issue or replied in the negative. Of the eight who answered "yes," Allen Tate believed in the Southern (United States) Agrarian Movement, Edwin Muir in the social credit theories of Major C. H. Douglas,* Roy Campbell in South African nationalism, Dylan Thomas in equal sharing, David Gascoyne in Left-wing revolutionary movements, and three in Communism. Hugh MacDiarmid was a party member; Gavin Ewart sympathized; and Norman Cameron believed it was "necessary and good, but I'm not eager for it." No respondent advocated Fascism or National Socialism, and only one, Marianne Moore, called herself a conservative.[61]

The first issue of *Left Review,* the journal of the London section of the Moscow-based International Union of Revolutionary Writers, exhibited a similar patchwork sample of the intellectual Left. Since the union's goal was to unite "working class journalists and writers who are trying to

---

*Government should control the entire money supply, and people should be paid only for work done on a product.

express the feelings of their class" with famous middle-class authors who would "use their pens and their infuence against imperialist war and in defense of the Soviet Union," the editors invited "some of the few living writers in England, whose names have power in more than one generation and more than one class, to express their opposition to the warlike plans of the Imperialist governments."[62] The cynical and pessimistic responses probably sent shudders through the CPGB Politburo and the ECCI. J. B. Priestley wrote that even though the "determined literary Left is inclined to be pretentious and tedious," he would support *Left Review* if it could convince people that they can do something to improve conditions. Siegfried Sassoon sent a satirical poem, "The Writing on the Wall," which began:

> Rats, decent people in their nibbling way
> Have read the notice on the churchyard wall
> "Rat Week next week!" They squeak. And that same day
> An urgent parish conference they call.
> "What can we do to check this inhumanity?"
> They ask; and twitch their whiskers in debate.

George Bernard Shaw professed strong support for "all the Powers making the very deadliest preparation they can afford for the next war," which they would do regardless of his opinion, and thereby make themselves "afraid to fire a shot or drop a bomb. Poison gas is a game they all can play at." Stefan Zweig's "Tower of Babel" depicted the problem peoples and nations have understanding one another.

Left Review followed a pro-Communist, pro-Soviet line. John Lehmann, disenchanted with what he called its low literary level and "doctrinaire Marxist purity," founded *New Writing* in the spring of 1936, which, by being more literary than political, would, he hoped, rally "the so rapidly growing anti-fascist and anti-war sympathies of my intellectual generation."[63]

Only the students seemed to be uniting. While the Federation of Student Societies and the University Labour Federation reached agreement in May 1935 to cooperate on specific issues, Labour's National Executive continued to reject appeals for anti-Fascist coalitions. Harry Pollitt agreed with Labour's analysis—that only a Labour electoral victory could reverse national and international trends—but not its conclusion. He told the Seventh CPGB Congress that it must lead "the fight to secure the defeat of the national Government by the organization of a broad united front movement, based upon a program of demands that every worker really believes can and must be carried through by a Labour Government."[64] Labour refused his offer to withdraw most Communist candidates if Labour stepped aside for a select few, but the CPGB ran only two candidates anyway (Pollitt lost in South Wales and William Gallacher won in West Fife), and worked hard to elect a Labour government.[65] Labour recouped almost all its 1931 losses, but the National Government coalition retained a comfortable majority.

Following the election, Communists were told to work in TUC-dominated trade councils and alongside Labour organizers and elected officials. Pressure was put on Wal Hannington to merge the National Unemployed Workers' Movement into Labour or dissolve it altogether.[66] The Agit-Prop Department established a network of professional groups of theater and film people, journalists, writers, artists, and musicians, and made few demands on their members.[67] The London section of the Writers' International changed its name to the British Section of the Association of Writers for the Defense of Culture and tried to form links with anti-Fascist groups such as For Intellectual Liberty and Friends of Europe.

It was, however, a non-Communist book publisher, Victor Gollancz, who succeeded in weaving together the various strands of British anti-Fascism. In January 1936, he heard about Strachey's long-standing and unfulfilled plan to start an anti-Fascist weekly.[68] Gollancz suggested "some sort of Left Book Club or something of that sort" that would print low-priced books on topical matters and discuss them in a monthly, *Left Book News*. When the club grew large enough, the monthly would be transformed into an anti-Fascist weekly. The editors, Gollancz, Strachey, and Harold Laski,* selected Maurice Thorez's *France Today and the People's Front* as the first offering in May 1936.

Although Strachey and Laski wrote the bulk of the reviews and did most of the speaking on behalf of the club, Gollancz was its heart. He wrote the editorials for *Left Book News* and worked ceaselessly to increase its subscription list. Yellow leaflets, pleading "Please use this leaflet to get a new member," were sent with every book and distributed at every

---

*Laski was, wrote Frederick Vanderbilt Field, "uncommonly articulate, brilliant, extraordinarily well informed; his memory seemed infallible . . . a man of small stature, flushed cheeks and eyes that seemed to radiate a fire burning inside him." *From Right to Left: An Autobiography* (Westport, Conn:. Lawrence Hill, 1983), p. 68.

meeting. Gollancz wanted to promote ideas and knowledge that would establish peace, defeat Fascism, and lead to "real Socialism," but he did not want the Left Book Club to serve as a people's front. "For what the Left Book Club is attempting to do is to provide the indispensable basis of *knowledge* without which a really effective United Front of all men and women of good will cannot be built."[69]

The club published and distributed inexpensive books that explained or supported Left-wing ideas and causes. Communists did not write the majority of the main selections, but only a tiny handful of club books diverged from the Comintern line. All sympathized with the Soviet Union, as did the *News*. Nevertheless, the club was neither a creation nor puppet of the CPGB or ECCI. John Lewis, who organized and coordinated the club groups, claimed that there was little contact between CPGB branches and club activities, that the majority of club members were newcomers to politics "worried and disturbed at the trend of events," and that those who did become active politically gravitated more toward Labour than Communism.[70]

Gollancz, in fact, offered Labour a regular, unrestricted column in the *News*. Labour officials rejected the offer and tried to start a rival club. That posed a dilemma for the editors, who believed that the Labour Party represented the "indispensable nucleus of a People's Front," but who also knew that if they deviated from the united front position they had originally announced they would both fail to conciliate Labour "and disappoint terribly the maximum majority of the Club membership."[71]

Nearly 60,000 people responded to the club, but a people's front did not materialize. Nevertheless, the Left-Book Club helped build a social and cultural home for a large number of people disturbed by social and political conditions. It sponsored large rallies at Albert Hall and Queen's Hall, sparked discussion on current issues, publicized the Chinese and Spanish struggles against aggression, collected money for China and Spain, established a summer school, compiled a songbook, and, in the arts, worked closely with Unity Theatre, Kino Films, and the Workers' Film and Photo League. Despite the activity, Strachey and Gollancz sounded discouraged by early 1937. The former wrote that "little progress is being made towards ranging Britain on the side of peace and democracy," while the latter complained about the astounding public indifference to Spain and the masses' lack of understanding and activity on its behalf.[72]

When the masses did act, as they did several times in 1936 against the

BUF, it displeased both the CPGB and Labour. London's East End had become the main focus of Mosley's activity and anti-Semitism his main theme. Anti-Jewish shopkeepers and workers in Stepney, Shoreditch, and Bethnal Green who claimed they were losing their jobs, their standards of living, and their neighborhood to the Jews sought BUF aid.[73] Signs of militancy and direct action among young Jews and local Communists met with resistance from Jewish leaders and Communist officials. The former preferred a dignified form of response, while the latter, not wanting to antagonize the government into passing civil disorder legislation, further alienate Labour, or stimulate mass activity it could not control, ordered its locals to concentrate on trade and tenant union work.[74]

Strachey's Coordinating Committee for Anti-Fascist Activities did, however, plan a counterdemonstration to a BUF meeting at Albert Hall on March 22. When the police sealed off the meeting from the public and ordered the anti-Fascists to separate their counterdemonstration by one-half mile, Strachey agreed. The forces did not clash, but the police, claiming the anti-Fascists were disorderly, charged them on foot and horse, cleared the area in ten minutes, and arrested twenty-four demonstrators.[75] That event strengthened the CP's efforts to focus anti-Fascist activity on the Spanish Civil War, which began in July, and away from the East End, where, according to Jacobs, BUF meetings and violence had become daily events. He and local organizers from other working-class areas targeted by Mosley (e.g., Manchester and Aberdeen) argued that the CP would lose its appeal if it either allowed the BUF space and time to make significant gains among anti-Semitic workers or did not side with the young Jewish workers determined to fight the Fascists.[76]

The two objectives clashed in September. Mosley planned a rally and march in the East End for October 4. East End anti-Fascists began to organize a massive counterdemonstration, but the Young Communist League had decided to hold a rally that day on behalf of Spanish workers. The District Party Committee refused to postpone the Young Communist League rally and ordered East London Communists to "avoid clashes," "keep order," and arrange an orderly meeting after the BUF had gone. Jacobs thought that those orders, if followed, would destroy the CP in East London. "How," he wondered, "could they be so blind to what was, happening in Stepney? The slogan 'They shall not pass' was already on everyone's lips and being whitewashed on walls and pavements."[77] The Politburo listened, and bent slightly; Communists would first attend the

Young Communist League rally in Trafalgar Square and then, after Mosley's march had ended, would themselves march through the East End protesting BUF support for Spanish Fascists.[78] This compromise failed to satisfy most East London Communists, who argued "that the best way to help the Spanish people was to stop Mosley marching," that a "victory for Mosley would be a victory for Franco," and that the anti-Fascists of East London "would oppose Mosley with their bodies, no matter what the Communist Party said."[79] Finally, party leaders paid attention, and on October 2, the *Daily Worker* announced that the London party branch and the Young Communist League, "reacting to the urgency of the situation . . . have decided to concentrate all their forces in support of the East London workers." The CPGB and ILP urged the workers of London to block the BUF march.[80]

A mass campaign of preparation followed. "Scores of meetings were held in all parts of London. . . . Thousands of posters, hundreds of thousands of gallons of whitewash were employed. . . . Approaches were made to trade councils, trade unions, and Labour parties."[81] The *Daily Herald* and *News Chronicle*, fearing the counterdemonstration would harm the anti-Fascist cause, implored their readers to stay home. Five East End mayors tried, unsuccessfully, to persuade Home Secretary Sir John Simon to ban the BUF march.

On Sunday morning, October 4, 300,000 anti-Mosley demonstrators blocked the main roads into East London. Six thousand foot police and a mounted division charged repeatedly at this crowd, trying to clear a space for the BUF marchers. With police assistance, the black shirts made slow progress eastward, shouting, "The Yids, the Yids, we are going to get rid of the Yids." Anti-Fascists responded, "They shall not pass!"[82] At Cable Street, the crush of counterdemonstrators, barricades, and a hail of missiles from the roofs halted all movement. The police commissioner told Mosley the march would have to be abandoned, and the police escorted the BUF marchers back to London.[83]

The next day, the *Daily Worker* jubilantly headlined its account of the battle of Cable Street: "Mosley Did Not Pass: East London Routs the Fascists," while the *Times* dryly noted that Fascists and Communists continued to engage in "a tedious and rather pitiable burlesque" that threatened public order.[84] BUF violence did not cease, and Parliament finally responded with a Public Order Act, banning the wearing of political uniforms in public and giving the police commissioner the authority to ban political processions that had disorderly potential. The BUF fared even less well in 1937: none of its candidates won a seat on the London County Council, and a demonstration in South London had to be rerouted by the police when nearly 100,000 anti-Fascist counterdemonstrators appeared.[85]

With Mosley's movement in sharp decline and Jacobs suspended from the party (for continuing to demand direct action against the BUF in East London), the CPGB could turn its full anti-Fascist attention to Spain. Some 3,500 men and women from the British Isles volunteered to fight or perform medical services for the Loyalists. Almost all had a political background, and over 80 percent were workers. Frank Graham, one of the volunteers, estimated that "a quarter to a third of those who went were [Communist] Party members and another quarter were closely connected, people who had been in the National Unemployed Workers' Movement. The other half were Labour Party and Trade Unionists and people without affiliation."[86]

Esmond Romilly was one of the first and youngest to travel to Spain, arriving there in October 1936. He was placed in the Thälmann Battalion of the XII International Brigade. It was sent into action south of Madrid on November 12, and on December 15 to Boadilla del Monte. It suffered "appalling losses" there, and within five days, only Romilly and one other British volunteer remained in action. The eighteen-year-old Romilly contracted dysentery and was sent to Barcelona on sick leave. The British consul there provided him with a ticket and a passport for England. As Esmond was returning home to recuperate, Giles was traveling to Spain to fight. Esmond spent several weeks in the hospital during January 1937. Though he expressed dissatisfaction with the disorganized war effort of the Loyalists and aspects of Communist behavior, he decided to return, this time as a correspondent (for the *News Chronicle*) and accompanied by Jessica Mitford. Though he could not get back into Spain, he spent five months in Bayonne dispatching news stories.[87]

Meanwhile, thousands of British people attended meetings promoting the Loyalist cause, contributed millions of pounds to it, and lobbied Parliament to scrap nonintervention and send arms to the republic. But British public opinion remained overwhelmingly pro-embargo. In fact, polls taken in March and October 1938 indicated that only 57 percent of the respondents favored the Popular Front government of Spain (although only 9 percent favored Franco).[88] Labour, at first, supported nonintervention and the embargo, but even when it shifted its position—to arms for

Spain, but no intervention—the National Executive "refused to inaugurate any national campaign in the Spanish cause, apart from collecting funds for the relief of the victims of the War."[89] Labour wanted no connection with mass activity, especially if it might involve Communists.

Undaunted, the CPGB fervently pursued unity (even proposing Communist affiliation to Labour), organized meetings, and dispatched its members to all manner of international congresses. Despite the activity, Philip Toynbee had come to the conclusion that the party was only "an exotic and impotent little growth whose perceptible effect was almost negligible."[90] In addition, the Moscow purge trials drove a large wedge between CPGB supporters and critics, while the Abyssinian and Spanish conflicts opened a gap between those favoring unarmed collective security and those beginning to think in terms of armed intervention on behalf of victims of aggression.

The darkening international skies did promote some alliances, however. The Federation of Student Societies and the University Labour Federation merged in February 1936, and in October, the CPGB, ILP, and Socialist League issued a "Unity Campaign Manifesto," designed to create a mass-based people's front to revitalize the Labour movement by waging a struggle against Fascism, war, reaction, and the National Government.[91] It was the brainchild of the Socialist League's Sir Stafford Cripps, perhaps the only person in Britain capable of arranging a semblance of unity among such divided forces. He radiated, said Fenner Brockway, "burning sincerity," "the earnestness of a crusader," "a simple enthusiasm," and "a spirt of human mission."[92] He needed all that and more, since the CPGB and ILP divided over the Abyssinian war, the purge trials, and the Spanish Popular Front's suppression of the Marxist Unity Workers' Party. In addition, only 48 percent of Socialist League members favored the unity campaign.[93]

Cripps, Maxton, and Pollitt launched the campaign at Manchester on January 24, 1937, but Labour's National Executive immediately disaffiliated the Socialist League, forcing Cripps to withdraw. The ILP and CPGB continued for three months, but gathered only 18,000 signed "pledge cards" and collected only £1,900. Cripps remarked to Brockway "on the irony of unity meetings when at the door members of the two parties were selling literature bitterly attacking each other."[94] Labour's National Executive avoided similar occurrences at its party's meetings by threatening to expel from the party any member who belonged to the Socialist

League after May 31. Cripps dissolved the league, leaving Labour's Left in disarray.

Doubt and despair accompanied disunity on the British Left in 1937, as news from China and Spain remained bad. To counteract the spreading disillusion, editors of journals supporting the people's front pursued a see-no-evil approach to information. *The Week*, for example, accurately reported the details of German and Italian intervention in Spain, but its commentary drew a "grossly misleading" picture of the situation as a whole.[95] The Left Book Club excluded from its selections any book that constituted a "Trotskyite" attack on the Soviet Union, because, as Laski wrote: "However sincere Trotskyites may be, 'declarations of war' on the Soviet Union cannot be held to fight against war and fascism—on the contrary they must be held to be strong allies of Nazi Germany in her militarist plans."[96] *Left Books News* also defended the procedure and substance of the Moscow trials and debunked the critical report prepared by the Dewey Commission in the United States (see chapter 8). Kingsley Martin, editor of *The New Statesman*, commissioned and then rejected George Orwell's review of Franz Borkenau's *The Spanish Cockpit*, because in it Orwell described Communist suppression of the Catalonian Anarchists and Marxist Workers' Unity Party and attempted to expose "the Soviet myth." Martin told Orwell that the review "too far controverted the political policy of the paper. It is very uncompromisingly said and implies that our Spanish correspondents are all wrong. . . . It is no use publishing reviews that too directly contradict conclusions that have been reached in the first part of the paper."[97]

As the people's front effort diminished and fell into increasing disrepute, non-Communist Leftists tried to fill the breach. At the end of 1937, forty-three resolutions urging unity on the Left were presented at Labour's National Conference; all were tabled. In March 1938, Sidney R. Elliott, editor of *Reynolds News*, the journal of the Cooperative movement,* proposed a Peace Alliance, to be led by Labour and to include "all parties who care for Peace and Democracy." It would campaign on a platform of collective security by means of a strengthened League of

---

*The Cooperative Party had been founded in 1919 by the Cooperative Union. By 1935, it had a membership of five million, and nine members of Parliament. It was allied to, but not affiliated with, Labour. Sidney R. Elliott, *The English Cooperatives* (New Haven: Yale University Press, 1937); G. D. H. Cole, *A Century of Cooperation* (Manchester: Co-Operative Union, 1944).

Nations, support for the national integrity of Czechoslovakia, an immediate halt to the "fascist rape of Spain," and national and international economic reforms.[98] The CPGB expressed approval, but the National Co-operative Congress voted 2–1 against it, and Labour's National Executive condemned the idea and threatened to disaffiliate any local branch that adhered.[99] Cripps' "Democratic Front" to "Save Spain, Save Britain, Save Peace" fared no better.[100] The Communist Party's Peace Front idea, a coalition of democratic, non-Fascist countries, was labeled "a capitalist war alliance" by the ILP.[101]

Only the student Left maintained its optimism and energy. While it promoted an Emergency Youth Campaign to preserve peace, the editors of *Left Review*, feeling overwhelmed by events, ceased publication in May, confessing they lacked the will and resources to answer the questions that so disturbed writers and artists: " 'What is my job?' and 'What can I do?' "[102] As the Czechoslovakian crisis worsened, remembers Brittain, "silent Londoners knelt before the Cenotaph in Whitehall to pray that Chamberlain would save them from war."[103]

When the Munich Conference ended the immediate danger of war, "an enormous wave of blind relief swept England," wrote Mitford.[104] In the wake of it, the divided Left tried to regroup on a platform of peace and opposition to Chamberlain's foreign policy, which, it was argued, only whetted the appetites of the makers of war. For the first time, the British Left's proposals seemed in tune with public opinion. Seven by-elections to Parliament in October and November focused on foreign events; two Conservatives lost and the five Conservative victors won by much narrower margins than their predecessors had in 1935.[105] A public opinion poll in March 1939 revealed that 84 percent of the respondents favored better relations with Russia.[106]

Nevertheless, the Left failed to build a unified movement on this growing opposition to Chamberlain. Strachey and Gollancz tried to broaden Left Book Club membership by changing the club from a collective of readers of Left literature to a moderate association of anti-Fascists.[107] The ever-prolific Cripps sponsored a unity petition that urged "the parties of progress to act together and at once for the sake of peace and civilization."[108] Labour reacted negatively to both, and expelled Cripps and three other prominent supporters of the petition. When the party's League of Youth defended Cripps, it was dissolved.

Feelings, attitudes, and posturing oscillated during the spring and summer of 1939, but only the students managed to maintain a semblance of initiative. They organized a National Youth Campaign, a Youth Pilgrimage to London, and resistance to conscription.

All anti-Fascists, youth and adult alike, had to confront two issues: if war came, would they fight for Britain? and what would they do if the Soviet Union attempted a rapprochement with Germany? Esmond Romilly probably spoke for the vast majority of anti-Fascists when he decided that he would fight "for the grey of British imperialism allied to Polish and Rumanian Fascism against the black of German-Italian Fascism."[109]* and John Strachey undoubtedly reflected the fears of that same vast majority when he wrote: "If the Soviet Union were to go into benevolent neutrality toward Germany, my whole political position would be shattered."[110]

With the exception of the *Tribune*, which argued that a German-Soviet treaty improved the prospects of peace in Eastern Europe,[111] the non-Communist anti-Fascist journals attacked the Nonaggression Treaty and the Soviet Union. The *Daily Herald* called it "a bigger betrayal of peace and of European freedom even than Munich"; "No good Can Come of the Nazi-Soviet Pact," the *New Leader* announced; *The New Statesman* accused the Soviet Union of precipitating a war; and *Reynolds News* called Russia's decision explicable but inexcusable.[112] The Left Book Club did not take a position, because the editors disagreed; Gollancz, Strachey, and Laski simply urged all club members "in their various ways to do all in their power to win the war and defeat Fascism."[113]

As far as British Communists knew, they, too, would be fighting a war to defeat Fascism. On the eve of the German invasion of Poland, Pollitt told the CPGB Central Committee that the party would support a declaration of war against Germany and launch a campaign for a broad-based, multiparty war government. A day after the invasion, the Central Committee announced it supported "all necessary measures to secure the victory of democracy over Fascism."[114] As Pollitt eloquently argued in his pamphlet "How To Win the War":

To stand aside from this conflict, to contribute only revolutionary-sounding phrases, while the Fascist beasts ride roughshod over Europe, would be a betrayal

---

*He volunteered for the Canadian Air Force in the summer of 1940. The airplane on which he was a navigator went down in the North Sea during a bombing raid in November 1941.

of everything our forbears have fought to achieve in the long course of long years of struggle against capitalism. . . . Whatever the motives of the present rulers of Britain and France, the action taken by them . . . is not only helping the Polish people's fight, but is actually, for the first time, challenging the Nazi aggression which has brought Europe into crisis after crisis for the last three years.[115]

Two weeks later, on October 2, the ECCI repudiated Pollitt's position, telling the CPGB this war was not one the working class could support. When Pollitt voted against the motion to rescind the national defense resolution of September 2, he was removed as party secretary. On October 12, the Central Committee announced that its earlier statement had been "incorrect," that Britain, France, and Poland bore equal reponsibility for the war, and that it was "unjust and imperialist."[116]

Chamberlain's foreign policy had placed the British people in a difficult situation. As France fell, the United States remained neutral, and the Soviet Union complied fully with the terms of the Nonaggression Treaty, Britain would soon confront, virtually alone, a rampaging German military machine. Few British citizens welcomed the war, but there was one bright note, at least, for those people's front supporters who rejected the Comintern's "imperialist war" line—they could now be patriotic anti-Fascists. The Communists, however, could be neither and spent, according to Claud Cockburn, two years "in a very cold cold."[117]

Chapter 8

"Premature" Anti-Fascism in the United States

America of the twenties and thirties seemed far removed from threats of external and internal aggression. The oceans were wide, organizations of Left and Right very small, and Franklin D. Roosevelt's New Deal administration proved solid, popular, and enduring. Nothing resembling French league or BUF demonstrations or violence occurred, and as a result, except among intellectuals in New York and movie writers, actors, and directors in Hollywood,[1] anti-Fascism did not become a significant factor in American political life.

The Left directed most of its energy toward unemployed and unorganized industrial workers. For a short period, during the mid-thirties, elections and Spain captured their attention, but Roosevelt's reforms, ideological and organizational divisions among workers and parties, and the lack of immediate threats defeated most national Left political efforts. The one national movement with which Leftists were involved, the peace movement, harmed rather than helped anti-Fascism by creating an atmosphere in which neutrality legislation could be passed, thereby rendering the United States government powerless against aggressor nations.

The bases on which the Left would try to unify during the thirties existed only as tiny nuclei during the twenties. The American Federation of Labor (AFL), the one worker group of size and stature, held itself aloof from Left-wing politics and refused to organize the semiskilled. Socialists (ASP) made feeble efforts to form national progressive coalitions and third parties, and feebler efforts to organize industrial workers and blacks. Communists tried to organize workers and blacks, but its words and methods did not appeal to most potential recruits or allies, and the party purged its leaders and splintered too frequently. Between 1919 and 1923, there was, at different times, a Communist Party, a Communist Labor Party, a United Communist Party, a Workers Party of America, and a United Toilers of America. By the time the ECCI imposed unity, discipline, a reliable cadre, and a permanent name (Communist Party USA) in 1929, the American Communist movement was a tiny sect.

The labor movement in the United States was moribund during the twenties. The AFL, reacting defensively to a probusiness set of Republican adminstrations, an antilabor judiciary, and an aggressive employer offensive on behalf of open shops and company unions, lost over one million members. The Communist Trade Union Education League, which tried to revolutionize the AFL by boring from within, succeeded only in having its organizers and fractions regularly purged. Communist efforts to organize workers involved in bitter strikes, at Passaic, N.J. in 1925, New Bedford, Mass. in 1928, and Gastonia, N.C. in 1929, did not translate into a mass union base, and its successor, the Trade Union Unity League, developed only a shadow of a dual union structure and a knot of experienced union organizers. The garment workers in the Socialist Party were far outnumbered by white-collar workers and intellectuals, who neither pressured the AFL nor its own membership to organize the unorganized. By 1930, only 10 percent of America's nonagricultural labor force and 12 percent of its industrial workers belonged to unions.[2]

Intellectuals and artists did not seem interested in politics, lending their names and efforts only to the Sacco-Vanzetti cause and Socialist Norman Thomas' 1928 presidential campaign. Although civil liberties had been placed in serious jeopardy by state criminal syndicalist laws, restrictions on immigration, the Ku Klux Klan, and antistrike injunctions, no substantial resistance movement arose in opposition.

Youth groups and movements were similarly limited in scope and impact. Young Socialists tended to confine their activity to ASP election campaigns; Young Communists disdained campus politics and "student" issues; the Student League for Industrial Democracy was very active on campus, but militantly anti-Russian.[3] Vague rumblings of a sexual revolution and new types of freedom and cynical jousts against cultural targets represented the major focus of student activism.[4] Only at City College of New York, Ohio State, and the University of Wisconsin did an antiwar political impulse take substantive shape in the form of a challenge to the ROTC programs on those campuses.[5]

Only the peace movement attracted large numbers of citizens. It consisted of dozens of organizations, broadly divided into two types. One, exemplified by the Carnegie Endowment for International Peace, had the funds and prominence to enable it to work through traditional channels of persuasion and issue regular publications. The other, more irregular type made up in zeal and energy what it lacked in numbers, money, and access. Less than 100 active, full-time workers utilized every known public relations device—fancy letterheads, petitions, news releases, and incessant congressional lobbying—to package the national antiwar feeling.[6] Most of the forty or so organizations of this crusading type had "Women" or "Christian" in their titles: the largest was the American Friends Service Committee; the most active the Women's International League for Peace and Freedom and the Fellowship of Reconciliation. They increased their impact by coordinating activities through a National Council for the Prevention of War, which in 1932 alone dispatched 2,615,000 pieces of antiwar literature.[7] At first, both types of the peace movement supported the League of Nations and favored disarmament, but in the later twenties, as the League of Nations weakened and hopes for disarmament dimmed, organizations like the Carnegie Endowment tended to develop a more nuanced stance toward national defense and military aid, while the others became increasingly pacifistic and embargo-oriented. None became mass or popular movements, but public opinion solidly aligned itself behind their efforts to avoid American involvement in another war.

Right-wing successes, either at home or abroad, failed to solidify the American Left. The parties barely noticed Mussolini and Italian Fascism, and writers and artists did not rally against an Italian Fascist threat to culture. Italian-American workers made the one solid effort to organize an American resistance to Fascism in Italy by forming, in April 1923, the Anti-Fascist Alliance of North America. It gained the support of the New York Federation of Labor, the Amalgamated Clothing Workers, the International Ladies Garment Workers, and, some said, the Communist Party. To stem accusations of Communist domination, the Anti-Fascist Alliance was renamed, in 1926, the Anti-Fascist Federation for the Freedom of Italy. The new group welcomed any "labor, radical, and liberal groups" opposed to Communist centralism as well as Fascist totalitarianism. The group provided aid to refugees and exiles, exposed Fascist propaganda lies, and organized demonstrations against visiting Italian dignitaries. It failed to attract broad support, because many Italian-Americans approved of Mussolini, and the United States government appreciated Mussolini's anti-Bolshevism and believed he would stabilize Italy politically and thereby enhance the prospects for general European economic recovery. The State Department did evidence concern in late 1922 that Fascist foreign policy contained potentially destabilizing territorial elements. In 1928, however, following Mussolini's strong support for the Kellogg-Briand Pact (renouncing war as an instrument of national policy), United States foreign policy makers relaxed.[8]

The Executive Council of the AFL, though keenly disappointed that yet another autocratic government had appeared, refused to consider a resolution endorsing and supporting the Anti-Fascist Alliance. It warned its members, though, that "there must be no Fascisti in our Republic."[9] The council reiterated that position in 1927: "We record our opposition to the practice and principle of dictatorship, holding that it is sufficient to emphatically record our own position without giving our endorsement to any organization."[10] The following year, President William Green equated Fascism with Communism and proclaimed AFL opposition to both.[11] With that pronouncement, Fascism disappeared from AFL convention agendas until 1933.

Left political activity awakened during the depression year of 1929. A. J. Muste formed the Conference for Progressive Labor Action to promote industrial unionism, trade union democracy, and active class struggle. A militant element arose within the Socialist Party and it attracted voters and members, but enrollment did not exceed 6,000, and deep cracks opened over theory and practice.[12] The Trotskyists, who had been expelled from Communist ranks in October 1928, held an organizing conference in Chicago in May. Thirty-one delegates met to create the Communist League of America (Opposition).[13] Their newspapers and speeches focused on the "Right Danger" in the Communist Party, the Third Period strategy, and the threat of imperialist war. None of these parties appeared concerned with a Fascist danger.

The Communist Party was also a tiny sect in 1929, but its ranks contained a sizable majority of young, energetic, dedicated, and disciplined activists. An "Americanized elite," led by Earl Browder, had begun to replace the foreign-born and -oriented founders of the party.[14] Browder, like Thorez and Pollitt, was ambitious, theoretically impoverished, tactically competent, and ready to swerve on Moscow's command. Frederick Vanderbilt Field found Browder "less doctrinaire . . . . and easier in give and take than a good many others in the Party leadership."[15] He "opened up secondary leadership positions throughout the party and its auxiliaries to the generation of politically talented young people who began entering the movement in the early 1930s through the Young Communist League, the Unemployed Councils, and various left-wing student organizations."[16] One of those young people, Dorothy Healey, then organizing field and cannery workers in California, believed the Browder generation were "human beings of extraordinary capacity and abilities." It did not occur to her to submit their words and thoughts to critical inquiry: "I can only remember reading those things with the idea that of course it was right."[17]

Very few non-CP Leftists would have agreed, and American Communists found it very difficult to broaden the base of their movement. They approached Muste with the idea of combining forces and seemed to accept his precondition for talks—no existing Communist Party units could "be regarded as the nucleus of the new unions." The talks collapsed, however, when the Communist negotiators insisted on Trade Union Unity League unions serving as the base for an organizing drive and Unity League leaders directing it.[18] Problems with non-Communists also bedeviled the main party front, the All-American Anti-Imperialist League. A CP memo revealed that non-Communists would be given "in appearance the concession that the League is not to be under Party control," but "our fraction can work it in an efficient manner."[19] Six months later, however, the Anti-Imperialist League was severely criticized for failing to confront "the revolutionary perspectives opened up before it."[20] On their own, Communists actively engaged in organizing the unemployed, the semiskilled, black people, and a hunger march on Washington in November 1931.

Their energy contrasted so sharply with the Socialist and Democratic parties that some fifty intellectuals, Langston Hughes, Sherwood Anderson, Lincoln Steffens, and Sidney Hook among them, openly supported the 1932 presidential campaign of William Z. Foster. They formed the League of Professional Groups for Foster and Ford. The league's pamphlet *Culture and Crisis* stated: "The Communist Party alone is working to educate and organize the classes dispossessed by the present system."[21] The dispossessed did not respond: Foster polled slightly over 100,00 votes (as compared with the 900,000 cast for Norman Thomas and the 22.8 million for Franklin D. Roosevelt).

The national significance of the American Left only began to improve markedly when it was stimulated by the spontaneous outbursts of militancy from students and workers. In 1932, a group of college students founded the New York Student League. They were, one of them has written, "alert and talented young men and women who had begun to perceive the devastation which economic disorder was bringing not merely to 'humanity' or some other vague quantity but to themselves as students."[22] For their first major effort at involvement in the nation's social problems, they sent three automobiles and two buses filled with students to Harlan, Kentucky, to investigate a coal strike and aid the strikers. Although sheriff's deputies turned them away, the experience made a powerful impact on the participants.[23] On their return, they created a National Student League, which helped organize a Student Congress Against War, in December. Both the Student League and its Chicago congress were dominated by those sympathetic to the Communist antiwar position, and the 600 delegates voted resolutions strikingly similar to those voted at Amsterdam the previous summer. The National Student League was the most active force on college campuses for the next few years; it advocated unity on the Left and student support for workers' strikes. "It was," James Wechsler wrote, "with these men and women— workers on the docks, in the factories, on the farms and in the mines— that the students' search for peace would have to be aligned."[24]

Though the students had approved an anti-Fascist plank, anti-Fascism per se still had not attracted many people to its banner, nor did the Socialist and Communist parties actively promote it. Though Hitler's appointment as Chancellor of Germany spurred activity, Communist determination to control the anti-Fascist groups that formed provoked division, fragmentation, and weakness. When Jane Addams, John Dewey, Oswald Garrison Villard, and William Allen White formed the American Committee Against Fascist Oppression as a vehicle for disseminating information about Fascism and collecting aid for refugees from Fascist countries, Communists joined, but only as a means of holding it to the Comintern anti-Fascist line. Two of them, Kyle Crichton and Joseph Freeman, asked Matthew Josephson to write a pamphlet on Nazi terror, but then rejected it because he "had neither stressed the immense efforts made by the 'heroic workers' of Germany to win their fight nor made it plain that their ultimate triumph was foreordained."[25]

The Communists in the League of Professional Groups for Foster and Ford rejected Sidney Hook's and James Rorty's proposals that the league be made into an independent, united Left front, including even Trotskyists and Lovestoneites.[26] "It was not long," wrote Hook, "before the rift between the Communist party and our group widened into a gulf and then became an unbridgeable abyss"; party leaders feared that this broad-based united front infection would spread and lead to the formation of a new political party on the Left.[27] The Professional Group disintegrated: some became outright Trotskyists, others worked with Trotskyists in the Non-Partisan Labor Defense (established by the Communist League, the American Workers Party, and an anarchist group), others wrote critical articles about Communists in *Modern Monthly*, the short-lived *Marxist Quarterly*, and, starting in 1937, *Partisan Review*. They continued to call for a broad-based united front and a new revolutionary party.[28] In April 1933, another group of Communists and independent Marxists shattered, when eight non-Communist members of the National Committee for the Defense of Political Prisoners resigned because of conflicts over the united front, the conduct of the Scottsboro case, and limits on free discussion.[29]

Undaunted, the CPUSA continued to build party-dominated fronts, notably, in 1933, the American League Against War and Fascism. Henri Barbusse toured the East and Midwest promoting the antiwar congress scheduled for New York on September 29. The names of Theodore Dreiser, Malcolm Cowley, Sherwood Anderson, Roger Baldwin, Franz Boas, Sidney Hook, Upton Sinclair, Lincoln Steffens, and Thornton Wilder adorned the letterhead, but a Communist, Donald Henderson, did the work. The Socialist Party refused to participate because the inclusion of the Trade Union Unity League removed any possibility of AFL affiliation,[30] but a wide range of non-Communist groups sent delegates: the Fellowship of Reconciliation, American Civil Liberties Union, League for Industrial Democracy, American Friends Service Committee, National Urban League, National Association for the Advancement of Colored People, and Women's International League for Peace and Freedom.

Despite a multiparty organizing committee, Communists fully controlled the congress. They did not, however, adroitly manipulate membership of the Presiding Committee. When non-Communists tried to nominate, first, the ex-Communist Jay Lovestone, and then Charles Zimmerman (head of an ILGWU local in New York) to the committee, Communist-orchestrated physical violence resulted. Finally, as the strains of "Solidarity Forever" rose from a piano in the hall, the delegates restored calm and voted a ten-point program to combat war and Fascism.[31] It became the largest anti-Fascist organization in the United States, claiming by 1939 20,000 dues-paying members and 1,023 affiliated organizations (with a combined membership in excess of 7 million people).[32] The league published a monthly magazine (*The Fight Against War and Fascism*), distributed millions of pamphlets and news releases, sponsored congresses, conferences, and demonstrations, and organized petitions to Congress. Herbert Solow wrote that next to the Communist Party itself, the league "is Stalin's most important American instrument" for spreading propaganda in support of Soviet foreign policy.[33]

Student activism also increased in 1933. As in Britain, politicized American students sounded stronger than they were (perhaps 2 percent of the campus population).[34] In March, students at Brown University adopted a peace pledge modeled on the Oxford "King and Country" resolution, stating that "war is only justified in case of invasion of the mainland of the United States by a hostile power."[35] They organized a nationwide campaign against war and presented an antiwar petition to Congress and the White House.[36] By May, antiwar committees existed on over ninety campuses, and a student poll taken at sixty-five colleges indicated that 8,415 of the 21,725 respondents were absolute pacifists and 7,221 would bear arms only in case of an invasion.[37] At a National Conference on Students in Politics in Washington that December, Eleanor Roosevelt delivered the keynote speech, but the resolutions followed the League Against War and Fascism line: antiwar, anti-Fascism, anti-racism, and pro–trade union and educational reforms.[38]

The AFL, though standing resolutely apart from the League Against War and Fascism, had, in October, condemned Hitler's treatment of German Jews, protested his destruction of the German labor movement, and recommended that its members boycott German goods and services.[39] It did not, however, relax its monetary and jurisdictional constraints against organizing industrial workers. No other Left organization would or could fill the gap. The Socialists, at their 1932 convention, defeated a motion urging the organization of industrial unions, while the Trade Union Unity League tried and failed. Muste's American Workers Party, the National Unemployed League it organized, and the Socialists' Unemployed Union spurred local organizing, but it took the National Industrial Recovery Act (June 1933) to release pent-up worker militancy.

Section 7(a)(1) of the act legalized employees' rights to organize, bargain collectively, and choose their own bargaining representatives, and prohibited employers from interfering with, restraining, or coercing union organizers. Although the CPUSA and ASP condemned the act's National Recovery Administration as a step toward a corporate or Fascist state, workers' frustrations exploded during the spring of 1934, partially in response to the promises of Section 7(a)(1). Four major strikes, unplanned and uncoordinated, broke out among electrical workers in Toledo, teamsters in Minneapolis, West Coast longshoremen, and Atlantic seaboard textile workers. When the Musteites (in Toledo), Trotskyists (in Minneapolis), and Communists (in the West) provided valuable organizing assistance, and the Roosevelt adminstration seemed squarely in management's corner, workers began to turn toward Left-wing organizers who, in turn, began to pressure their parties to form national political alliances.

Students also moved toward unified activity. The National Student League joined with the Student League for Industrial Democracy to organize a "peace strike" on April 13, to commemorate American entry into World War I. Though 15,000 of the 25,000 strikers congregated in New York, it drew national attention and spurred liberal student organizations to form the American Youth Congress. Though the congress was never more than a letterhead organization, it marked the first time Young Communists had joined an organization dominated by non-Communists. The Communists were able to engineer the adoption of an antiwar resolution similar to that of the League Against War and Fascism.[40]

Some Socialists wanted limited cooperation with Communists on selected issues, but at the party's June convention, the moderates reacted angrily. They also rejected the idea of a general strike as a means of defeating an attempted Fascist counterrevolution, calling it "incitement to unlawful acts" that would turn the ASP into an "underground organization . . . avowing illegal purposes."[41] More controversy erupted in December, when the party's National Executive voted to allow members to arrange limited actions with Communists and Marxist splinter groups at the state and local level.[42]

Communist opponents did not lack ammunition for their resistance to coalitions with the CPUSA. In February 1934, when the ASP tried to hold a rally in Madison Square Garden to condemn the Austrian government's attack on the Austrian Left and congratulate Austrian Socialists for their resistance, some 5,000 Communists invaded the meeting and, according to the New York Times, "shouted down the speakers, threw folding chairs from the balcony, and started fights all over the floor."[43] Twenty-five non-Communist writers and intellectuals sent a protest letter to *New Masses*, an American Civil Liberties Union investigating committee condemned the CPUSA for its behavior, and organizations sympathetic to the Socialist Party disaffiliated from the League Against War and Fascism.[44] In an "Open Letter to American Intellectuals," Hook, Muste, V. F. Calverton, and James Burnham, among others, urged a wholesale resignation from the CP and its auxiliary organizations. They argued that the Madison Square Garden episode "and the recent course of the Communist Party which led to the incident gives a lurid and unforgettable picture of the degeneraiton which has taken place in the Communist movement and its inability to cope with the problems raised by the world threat of Fascism."[45] The league withstood the assault: Roger Baldwin of the ACLU chose not to resign, Harry F. Ward of the Union Theological Seminary accepted the post of national chairman, and several new pacifist and church groups affiliated.

Jewish Socialists, however, established a rival to the Communist-dominated Jewish People's Committee Against War and Fascism, which had been established in 1933. The new group, the Jewish Labor Committee, was closely linked to Jewish trade unions and to the American Jewish Congress, and steadfastly refused to cooperate with the Jewish People's Committee, or any other Communist-influenced group. Although both Jewish groups were very active for the next four years, organizing demonstrations and boycotts, the Jewish Labor Committeee had a wider agenda, involving aid to refugees and campaigns against anti-Semitism.[46]

In March, a chorus of liberals voiced a strong protest against Nazism. In an anthology, *Nazism: An Assault on Civilization*, Senator Robert F. Wagner (D-NY), Alfred E. Smith, Dorothy Thompson, John Haynes Holmes, William Green, and Rabbi Stephen S. Wise, among others, passionately discussed the nature of the Third Reich, its menace to the world, and "the challenge to America." The articles were informative, but aside from Green's mention of the AFL boycott of German goods, no anti-Fascist program or format was presented.[47]

The Communists held the key to organized anti-Fascism in the United States, but even though there was perceptible movement away from their divisive "class-against-class" tactic, party leadership failed to take advantage of the most salient example of a mass political movement in the United States during the 1930s. A Politburo directive of January 1934 called on Communists to increase their work within the AFL and independent unions, and key Communist autoworker organizers left the Trade Union Unity League to work within non-Communist groups.[48] At the party's April convention, James Ford, who advocated uniting blacks with liberals and Left-leaning intellectuals, was given control of CP organizing efforts among blacks.[49] Nevertheless, when Upton Sinclair launched his third campaign for the California governorship, the CPUSA bombarded him and it with the full-force of party polemics.

Sinclair, a lifelong Socialist, had begun early in 1933 to rethink his politics. He had run as a Socialist for Senator once and governor twice, but he had grown disappointed with the ASP's failure to attract members, especially from the middle class, and world Socialism's weakness toward Fascism. He was fifty-four, feeling old, exhausted, and ready to retire from politics. "But then came Hitler; to me the most hideous phenomenon since the days of the Inquisition. . . . I saw around me all the little incipient Hitlers—the Californazis. I put to myself the question: what is the use of taking a life-time to build a Socialist movement, when our enemies can destroy it in twenty-four hours?"[50]

Politically naive—he believed he had Roosevelt's support and that the President intended to adopt production for use as a national policy*— Sinclair possessed a near-bottomless reservoir of stubborn determination. His "whole being," he wrote, became "concentrated upon the idea that there shall be no fascism in the United States," and that he would build a new social order, in a "democratic" and "American way," to stop it.[51] The campaign to End Poverty in California (EPIC) resulted.

Upton Sinclair's Paper: End Poverty appeared on December 26, 1933, carrying the headline "Noted Author Renews Battle for Humanity." Its editor, Reuben Borough, "wondered how in the world we would ever get those 20,000 copies circulated." By the time of the November election, 1,000 EPIC clubs and 100,000 EPIC members were financing and distributing one million free copies each week of *EPIC News*.[52] The Epic plan, published in the July 30 issue of the paper, contained twelve proposals: a California Authority for Land (to create land colonies where the unemployed could become self-sustaining), a California Authority for Production (to acquire factories the unemployed could use to produce goods for themselves), a California Authority for Money (to handle financing),

---

*A system in which factory workers produce goods for their own consumption, not for the market.

various tax reform measures, and payments of fifty dollars per month to needy people. It had an immediate impact, Borough remembered, especially in southern California, among "the elements on the fringes who were actually unemployed and depended upon relief and on the co-op, or who were pretty near it and who were afraid they were going to get into these groups."[53] The campaign catalyzed a spontaneous, near-frenzied response from thousands of people primed for action. "It was," wrote Sinclair, "like living on board a ship in a hurricane."[54]

Sinclair tried to bar groups that were "anti-democratic in character and which look to force as the means of bringing about the changes they desire." Communists and Fascists were engaged in a struggle that was "tearing one nation after another to pieces," and EPIC respresents "the effort to avoid this conflict in our state of California."[55] Communists reponded by heckling his speeches and branding him with their "Social-Fascist" label. Browder told the Central Committee in September that "the fight against the Sinclair illusions is an essential feature of our whole struggle against social-fascism," and a *New Masses* editorial called the basic ideology of Sinclair's program "the fascist objective of saving the dying capitalist system by force."[56]

The Socialist Party also kept its distance, claiming that Sinclair, by running in the Democratic Party primary, was not advancing the cause of Socialism. Nor did organized labor lend its support to his campaign. On its own, then, EPIC captured the California Democratic Party, nominating, in addition to Sinclair, over fifty candidates. California businessmen spent a fortune to defeat him, using every means available to them, from phony newsreel features to legal action. Sinclair lost—he polled 879, 537 votes (37.3 percent) or 250,000 less than the Republican winner (albeit 870,000 more than the combined vote total of the Socialist and Communist candidates)[57]—but twenty-nine EPIC candidates were elected to the state assembly and one to the state senate. Sinclair envisioned EPIC as an independent group which would use the initiative process to advance its program, but Borough and many of the newly elected legislators wanted to broaden the political base of EPIC and maintain control of the state Democratic organization. At a time when most American Leftists were gravitating toward some version of a united front, EPIC was in the process of splitting over it.

The Communist League (Trotskyists) and the American Workers Party (Musteites), merged to form the Workers Party of the United States and, several months later, joined the Socialist Party (the "French turn"). The student peace strike of April 12, 1935, far surpassed its predecessors in numbers (175,000), schools (150), and scope (from Harvard to UCLA).[58] Later that year, New York students organized an Anti-Fascist Conference at Columbia University. And the CPUSA, moderating its tone and tactics, also began moving toward a coalition of Left forces. A Central Committee resolution ordered members to persuade and convince rather than abuse Socialists, and to form local united front committees with them.[59] In California, for example, Communists joined EPIC and Young Democrat clubs. The party then convened a meeting in Washington, D.C., to form a national farm workers union, and a drought conference in South Dakota.[60] Browder spoke in favor of a national labor party, a formal united front with the ASP, and the value of intellectuals.

At the end of 1934, following a Comintern decision that famous writers and artists would be more valuable to Communism than the "social-realist" output of proletarian writers, the American party created a Cultural Commission to organize well-known writers and artists into the League of American Writers and the American Artists' Congress. They were designed to rally support for Soviet foreign policy under the banner of the struggle against war and Fascism. At the first American Writers Congress in April 1935, Browder assured his listeners that the party had no intention of telling them how to write, and that there was "no fixed 'Party line' by which works of art can be automatically separated into sheep and goats."[61]*

Suspicion of Communist motives did not dissipate, however. In March 1935, Sinclair condemned the united front, calling it "a very silly pretense," and warned EPIC members that "if any Communist comes into our movement he comes for the sole purpose of destroying the movement."[62] At the EPIC convention in May, a heated debate over the united front occurred. Sheridan Downey called it "a dagger in the hands of the Communist Party held at the heart of the liberal movement in California," John Packard predicted it would lead to "a dictatorship in America like Hitler's in Germany," and Sinclair likened EPIC to "a mother nursing an infant at her breast [dealing] with those who wish to cut the infant's throat." United

*The First Artists' Congress met on February 14–16, 1936, in New York City, but no CPUSA hierarchs delivered major speeches there. Matthew Baigell and Julia Williams, eds., *Artists Against War and Fascism: Papers of the First American Artists' Congress* (New Brunswick: Rutgers University Press, 1986).

front advocates responded that EPIC, by itself, could not win the battles against war and Fascism and for a collective society. A compromise resolution approved united fronts based on "true democratic principles."[63] The ASP's 1935 convention voted to postpone considerations of the united front, the AFL convention condemned it altogether, and the Trotskyists labeled the people's front a "united front not of the working class, but with the bourgeois political state," representing not a struggle for power but one on behalf of "national recovery."[64]

The bulk of unified Left activity that did develop came from the ranks of workers and students. "Every major center of industrial unrest in 1934 witnessed the rise of labor party activity the following year."[65] Conventions of workers in Connecticut, Wisconsin, Oregon, Toledo, Ohio, and Paterson, N. J. endorsed the idea of a labor party. Labor party tickets were nominated in San Francisco, Chicago, and Springfield, Massachusetts. Farmer-labor movements formed and won victories in Minnesota, Washington, Wisconsin, and South Dakota. In California, Borough and other EPIC organizers broke with Sinclair and formed United Organizations for Progressive Political Action, a coalition of fourteen liberal and progressive groups, which helped elect three judges and five city council candidates in Los Angeles.

In December 1935, the National Student League and the Student League for Industrial Democracy merged to form the American Student Union. Stressing antimilitarism and collective security against aggression, the American Student Union enrolled 20,000 members and organized antiwar strikes in 1936 and 1937 that far surpassed those of 1934 and 1935. Communist members proved very conciliatory, even allowing the anti-Fascist plank to be placed sixth among the demands.[66] They were so accommodating, in fact, that the more revolutionary-inclined members of the student movement, such as Harold Draper, accused them of sapping the movement's militancy. The virus of people's front opportunism, he argued, was debilitating the union and restricting it to tactics that did not antagonize liberals or polarize students. In place of picketing and striking, he wrote, the Communists wanted the American Student Union to tag along "in the wake of middle class prejudice."[67]

The Communist people's front movement moved into a higher gear at the end of 1935. The party dissolved its United Farmers League and sent its members into the Farm Holiday Association and the National Farmers Union, merged its unemployed groups with the Workers' Alliance, opened the third congress of the League Against War and Fascism to unaffiliated groups, and tried to place itself in the mainstream of radical American patriotism. William Z. Foster wrote that Communists should link their effort to build an anti-Fascist movement "with the historical traditions of the American masses against capitalist oppression," and Browder, at a Madison Square Garden rally, recited parts of the "Star-Spangled Banner."[68] Although many Leftists regarded the CP's adoption of "Tom" Paine and "Tom" Jefferson with marked skepticism, Dorothy Healey has attributed the party's remarkable growth (from 7,500 in 1930 to 75,000 in 1938) to its decision "to reckon with the American heritage."[69]

The massive sit-down strikes of 1936 seemed as if they would increase the power and unity of the Left, but, as in France, worker militancy did not get translated into political effectiveness. The strength of organized labor grew tremendously—union membership totals tripled by 1941—but the antiwar and anti-Fascist causes did not keep pace, and the Italian invasion of Abyssinia did not awaken much interest.

Nearly two million workers went on strike in 1936. They were spearheaded by Ohio rubber workers and Michigan autoworkers, and spurred by their anger at employer resistance to their demands, the passage of the National Labor Relations Act in June 1935, the election of Frank Murphy as governor of Michigan, and John L. Lewis' determination to ignore the AFL's repudiation of his Committee for Industrial Organization.*

Although Murphy and Roosevelt, like Blum in France, believed that sit-down strikes were illegal interferences with private property rights, they refused to use force to evict the workers. To take greater advantage of this surge of militancy, Lewis and Sidney Hillman (Amalgamated Men's Clothing Workers) created Labor's Non-Partisan League as a means of broadening labor's political strength and eliminating its dependence on the Democratic Party. Funded and controlled by Lewis' mine workers and Hillman's garment workers, the league took firmest root in West Virginia, Ohio, Pennsylvania, and New York. It supported Roosevelt's reelection and progressive candidates of any party in local, state,

---

*Lewis had formed the committee in November 1935, one month after the AFL convention had voted against organizing unions on an industrial basis. The AFL Executive Council the following August accused the unions belonging to the committee of engaging in "dual unionism," and ordered them to withdraw. One month later they were suspended, and in March 1937, their delegates were expelled from AFL bodies. The committee transformed itself into the Congress of Industrial Organizations at its constitutional convention, October 1938.

and congressional elections, but resolutely refused to become or support a third national party.[70]

Communist leaders did likewise, but without announcing it. Fearing that open support for the league or Roosevelt would weaken them both, Alexander Bittleman accused the CIO and the league of seeking Roosevelt's reelection at the expense of "the most vital economic and political interests of the toiling masses of this country," Browder argued that only a national farmer-labor party could usefully serve as a "foundation for the people's front," and the CPUSA ran its own people as vehicles for Communist propaganda. Communists, however, devoted their time, and energy to securing the election of pro–New Deal candidates.[71]

Clearly, the people's front was a Communist maneuver to open doors to organizations and constituencies previously closed. Because Communists worked for undeniably important Left causes—organizing workers, blacks, anti-Fascists—and because Communist organizers were only too willing to "hide the Party face" in the interest of building mass organizations, organizations joined and built by Communists attracted unprecedented numbers of workers, blacks, intellectuals, artists, and liberals to political causes. But even though Upton Sinclair approved Browder's 1936 presidential platform and opened the pages of *EPIC News* to announcements from the League Against War and Fascism, the ASP and AFL continued to remain aloof, the Trotskyists continued to criticize, and, according to Healey: "When it came to an issue like Spain, when we came into head-on conflict with the Catholic Church, or in other big social issues, then even in the unions and organizations that the Left had organized and influenced and dominated, there was always a very great limitation on how far that influence extended."[72]

It did not extend to effective anti-Fascism. Mussolini and Hitler were too distant, and the domestic radical Right did not present a serious threat. Its motley ranks—the Liberty League, Silver Shirts Legion, German-American Bund, Ku Klux Klan, Father Coughlin, Huey Long, etc.—lacked the programs, funding, organizers, and conditions to develop a substantial following. Native Fascists remained on the periphery of American politics.[73] Even the 892,378 people who voted for the National Union Party in 1936 cared much less for the demagogues who organized it (Coughlin, Dr. Francis Townsend, and Gerald L. K. Smith) and much more for the opportunity to express their disapproval of Roosevelt's failure to end the depression.[74]

When a potent rallying symbol did arise, in the form of the Spanish

Civil War, solidarity and fissuring ran parallel courses in anti-Fascist ranks. Part of the problem was the CPUSA's polemical response to criticism of the Moscow trials and Communist behavior in Spain, but even if Communists had remained silent, Spain would have divided the American Left. Hostility to Roosevelt's decision to embargo arms shipments to Spain was nearly unanimous, but opinions diverged on the best means to support the republic and maintain peace in the world. The Communists sent 3,000 volunteers to the Abraham Lincoln Battalion,[75] the Socialists recruited 500 for the Eugene V. Debs Column, while the Trotskyists demanded that arms should be sent to Spanish workers and peasants, rather than to the Popular Front government. The AFL's Executive Council blocked a resolution advocating support for the republic and cooperation with groups aiding it, and John L. Lewis maneuvered to avoid the issue in order not to split Catholics from Protestants in the CIO.[76] Labor support for the Loyalists came from individual locals' contributions to the North American Committee to Aid Spanish Democracy.[77]

Disputes over the Spanish Civil War led to the expulsion of the Trotskyists from the ASP* and a major rift in the American Student Union. In the former case, Trotskyist refusal to follow the majority's uncritical support of the Spanish Popular Front government caused the schism; in the latter instance, the question of the nature of student support for the republic sparked a bitter debate. The national officers each took a different position on the relationship between Spain and peace, while the editors of *The Student Advocate*, the union's newspaper, moved closer to the Communist position and farther from that of the rank and file. Though the delegates to the December 1936 national convention agreed to avoid the question of collective security and reaffirm the peace pledge, the editors unequivocally stated, on the eve of the fourth student peace strike in April 1937, that "the cause of peace is being most valiantly defended by the Spanish Loyalists."[78] The editor's criticism of the strike's organizers caused such restiveness in the American Student Union that it withdrew from official support in order to preserve unity.[79] In November, the Administrative Committee, by a vote of 6–5, dumped the Oxford pledge. When the December convention ratified that move, 282–108, the Young Socialists withdrew and formed their own antiwar organization.[80]

The peace movement breach also widened during 1937. The President's

---

*The Trotskyists then formed the Socialist Workers Party.

decision not to invoke the Neutrality Act against the participants in the Far Eastern war led the pacifist wing to launch a vigorous campaign to get America out of the Orient and to pass the Ludlow Amendment, requiring a national referendum before war could be declared (except in case of invasion). The collective security advocates, on the other hand, formed the Committee for Concerted Peace Efforts to revise the neutrality laws so that the President would have the power to favor "peace-loving" nations and democracies involved in wars with dictators, aggressors, and treaty violators.[81] The people's front groups remained solidly pro–collective security.

Although Communists in organizations like the CIO were careful not to make an issue of Spain or collective security, their position was becoming precarious for other reasons. The national tide had begun to turn against labor. A recession and a determined employer counteroffensive brought defeat to strikes at Republic Steel and Ford Motor, forced the United Electrical Workers to fight fifty lockouts and strikes, and led to unemployment, a decrease in union membership and dues paying, and layoffs of union organizers. Major unions, such as the United Auto Workers, began to remove Leftists from prominent positions.

At the same time, American Trotskyists, seeing a grand opportunity to defend their leader, put the Soviet Union on the defensive, and undermine the people's front, launched a frontal assault on the verdicts in the Moscow trials. A Provisional Committee for the Defense of Leon Trotsky was formed in November 1936, and made permanent in December. It created a Preliminary Commission of Inquiry Into the Charges Made Against Leon Trotsky in the Moscow Trials. The commission then appointed a subcommittee, chaired by John Dewey, which traveled to Coyoacan, Mexico, in April to record Trotsky's testimony.[82] Even had the committee and commission not been packed with pro-Trotsky people, the Communists would have blasted it. Since it was, they unlimbered all their polemical and abusive guns, labeling the inquiry's backers allies of Fascism, agents of reaction, "scabs, splitters, and assassins."

Some non-Communists expressed dismay with the inquiry, because, they argued, the anti-Fascist cause was more important than the behavior of the one country in the world actually aiding that movement. Other Leftists simply preferred not to have to examine too closely the vehicle (people's front) of a cause (the Spanish Civil War) they did not question. *The New Republic*, for example, opposed the Commission of Inquiry because it intensified confusion on the Left, and because Spain, the CIO, and unity were more important issues than the guilt of Trotsky.[83] A large group of "American Progressives"—137—sent a statement to *New Masses* declaring that "anti-Soviet propaganda" was being used "to mask the international aspects of fascism, and to destroy the unity of workers, liberals, and progressives. Much of their propaganda is supplied by Trot-skyist sources, and is used in attempts to weaken the anti-fascist fight."[84]

Communist Party leaders were far more worried about the inquiry's impact on people's image of the Soviet Union than they were about its effects on anti-Fascism. Party spokespeople were already moving away from the people's front. Browder was promoting a peace front of the Western democracies and the Soviet Union, and Alexander Trachtenberg was introducing the idea of a "democratic front" within the United States.[85] The democratic front was adopted at the May 1938 CPUSA convention. It was a broader, looser, more general, less doctrinaire approach to Left unity than the people's front. Party ideologues, such as Clarence Hathaway and Eugene Dennis, argued that the democratic front was the 'building block" of the people's front and *"the concrete application of the people's front policy in the conditions of a rising democratic movement."*[86] In fact, it was part of the CPUSA campaign to implant itself more firmly in the New Deal coalition in order to push that coalition toward support of national rearmament. The American League Against War and Fascism was renamed the American League for Peace and Democracy. The Young Communist League won control of the American Student Union, dissolved *The Student Advocate,* and turned the union into a virtual Young Democratic Club, replete with fulsome praise for Roosevelt's domestic and foreign policies.[87] The platform the California state party section developed for the 1938 state elections—with its call for putting Americans back to work, guaranteed social security, protection of farmers, and full rights for blacks[88]—was less radical than EPIC's in 1934, and Malcolm Cowley accused *New Masses* of becoming conventional and timid.[89] Browder capped this move in the months following Munich (and his October 1938 trip to Moscow) by adopting a national defense and war preparedness posture, while *The Communist* suggested that Roosevelt's America was not an "imperialist power."[90]

Other components of militant anti-Fascism also fell by the wayside in late 1938, distraught over the news of Munich and the impending fall of the Spanish Republic, weakened by the economic recession, or, as in the case of the Jewish Labor Committee, stifled by a resolution passed at the December 18, 1938 meeting of a newly organized umbrella group, the General Jewish Council: "Resolved that it is the present sense of the General Jewish Council that there should be no parades, public demonstrations, or protests by Jews."[91] Workers were markedly less militant and thought much more about jobs and wages than international events. The AFL and CIO fought each other to the point that they backed opposing candidates in several November elections,[92] while members, votes, and leaders hemorrhaged from the Socialist Party.

Only in California did the progressive forces remain unified and victorious. EPIC veterans, under the leadership of Reuben Borough and Oliver Thornton, had used a newspaper, *United Progressive News,* and a coalition, the Federation for Political Unity, to rally labor unions and civil rights and civil liberties groups. They dominated the state Democratic Party convention and, with the assistance of Labor's Non-Partisan League, elected Culbert Olson governor, Ellis Patterson lieutenant governor, and Sheridan Downey United States Senator.

Elsewhere, however, a strong conservative resurgence was evident, and the Right began to mount a counteroffensive against the New Deal and what would come to be called "premature anti-Fascists." At the same time, non-Communist anti-Fascists launched their own offensive against people's front anti-Fascists. Scattered attacks had been launched before, by liberals (Charles Beard, John Dewey, Walter Lippmann, among others), the AFL, *Partisan Review, Modern Monthly, The New Leader,* and *Common Sense,* but in 1939 two groups of intellectuals—the Committee for Cultural Freedom and the League for Cultural Freedom and Socialism—delivered a collective, organized fusillade. At the end of May, Sidney Hook sent the committee's statement of principles and a list of its signers to *The Nation* and *The New Republic.* Both journals printed large parts of the statement, and editorials critical of it. The statement lumped together under the rubric of totalitarian societies Italy, Germany, Japan, Spain, and the Soviet Union, and stated that Communists could not be reputable anti-Fascists. Freda Kirchwey, editor of *The Nation,* replied that the Communists' American fronts served not the "cause of 'totalitarian doctrine,' " but instead that of "a more workable democracy." Hook responded that the primary loyalty of Communists "is to the Kremlin and not to peace, democracy, or intellectual freedom."[93] John Dewey wrote *The New Republic,* on behalf of the committee, that "there is danger that we shall embrace a large part of fascism, while probably calling it anti-fascism," and that true anti-Fascists must be antitotalitarian as well.[94] Editorials in both journals warned the Committee for Cultural Freedom that it would weaken and divide the progressive movement.[95]

The League for Cultural Freedom, created by the editors and writers of *Partisan Review*, condemned the anti-Fascism of the people's front, claiming that it promoted war as a means to stop Hitler. American entry into such a war, they argued, would not help free Germans from the Fascist yoke, but destroy American liberties and lead to a totalitarian United States. Only a "militant struggle for socialism" in each country, the league's manifesto concluded, could defeat Fascism.[96]

The German-Russian Nonaggression Treaty strengthened the case of these anti-Communists, especially when the CPUSA's National Committee announced, on September 19: "The war that has broken out in Europe is the Second Imperialist War. . . . It is not a war against fascism."[97] People's front groups disintegrated as liberal, Socialist, and Trotskyist journals heaped diatribes on the Soviet Union, and Communists loudly defended the treaty and the subsequent invasions of Poland and Finland. The American Student Union, the Hollywood Anti-Nazi League, the American League for Peace and Democracy became Communist rump groups, campaigning not against Fascism but to keep America out of war. Browder claimed that Communists were still fighting Fascism, that party policy had not changed, but Communist veterans like Steve Nelson claim they knew better.[98] So did party critics. A Socialist noted, "In a total of 26 slogans issued by the Party Central Committee [since the treaty], there is *not one* calling for the *defeat* of Germany."[99]

Most of those who had been critical or wary of Communism could not take much solace from the accuracy of their warnings. The anti-Fascist movement collapsed along with what had remained of Soviet and Communist reliability, leaving the American Left vulnerable to a new "Red scare" campaign. The AFL and ASP maintained their consistent opposition to American involvement in a war, but from a position far distant from that of the CPUSA. The tiny Trotskyist party split into tinier parties when the "Old Man" approved the Red Army's invasion of Eastern Europe and Finland.[100] Independent Leftists tried to form a new, neo-Marxist movement, divorced both from Stalinists and anti-Stalinists, but could not find solid ground on which to cohere. After several months of trying, they went the way of all Left politics between the wars—their separate ways.[101]

Epilogue

The emotions and the arguments used
by the anti-Fascists were taken over
by the democratic governments in their
war against Hitler. . . . But the fact was
that the anti-Fascist battle had been lost.
—Stephen Spender[1]

Where Are the War Poets?
It is the logic of our times,
No subject for immortal verse—
That we who lived by honest dreams
Defend the bad against the worse.
—C. Day Lewis[2]

War in '38 could have been the occasion for a revolution—in '40 it's
the occasion for a counter-revolution.
—Jean-Paul Sartre[3]

The second great war of the century ended with the defeat of Fascist Italy
and Nazi Germany and the dismantling of their movements and institutions in all the countries they occupied. Though united front anti-Fascism
made a reappearance in modified form following the German invasion of
the Soviet Union in June 1941, it was a shell of its former self, devoted to
victory over the Axis to the virtual exclusion of its basic prewar social and
political concerns: improvement of workers' rights and conditions, fair
treatment of racial minorities, wider democratic practices.

During the period between August 1939 and June 1941, the gap separating the Soviet Union from the democratic West and Communists from

the Left grew wider as Stalin, seeking to take full advantage of the Secret Additional Protocol, sent the Red Army into Poland, Finland, Estonia, Latvia, Lithuania, and Bessarabia, and negotiated with Hitler for Bucovina and Bulgaria. Stalin was not cunningly biding his time or secretly preparing to open a second front against Germany. He was prepared to maintain a working relationship with Hitler, watch the defeat of the democracies, and adhere to the Tripartite Pact (with Germany, Italy, and Japan) if the necessary guarantees could be arranged. As late as April 1941, with Operation Barbarossa pending against it, the Russians continued to observe their commercial arrangements with Germany and deliver considerable amounts of raw materials to it.[4]

The extent and depth of obloquy directed at Soviet behavior and Communist Party activity convinced Ivan Maisky that the outcries were a cover for "the desire of the ruling British (and French) circles to 'switch' the war, i.e. to replace the war with Hitler which was so unpleasant for them by the much more attractive war with 'Soviet Communism.' "[5] In fact, the strength of the criticism simply allowed the governments of Great Britain, France, and the United States to undertake an "attractive war" against Communists within their borders.

In the United States, the Alien Registration Act (June 1940) made it a criminal offense to advocate or organize the forceful overthrow of any government in the United States "or to be or become a member of, or affiliate with, any such society, group, or assembly of persons, knowing the purposes thereof."* The House Committee on Un-American Activities and several state versions of it launched investigations of "Communist subversion," the Federal Bureau of Investigation began compiling massive dossiers of "subversives," and several states removed the CPUSA from their ballots and fired suspected Communists from government employment. Earl Browder and three other CP leaders were charged with passport fraud at the end of 1939. Browder was convicted and began serving a four-year sentence in March 1941.

In Britain, Communist MP William Gallacher "became a sort of pariah

---

*Minneapolis Trotskyists were the first victims of this crime of guilt by association. The *Daily Worker* applauded this effort "to exterminate the Trotskyite Fifth Column from the life of our nation." Quoted in Art Preis, *Labor's Giant Step* (New York: Pioneer, 1964), p. 141. Many Communists who refused to defend the civil liberties of the Trotskyists would themselves be needing—and not getting—such a defense effort when they were indicted, tried, and imprisoned, after the war, under the same act.

in the House of Commons. Each time I got up to speak in defence of the Soviet Union . . . there was pandemonium. . . . Sometimes it looked as if I would be the subject of physical attack."[6] Demands to ban the CPGB and intern its members did not succeed, but in January 1941, the *Daily Worker* was banned for allegedly receiving subsidies from the Soviet Union.

The French government, under much more immediate duress than its counterparts in the United States and Great Britain, dissolved the PCF and arrested or drafted its leaders. In April 1940, a military tribunal condemned forty-four former Communist deputies (nine *in absentia*) to prison sentences. Foreign Leftists also received summary treatment. Loyalist supporters fleeing Spain, like Arthur Koestler, had been incarcerated in large camps in the south of France during 1939. Now, those who had fled Austria, Germany, and Czechoslovakia, were being interned in the north. Joseph Buttinger, an Austrian Social Democrat, wrote his wife: "We anti-fascists, who were received in this country as political exiles, are now treated exactly like the German Fascists in France, as 'enemy aliens.' We are all here together."[7] Willi Münzenberg was sent to Camp Chambarran in May, as the German army invaded France, and released on June 21, the day before the French-German armistice was signed. Four months later, his body was discovered in a forest near the camp. It remains unclear if he committed suicide or was murdered by Stalin's agents.[8] (Leon Trotsky was murdered by a Soviet assassin on August 20, 1940.)

In a macabre twist of fate, the man responsible for most of the arrests of France's anti-Fascists, Edouard Daladier, was himself arrested and imprisoned (along with Léon Blum, General Gamelin, and other prominent former ministers) by the Vichy government. They were charged with betraying "the duties of their office by acts which contributed to the passage from a state of peace to a state of war before September 4, 1939," and by acts "which subsequently aggravated the consequences of the situation thus created."[9]

In the United States and Great Britain, meanwhile, people's front groups were reduced to their Communist nuclei, and efforts to reconstruct them on anti-imperialist war lines—the People's Convention in Britain and the American Peace Mobilization—failed. It was Hitler who provided the Communists their path back to respectability. The German attack on Russia allowed Communists to act patriotically in the nonoccupied countries and heroically in the occupied ones. A united war front emerged, and Russian popularity reached unprecedented levels. But even as anti-Fascists relinked arms to defeat the Axis, many, like George Orwell, felt deeply divided. Out loud he said, "I never thought I should live to say 'Good luck to Comrade Stalin,' but I do"; in his diary, however, he wrote: "One could not have a better example of the moral and emotional shallowness of our time, than the fact that we are now all more or less pro-Stalin. This disgusting murderer is temporarily on our side, and so the purges etc. are suddenly forgotten."[10] As it turned out, they were only temporarily shelved by some, while others continued to harbor their memories and add material to them.

A much more horrifying, and destructive, example of the moral shallowness of the war against Fascism was provided by the Allied governments, who made only token efforts to save the lives of the Jewish people of Europe.[11] As early as the July 1938 conference at Evian-les-Bains, the delegates of the thirty-two countries that sent representatives retreated from concrete action to facilitate the emigration of political refugees from Germany or Austria. They simply recommended that an Intergovernmental Committee be established in London with the authority to negotiate with Germany (to get it to handle its expulsions in a less chaotic manner and allow the expelled to take some of their property with them) and to approach potential receiving countries "with a view to developing opportunities for permanent settlement."[12] During the war, American and British leaders refused to countenance substantive rescue or refugee operations or military measures against the death camps.

As they had in the prewar period, the democratic governments reflected the attitudes of their populations. A survey published in *Fortune* in July 1938 indicated that 67 percent of the respondents did not want the United States government to expand its immigrant quotas, and American newspaper coverage of the persecution of German Jews during the thirties, and the annihilation of European Jewry during the forties, did not fully convey the scope of the atrocity.[13] In Britain, an Austrian Jewish refugee, George Clare, discovered that the stories of his escape shocked his listeners and engendered kindness from them. "But it was rare to be asked a second time. By December 1938 there were so many refugees, so many harrowing stories in the newspapers. . . . these cruelties were happening in a world which for most of them, emotionally, was on the other side of the moon."[14]

The Soviet Union, for its part, convinced a number of its most prominent Jews to organize a Jewish Anti-Fascist Committee, but would not allow it to promote Jewish causes. The committee became a vehicle for influencing American Jews to support Soviet foreign policy and contribute money to Soviet causes. (The committee's organizers would be arrested and executed after the war.)[15]

People's front anti-Fascism, with few exceptions, had proved equally insensitive, and people's front organizations had not campaigned to save the Jews. Most Marxists believed that anti-Semitism was a symptom of a greater disease that could only be defeated by the overthrow of capitalism in the long run and the defeat of Hitler in the short run. Thus, in victory there was defeat. The instrumental quality of official and popular anti-Fascism prevented both from raising significant obstacles to one of Nazism's most integral goals—the destruction of European Jewry.

Marxist anti-Fascists had politically educated many people; they had aided many refugees from and victims of fascism; they had helped elect two governments in Spain and France that promised important social and economic reforms; they had bodily defended the Spanish Republic against a coalition of reactionaries, Fascists, and Nazis; and they had clearly, repeatedly, and accurately predicted the end results of unchallenged Fascist aggression. The Communist turn toward an anti-Fascist people's front had produced a mass Communist Party in France and the blueprints for one in Italy. But Marxists failed to find a way to use anti-Fascism effectively, to create from it a force to counteract the course of events and decisions leading toward war. The fault lay both in the stars and in themselves. Marxist party leaders constantly acted as though they did not believe the words of their own spokespeople, that Fascism was the worst evil imaginable, behaving instead as if rival parties were. Rival parties and unaligned citizens, on the other hand, refused to believe and act on the obvious. What Fascists had been promising for two decades, and anti-Fascists had been warning against for ten years, came to pass in 1939—Fascism *was* war.

These failures of belief helped prepare the path to death, destruction, and suffering of an unprecedented magnitude. But as the carnage ended, and the seeds of mistrust and alienation that had been planted before the war began to bloom, those who circumstances had thrown together as allies squared off against each other, inaugurating a new era under the shadow of an infinitely more devastating war.

Notes

Introduction

1. Pierre Ayçoberry, *The Nazi Question: An Essay on the Interpretations of National Socialism, 1922–1975*, Robert Hurley, tr. (New York: Pantheon paperback, 1981), p. vii.

2. Arno Mayer, *Dynamics of Counterrevolution in Europe, 1870–1956: An Analytical Framework* (New York: Harper Torchbooks, 1971), pp. 48–50 and 86–93.

3. *Ibid.*, pp. 60–68.

4. Pierre van Paassen and James Waterman Wise, eds., *Nazism: An Assault on Civilization* (New York: Smith and Haas, 1934), p. xi.

1. Revolutions, Counterrevolutions, and the First Fascist State

1. Renzo De Felice, *Interpretations of Fascism*, Brenda Huff Everett, tr. (Cambridge: Harvard University Press, 1977), p. 181.

2. Arno Mayer, *Dynamics of Counterrevolution in Europe, 1870–1956: An Analytical Framework* (New York: Harper Torchbooks, 1971), pp. 90–91.

3. *Ibid.*, p. 91.

4. De Felice, *Interpretations of Fascism*, p. 181.

5. J. Erös, "Hungary," in S. J. Woolf, ed., *Fascism in Europe* (London: Methuen, 1981), pp. 125–126; John Weiss, *The Fascist Tradition: Radical Right Wing Extremism in Modern Europe* (New York: Harper and Row, 1967), p. 87.

6. K. R. Stadler, "Austria," in Woolf, *Fascism in Europe*, p. 99.

7. F. L. Carsten, *The Rise of Fascism* (Berkeley and Los Angeles: University of California Press paperback, 1971), pp. 224–225.

8. Basil Dmytryshyn, *USSR: A Concise History*, 4th ed. (New York: Scribner's paperback, 1984), p. 92.

9. *Ibid.*, p. 93.

10. Arno J. Mayer, *The Politics and Diplomacy of Peacemaking: Containment and Counterrevolution at Versailles, 1918–1919* (New York: Knopf, 1967), pp. 245, 247, and 252.

11. *Ibid.*, pp. 98 and 102.

    12. Isaac Deutscher, *The Prophet Armed: Trotsky, 1879–1921* (New York: Vintage, 1954), pp. 463–466.
    13. Julius Braunthal, *History of the International,* vol. 2: *1914–1943,* John Clark, tr. (New York: Praeger, 1967), p. 35.
    14. Robert G. L. Waite, *Vanguard of Nazism: The Free Corps Movement in Postwar Germany, 1918–1923* (New York: Norton paperback, 1969), pp. 5 and 13; Hajo Halborn, *A History of Modern Germany, 1840–1945* (New York: Knopf, 1969), p. 529.
    15. Henry Ashby Turner, Jr., *German Big Business and the Rise of Hitler* (New York: Oxford University Press, 1985), p. 9.
    16. David W. Morgan, *The Socialist Left and the German Revolution: A History of the German Independent Social Democratic Party, 1917–1922* (Ithaca, N.Y.: Cornell University Press, 1975), p. 214.
    17. Helmut Gruber, *International Communism in the Era of Lenin: A Documentary History* (New York: Fawcett, 1967), pp. 170–173.
    18. Rudolf L. Tőkés, *Béla Kun and the Hungarian Soviet Republic: The Origins and Role of the Communist Party of Hungary in the Revolutions of 1918–1919* (New York: Praeger, 1967), pp. 163–164.
    19. Mayer, *Politics and Diplomacy,* pp. 578 and 583.
    20. *Ibid.,* p. 591.
    21. Alfred D. Low, "The First Austrian Republic and Soviet Hungary," in Gruber, *International Communism,* pp. 245–261.
    22. Tőkés, *Béla Kun,* pp. 192–193.
    23. Nicholas M. Nagy-Talavera, *The Green Shirts and the Others: A History of Fascism in Hungary and Rumania* (Stanford: Hoover Institution Press, 1970), pp. 52–55.
    24. B. Mussolini, "The Political and Social Value of Fascism," written for the *Enciclopaedii Italiana,* reprinted in Eugen Weber, *The Western Tradition: From the Enlightenment to the Present,* 3d ed. (Lexington, Mass.: D.C. Heath, 1972), p. 839.
    25. Reprinted in S. William Halperin, *Mussolini and Italian Fascism* (Princeton: D. Van Nostrand, 1964), pp. 97–98.
    26. G. D. H. Cole, *A History of Socialist Thought,* vol. 4: *Communism and Social Democracy, 1914–1931,* part 1 (London: Macmillan, 1958), p. 372.
    27. Jane Degras, ed., *The Communist International, 1919–1943: Documents* (New York: Oxford University Press, 1960), 1:188.
    28. August 27, 1920, *ibid.,* p. 191.
    29. Gruber, *International Communism,* pp. 294–295 and 301–302.
    30. *Ibid.,* pp. 296 and 299.
    31. January 21, 1921, in Degras, *The Communist International,* 1:209.
    32. John M. Cammett, *Antonio Gramsci and the Origins of Italian Communism* (Stanford: Stanford University Press paperback, 1969), p. 151.
    33. *Ibid.,* p. 153.
    34. Daniel L. Horowitz, *The Italian Labor Movement* (Cambridge: Harvard University Press, 1963), pp. 164–165 and 168–169; A. Rossi [Angelo Tasca], *The*

Rise of Italian Fascism, 1918–1922, Peter and Dorothy Wait, trs. (New York: Fertig, 1966), p. 157.

35. Carsten, *The Rise of Fascism,* p. 56.

36. *Ibid.,* p. 57.

37. Articles in *L'Ordine Nuovo,* February 21 and 23, 1922, reprinted in Antonio Gramsci, *Selections from Political Writings, 1921–1926,* Quintin Hoare, tr. and ed. (New York: International, 1978), pp. 83–84 and 469, n.50.

38. *Ibid.,* p. 120.

39. Reprinted *ibid.,* pp. 115 and 99.

40. Adrian Lyttelton, *The Seizure of Power: Fascism in Italy, 1919–1929* (New York: Scribner's, 1973), p. 80.

41. *Internationale Presse-Korrespondenz,* July 25, 1922, reprinted in Theo Pirker, ed., *Komintern und Faschismus: Dokumente zur Geschichte und Theorie des Faschismus* (Stuttgart: Deutsche, 1965), pp. 75–76.

42. Horowitz, *The Italian Labor Movement,* p. 171.

43. "The Victory of the Communist International," *Internationale Presse-Korrespondenz,* October 10, 1922, in Pirker, *Komintern und Faschismus,* p. 83.

44. *L'Ordine Nuovo,* October 29, 1922, in Gramsci, *Selections from Political Writings,* pp. 85–87.

45. Lyttelton, *The Seizure of Power,* p. 104.

46. Max Gallo, *Mussolini's Italy: Twenty Years of the Fascist Era,* Charles L. Markmann, tr. (New York: Macmillan, 1973), p. 189.

47. *L'Ordine Nuovo,* September 1, 1924, in Gramsci, *Selections from Political Writings,* p. 259.

48. *L'Unitá,* July 3, 1925, *ibid.,* pp. 279–282.

49. "The Italian Communist Party After the Fifth Congress," *L'Unitá,* August 26, 1925, reprinted in *The Communist International,* n.s., no. 10, pp. 43–44.

50. Horowitz, *The Italian Labor Movement,* p. 179.

51. Reprinted in Halperin, *Mussolini and Italian Fascism,* p. 130.

52. Alan Cassels, *Mussolini's Early Diplomacy* (Princeton: Princeton University Press, 1970), p. 12.

53. *Ibid.,* pp. 188 and 192–193.

54. Lyttelton, *The Seizure of Power,* p. 428; H. Stuart Hughes, "The Early Diplomacy of Italian Fascism, 1922–1932," in Gordon A. Craig and Felix Gilbert, eds., *The Diplomats, 1919–1939* (Princeton: Princeton University Press, 1953), p. 223.

55. Cassels, *Mussolini's Early Diplomacy,* pp. 173–174 and 367–370.

56. *Ibid.,* pp. 195–198 and 379–380.

57. Hughes, "The Early Diplomacy of Italian Fascism," p. 231.

2. *The Foundations of Marxist Anti-Fascism*

1. "Theses for the Second Comintern Congress," June 5, 1920, in V. I. Lenin, *On the Unity of the International Communist Movement* (Moscow: Progress, 1971), p. 201.

2. "On the Struggle in the Italian Socialist Party," November 4, 1920, printed in *Pravda*, November 7, and reprinted in V. I. Lenin, *Collected Works* (Moscow: Progress, 1966), 31:383.

3. Ruth Fischer, *Stalin and German Communism: A Study in the Origins of the State Party* (Cambridge: Harvard University Press, 1948), p. 115.

4. "Five Years of the Russian Revolution and the Prospects of World Revolution: Report to the Fourth Congress of the Communist International," November 13, 1922, in V. I. Lenin, *Speeches at Congresses of the Communist International* (Moscow: Progress, 1972), p. 144.

5. "On the United Front: Material for a Report on the Question of French Communism," Enlarged Plenum of ECCI, March 2, 1922, in Leon Trotsky, *The First Five Years of the Communist International* (New York: Monad, 1972), 2:92.

6. Alain Bergounioux, "L'Internationale Ouvrière Socialiste Entre les Deux Guerres," in Hugues Portelli, ed., *L'Internationale Socialiste* (Paris: Editions Ouvrières, 1983), pp. 29, 33, 38, and 42.

7. *Bulletin of the Labor and Socialist International* (June 1924), 1(3):8.

8. Claud Cockburn, *The Devil's Decade* (London: Sedgwick and Jackson, 1973), p. 55.

9. Aino Kuusinen, *Before and After Stalin: A Personal Account of Soviet Russian from the 1920s to the 1960s*, Paul Stevenson, tr. (London: Joseph, 1974), pp. 38, 59–60, and 78.

10. A. Rossi [Angelo Tasca], *The Rise of Italian Fascism, 1918–1922*, Peter and Dorothy Wait, trs. (New York: Fertig, 1966), p. 157.

11. Jane Degras, ed., *The Communist International, 1919–1943: Documents* (New York: Oxford University Press, 1960), 1:3.

12. "The Third International and Its Place in History," April 15, 1919, in Lenin, *On the Unity*, pp. 111 and 115.

13. Jane Degras, "United Front Tactics in the Comintern, 1921–1928," in David Footman, ed., *International Communism*, St. Antony's Papers, no. 9 (Carbondale: Southern Illinois University Press, 1960), pp. 12–13.

14. Marie-Luise Goldbach, *Karl Radek und die deutsch-sowjetischen Beziehungen, 1918–1923* (Bonn: Neue Gesellschaft, 1973), p. 32.

15. "Radek's 'Political Salon' in Berlin, 1919," E. H. Carr's translation of excerpts from Karl Radek, "November," *Krasnaya Nov'* (1926), no. 10, *Soviet Studies* (April 1951), 3:422–423.

16. David W. Morgan, *The Socialist Left and the German Revolution: A History of the German Independent Social Democratic Party, 1917–1922* (Ithaca, N.Y.: Cornell University Press, 1975), p. 293.

17. Helmut Gruber, "Paul Levi and the Comintern," *Survey* (October 1964), no. 53, p. 74.

18. E. H. Carr, *The Bolshevik Revolution, 1917–1923* (Harmondsworth: Penguin 1966), 3:226.

19. *Die Rote Fahne*, January 8, 1921, quoted *ibid.*, pp. 332–333.

20. Lenin, letter to Klara Zetkin and Paul Levi, April 16, 1921, in *Collected Works* (1970), 45:124.

21. Levi's report to the ECCI, January 20, 1921, is in Milorad M. Drachkovitch and Branko Lazitch, eds., *The Comintern: Historical Highlights. Essays, Recollections, Documents* (New York: Praeger, 1966), pp. 275–282.

22. ECCI Resolution, March 1921, in Degras, *The Communist International*, 1:212.

23. Lenin, *Collected Works*, 45:125.

24. Goldbach, *Karl Radek*, pp. 85–86; Carr, *The Bolshevik Revolution*, 3:334–336.

25. Paul Levi, *Zwischen Spartakus und Sozialdemokratie: Schriften, Reden, und Briefe*, Charlotte Beradt, ed. (Frankfurt: Europäische, 1969), pp. 40–43.

26. *Ibid.*, p. 44.

27. Lenin, *Collected Works*, 45:124–125.

28. Victor Serge, *Memoirs of a Revolutionary, 1901–1941*, Peter Sedgwick, tr. (New York: Oxford University Press paperback, 1963), p. 140.

29. Lenin, *Collected Works*, 42:319–323; see also Lenin, "A Letter to the German Communists," August 14, 1921, in *Collected Works* (1965), 32:516–520.

30. Carr, *The Bolshevik Revolution*, 3:389.

31. "Directives on United Front," issued December 18, 1921, in Degras, *The Communist International*, 1:311 and 316.

32. *Ibid.*, 1:308–309.

33. Lenin, *Collected Works*, 42:401 and 394.

34. *The Second and Third Internationals and the Vienna Union: Official Report of the Conference Between the Executives, Held at the Reichstag, Berlin, on the 2nd April 1922, and following Days* (London: Labour, 1922), pp. 11, 15, 27, and 83–85.

35. Lenin, "We Have Paid Too Much," *Pravda*, April 11, 1922, in *Collected Works*, 33:330–334.

36. May 19, 1922, in Degras, *The Communist International*, 1:347.

37. *Ibid*, 1:351.

38. *Bulletin of the International* (June 1922), no. 3, pp. 2 and 10.

39. Degras, *The Communist International*, 1:363.

40. Rossi, *The Rise of Italian Fascism*, p. 321.

41. Degras, *The Communist International*, 1:376.

42. Serge, *Memoirs*, pp. 162–163.

43. Lenin, letter of December 11, 1922, in *Collected Works*, 45:600.

44. Lenin, letter of November 8, 1922, *ibid.*, 45:592.

45. E. H. Carr, *Socialism in One Country*, vol. 3, part 1, p. 82.

46. Reprinted in Theo Pirker, ed., *Komintern und Faschismus: Dokumente zur Geschichte und Theorie des Faschismus* (Stuttgart: Deutsche, 1965), pp. 108–109.

47. Degras, *The Communist International*, 1:435–436.

48. *Ibid.*, pp. 448–449.

49. Trotsky to Lenin, November 24, 1922, in *The Trotsky Papers, 1917–1922*,

Jan M. Meijer, ed. (The Hague: Mouton, 1971), 2:769–771; Lenin to Trotsky, November 25, 1922, in *Collected Works*, 45:593.

50. Degras, *The Communist International*, 1:424–426.

51. John M. Cammett, *Antonio Gramsci and the Origins of Italian Communism* (Stanford: Stanford University Press paperback, 1967), p. 165.

52. Humbert-Droz, *Archives de Jules Humbert-Droz*, vol. 2: *Les Partis Communistes des Pays Latins et l'Internationale Communiste dans les Années 1923–1927*, Siegfried Bahne, ed. (Dordrecht, Holl.: D. Reidel, 1983), pp. 123, 153–156, and 206.

53. *Ibid.*, pp. 339, 355, and 652, n.7.

54. Paul Guichonnet, "Le Socialisme Italien," in Jacques Droz, ed., *Histoire Générale du Socialisme*, vol. 3: *De 1919 à 1945* Paris: Presses Universitaires de France, 1977), p. 189.

55. Antonio Gramsci, *Selections from Political Writings, 1921–1926*, Quintin Hoare, tr. and ed. (New York: International, 1978), p. 317.

56. Humbert-Droz, "Mussolini's Labor Charter," *The Communist International*, September 15, 1927, p. 256.

57. The paragraphs on the Italian Left in exile are based on W. Hilton-Young, *The Italian Left: A Short History of Political Socialism in Italy* (Westport, Conn.: Greenwood Press, 1975), p. 154; Guichonnet, "Le Socialisme Italien," pp. 190 and 192; Charles F. Delzell, *Mussolini's Enemies: The Italian Anti-Fascist Resistance* (New York: Fertig, 1974), pp. 56–63.

58. E. J. Hobsbawm, *Revolutionaries* (New York: New American Library, 1973), p. 34.

59. *International Press Correspondence*, January 22, 1930, p. 73.

60. E. Ercoli [Togliatti], "Communists and the *Confederazione del Lavoro*," *The Communist International*, November 30, 1926, p. 17.

61. Grieco, "The Situation and Prospects in Italy," *The Communist International*, December 15, 1928, pp. 48–49.

62. "Letter from Presidium of ECCI and RILU Bureau to IFTU and Second International," January 15, 1923, in Degras, *The Communist International*, 2:8–9.

63. *Ibid.*, 2:14.

64. Reprinted in Pirker, *Komintern und Faschismus*, pp. 116–118.

65. Reprinted *ibid.*, p. 120.

66. Degras, *The Communist International*, 2:42–43.

67. Radek, "Leo Schlageter: Der Wanderer in Nichts," reprinted in Hermann Weber, ed., *Der deutsche Kommunismus: Dokumente* (Cologne: Kiepenheuer and Witsch, 1963), p. 147.

68. Lionel Kochan, *Russia and the Weimar Republic* (Cambridge: Bowes and Bowes, 1954), pp. 80–81.

69. Degras, *The Communist International*, 2:52–53.

70. *Ibid.*, 2:62–64; E. H. Carr, *The Interregnum, 1923–1924* (New York: Macmillan, 1954), pp. 201–242.

71. *Internationale Presse-Korrespondenz* (1923), 3:1076–1077, reprinted in David Beetham, *Marxists in Face of Fascism: Writings by Marxists on Fascism, from the Inter-War Period* (Manchester: Manchester University Press, 1983), pp. 149 and 151.

72. Julius Braunthal, *History of the International*, vol. 2: *1914–1943*, John Clark, tr. (New York: Praeger, 1967), pp. 298–300.

73. Zinoviev, "Lessons of German Events and United Front Tactics," *The Communist International* (1924), n.s., no. 2, p. 93.

74. Degras, *The Communist International*, 2:77.

75. *Ibid.*, 2:151–152.

76. *Ibid.*, 2:138–140.

77. *Ibid.*, 2:147 and 139.

78. Stalin, "On the International Situation," *Bolshevik*, September 9, 1924, reprinted in Weber, *Der deutsche Kommunismus*, p. 181, and in *The Communist International* (November 1924), no. 6, p. 4.

79. "Theses of the Seventh ECCI Plenum on the International Situation and the Tasks of the Communist International," December 13, 1926, in Degras, *The Communist International*, 2:324.

80. *Ibid.*, 2:256.

81. Fenner Brockway, *Inside the Left: Thirty Years of Platform, Press, Prison, and Parliament* (London, Allen and Unwin, 1942), p. 167.

82. Summary of the 1927 Congress (in French), League Against Imperialism Archive, file 51, International Instituut voor Sociale Geschiedenis, Amsterdam.

83. Deutscher, *Stalin: A Political Biography*, 2d ed. (New York: Oxford University Press paperback, 1967), pp. 403–404.

84. Theodore Draper, "The Strange Case of the Comintern," *Survey* (Summer 1972), 18:101–103.

85. Humbert-Droz, letters of February 26 and April 8, 1927, in *Archives Jules Humbert-Droz*, 2:376 and 401.

86. Draper, "The Strange Case," pp. 103–104.

87. E. H. Carr, *Foundations of a Planned Economy, 1926–1929* (London: Macmillan, 1976), vol. 3, part 1, p. 188.

88. *International Press Correspondence*, July 19, 1928, p. 689.

89. Degras, *The Communist International*, 2: 455–456.

90. *Ibid.*, 2:484–485.

91. *International Press Correspondence*, August 23, 1928, p. 941; September 4, 1928, p. 1039; September 25, 1928, p. 1197.

92. Trotsky, "Summary and Perspectives of the Chinese Revolution," June 1928, in *The Third International After Lenin* (New York: Pathfinder, 1970), p. 228.

93. Quoted in Donald Sassoon's introduction to Palmiro Togliatti, *On Gramsci and Other Writings* (London: Lawrence and Wishart, 1979), pp. 9–10.

94. Lukács, *Political Writings, 1919–1929*, Michael McColgan, tr. (London: NLB, 1972), p. 249.

95. *Bulletin of the Labour and Socialist International* (September 1928), series 2, p. 4.

96. *Ibid.* (April 1929), p. 3.

97. *International Press Correspondence,* February 23, 1929, pp. 169–170; February 27, 1929, p. 207; March 27, 1929, pp. 368–369.

98. *The Communist International* 6(8): 239–240 and 6(24): 969 and 973.

3. The Nazi Phenomenon

1. Erich Eyck, *A History of the Weimar Republic,* Harlan P. Hanson and Robert G. L. Waite, trs. (Cambridge: Harvard University Press, 1962), pp. 278–282.

2. Robert G. L. Waite, *Vanguard of Nazism: The Free Corps Movement in Postwar Germany, 1918–1923* (New York: Norton paperback, 1969), pp. 177–181; Julius Braunthal, *History of the International,* vol. 2: *1919–1943,* John Clark, tr. (New York: Praeger, 1967), p. 35; Richard Breitman, *German Socialism and Weimar Democracy* (Chapel Hill: University of North Carolina Press, 1981), pp. 52–56.

3. Hajo Holborn, *A History of Modern Germany, 1840–1945* (New York: Knopf, 1969), p. 603.

4. Dietrich Orlow, *The History of the Nazi Party: 1919–1933* (Pittsburgh: University of Pittsburgh Press, 1969), pp. 42–45; Holborn, *A History of Modern Germany,* pp. 609–611; Alan Bullock, *Hitler: A Study in Tyranny,* abr. ed. (New York: Harper and Row paperback, 1971), pp. 55–60.

5. *Internazionale Presse-Korrespondenz,* December 27, 1922, reprinted in Theo Pirker, ed., *Komintern und Faschismus: Dokumente zur Geschichte und Theorie des Faschismus* (Stuttgart: Deutsche, 1965), p. 141.

6. *Ibid.,* November 3, 1923, pp. 144–145.

7. *Ibid.,* March 29, 1924, pp. 150–151.

8. Holborn, *A History of Modern Germany,* pp. 590, 617, and 621.

9. Istvan Deak, *Weimar Germany's Left-Wing Intellectuals: A Political History of the Weltbühne and Its Circle* (Berkeley and Los Angeles: University of California Press, 1968), pp. 159–160.

10. Jacques Droz, "Le Socialisme en Allemagne," in *Histoire Générale du Socialisme* (Paris: Presses Universitaires de France, 1977), 3: 215–216.

11. Orlow, *The History of the Nazi Party,* pp. 61, 84, 87, 95, 117–120, 129, and 137.

12. M. Feuchtwanger, *An Emigré Life: Munich, Berlin, Sanary, Pacific Palisades,* UCLA Oral History Program, 1976, 2:769.

13. G. Regler, *The Owl of Minerva* (London: Hart-Davis, 1959), p. 149.

14. Eve Rosenhaft, *Beating the Fascists? The German Communists and Political Violence, 1929–1933* (Cambridge: Cambridge University Press, 1983), pp. 88–93.

15. Erich Matthias, "The Downfall of the Old Social Democratic Party in

1933," in Hajo Holborn, ed., *Republic to Reich: The Making of the Nazi Revolution* (New York: Pantheon, 1972), p. 55.

16. Rosenhaft, *Beating the Fascists?* pp. 64 and 67.

17. Jan Valtin [Richard Krebs], *Out of the Night* (New York: Alliance, 1941), p. 357.

18. Droz, "Le Socialisme en Allemagne," p. 226; Carola Stern, *Ulbricht: A Political Biography*, Abe Farbstein, tr. (New York: Praeger, 1965), p. 40; Valtin, *Out of the Night*, p. 365.

19. Rosenhaft, *Beating the Fascists?* pp. 81 and 54.

20. Zetkin, *Clara Zetkin: Selected Writings*, Philip S. Foner, ed. (New York: International 1984), p. 174.

21. Matthias, "The Downfall," p. 56.

22. Orlow, *The History of the Nazi Party*, pp. 269–271 and 297–298; Holborn, *A History of Modern Germany*, pp. 692–693 and 703–709; Bullock, *Hitler*, pp. 127–136.

23. Reprinted in Jeremy Noakes and Geoffrey Pridham, eds., *Documents on Nazism, 1919–1945* (New York: Viking, 1974), pp. 173–174.

24. Gerald D. Anderson, *Fascists, Communists, and the National Government: Civil Liberties in Great Britain, 1931–1937* (Columbia: University of Missouri Press, 1983), pp. 3–4.

25. Martin Kitchen, *The Coming of Austrian Fascism* (London: Croom Helm, 1980), pp. 16–17.

26. Peter Loewenberg, "Otto Bauer as an Ambivalent Party Leader," in Anson Rabinbach, ed., *The Austrian Socialist Experiment: Social Democracy and Austromarxism, 1918–1934* (Boulder, Colo.: Westview Press, 1985), p. 75.

27. Julius Braunthal, *The Tragedy of Austria* (London: Gollancz, 1948), p. 93.

28. Anson Rabinbach, *The Crisis of Austrian Socialism: From Red Vienna to Civil War, 1927–1934* (Chicago: University of Chicago Press, 1983), p. 91.

29. Karl R. Stadler, "Austrian Social Democracy: The Image and the Facts," in Rabinbach, ed., *The Austrian Socialist Experiment*, pp. 86–87.

30. Rabinbach, *The Crisis of Austrian Socialism*, p. 161.

31. E. H. Carr, *Twilight of the Comintern, 1930–1935* (New York: Pantheon, 1982), p. 280.

32. Bruce F. Pauley, *Hitler and the Forgotten Nazis: A History of Austrian National Socialism* (Chapel Hill: University of North Carolina Press, 1981), pp. 104–109.

33. *Ibid.*, pp. 133, 138, and 192.

34. Nicholas Nagy-Talavera, *The Green Shirts and the Others: A History of Fascism in Hungary and Rumania* (Stanford: Hoover Institution Press, 1970), pp. 94–99.

35. *Ibid.*, pp. 137, 140, and 141.

36. *Ibid.*, pp. 285 and 293.

37. *Ibid.*, pp. 295–299 and 302.

38. H. Stuart Hughes, "The Early Diplomacy of Italian Fascism, 1922–1932,"

in Gordon A. Craig and Felix Gilbert, eds., *The Diplomats, 1919–1939* (Princeton: Princeton University Press, 1953), p. 232.

39. Michael Arthur Ledeen, *Universal Fascism: The Theory and Practice of the Fascist International, 1928–1936* (New York: Fertig, 1972), pp. 63 and 67.

40. *Ibid.*, pp. 99–101.

41. *Ibid.*, pp. 82–83; Denis Mack Smith, *Mussolini's Roman Empire* (New York: Viking, 1976), p. 46.

42. Ledeen, *Universal Fascism*, pp. 84, 99, and 114–123.

43. Max Gallo, *Mussolini's Italy: Twenty Years of the Fascist Era*, Charles L. Markmann, tr. (New York: Macmillan, 1973), p. 252.

44. Smith, *Mussolini's Roman Empire*, p. 66.

4. The Contradictions of Marxist Anti-Fascism

1. Jan Valtin [Richard Krebs], *Out of the Night* (New York: Alliance, 1941), p. 202.

2. *Die Rote Fahne*, June 15, 1930, reprinted in Hermann Weber, ed., *Der deutsche Kommunismus: Dokumente* (Cologne: Kiepenheuer and Witsch, 1963), p. 151.

3. Valtin, *Out of the Night*, p. 252.

4. *Bulletin of the Labour and Socialist International* (*April 1931*) series 2, no. 11, p. 2; (August 1931), series 3, no. 1, p. 9; (June 1932), series 3, no. 3, p. 39.

5. Annette Vidal, *Henri Barbusse: Soldat de la Paix* (Paris: Editeurs Français Réunis, 1953), pp. 239–240.

6. Rolland, letter of July 14, 1932, Romain Rolland Folder, Hoover Institution Archives, Stanford University.

7. *Monde*, June 4, July 16, and September 24, 1932.

8. Babette Gross, *Willi Münzenberg: A Political Biography*, Marian Jackson, tr. (East Lansing: Michigan State University Press, 1974), p. 240.

9. Vidal, *Henri Barbusse*, pp. 253–255; *Monde*, June 4 and July 16, 1932.

10. *The World Congress Against War: Report on the Congress, Opening Address by Romain Rolland and the Manifesto Adopted at Amsterdam, August 27–29, 1932* (New York: American Committee for Struggle Against War, 1932), pp. 4, 9, and 12.

11. E. H. Carr, *Twilight of the Comintern, 1930–1935* (New York: Pantheon, 1982), p. 391.

12. Victor Basch, "Le Congrès Mondiale Contre la Guerre Impérialiste," *Les Cahiers des Droits de l'Homme*, August 30, 1934, p. 484.

13. *Le Populaire*, September 4, 1932, p. 3; September 18, 1932, p. 1.

14. *La Vérité*, September 5, 1932, p. 1; *Déclaration des Bolcheviks-Léninistes Opposition de Gauche Internationale au Congrès Internationale Contre la Guerre* (Paris: n.d.), in League Against Imperialism Archive, International Instituut voor Sociale Geschiedenis, Amsterdam; Leon Trotsky, "Letter to All Members of the Spanish Opposition," April 24, 1933, in *The Spanish Revolution* (*1931–39*) (New York: Pathfinder, 1973), p. 195.

15. *La Révolution Prolétarienne*, September 25, 1932, p. 13.

16. Zdenek L. Suda, *Zealots and Rebels: A History of the Ruling Communist Party of Czechoslovakia* (Stanford: Hoover Institution Press, 1980), p. 133.

17. Jacques Rupnik, *Histoire de Parti Communiste Tchécoslovaque: Origines à la Prise du Pouvoir* (Paris: Presses de la Fondation Nationale des Sciences Politiques, 1981), pp. 94–97.

18. A. Gide, entry of July 29, 1932, *Journal, 1889–1939* (Paris: Gallimard, 1948), p. 1142.

19. Trotsky, "The Draft Program of the Communist International: A Criticism of Fundamentals," June 1928, in *The Third International After Lenin* (New York: Pathfinder, 1970), pp. 113–114.

20. Trotsky, "The Turn in the Communist International and the Situation in German," September 26, 1930, in *The Struggle Against Fascism in Germany* (New York: Pathfinder, 1971), pp. 60 and 67.

21. *Ibid.*, p. 70; "Against National Communism! (Lessons of the 'Red Referendum')," August 25, 1931, *ibid.*, p. 109; "For a Workers' United Front Against Fascism," December 8, 1931, *ibid.*, pp. 138–139.

22. Jane Degras, ed., *The Communist International, 1919–1943: Documents* (New York: Oxford University Press, 1965), 3:249–250.

23. Julius Braunthal, *History of the International*, vol. 2: *1919–1943*, John Clark, tr. (New York: Praeger, 1967), pp. 391–392.

24. Degras, *The Communist International*, 3:250.

25. *International Press Correspondence*, March 8, 1933, pp. 289–290.

26. "Resolution of the ECCI Presidium on the Situation in Germany," April 1, 1933, in Degras, *The Communist International*, 3:267.

27. Alain Bergounioux, "L'Internationale Ouvrière Socialiste Entre les Deux Guerres," in Hugues Portelli, ed., *L'Internationale Socialiste* (Paris: Editions Ouvrières, 1983), pp. 35–36; Jacques Droz, *Histoire de l'Antifascisme en Europe, 1923–1939* (Paris: Editions la Découverte, 1985), pp. 19–20.

28. Suda, *Zealots and Rebels*, p. 134.

29. Rupnik, *Histoire du Parti Communiste Tchécoslovaque*, pp. 98–101.

30. Reprinted in *Revue Française de Science Politique*, Jacques Rupnik, tr. (August 1976), 26: 794–796.

31. Gide, *Journal*, p. 1172.

32. Trotsky, "Platform of the International Left Opposition: A Declaration to the Congress Against Fascism," April 1933, in *Writings of Leon Trotsky*, vol. 5: *1932–1933* (New York: Pathfinder, 1972), pp. 180–181.

33. *International Press Correspondence*, June 10, 1933, p. 560.

34. *Ibid.*, September 8, 1933, p. 560.

35. Fritz Tobias, *The Reichstag Fire*, Arnold J. Pomerans, tr. (New York: Putnam's, 1964), pp. 120 and 123; Aino Kuusinen, *Before and After Stalin: A Personal Account of Soviet Russia from the 1920s to the 1960s*, Paul Stevenson, tr. (London: Joseph, 1974), p. 80.

36. *Bulletin of the Labour and Socialist International* (October 1933), series 3, no. 5, pp. 103–104.

37. Fenner Brockway, *Inside the Left: Thirty Years of Platform, Press, Prison, and Parliament* (London: Allen and Unwin, 1942), pp. 276–278.

38. Trotsky, "It Is Necessary to Build Communist Parties and an International Anew," October 1933, in *The Struggle Against Fascism in Germany*, pp. 421–422.

39. Carr, *Twilight*, p. 275.

40. *Ibid.*, p. 278.

41. I. Ehrenburg *La Guerre Civile en Autriche* (Paris: Editions du Comité Mondiale contre la Guerre et le Fascisme, 1934), p. 22.

42. G. D. H. Cole, *A History of Socialist Thought*, vol. 5: *Socialism and Fascism, 1931–1939* (London: Macmillan, 1960), p. 61; Adolf Sturmthal, "Austromarxism on the International Scene," in Anson Rabinbach, ed., *The Austrian Socialist Experiment: Social Democracy and Austromarxism, 1918–1934* (Boulder, Colo.: Westview Press, 1985), p. 182.

43. Jonathan Haslam, "The Comintern and the Origins of the Popular Front, 1934–1935," *The Historical Journal* (1979), 22:680–688.

44. G. Dimitrov, "Press Conference with Representatives of Communist Press Abroad in Moscow," April 1934, in *Dimitroff's Letters from Prison*, Alfred Kurella, ed. (London: Gollancz, 1935), pp. 146–147.

45. Degras, *The Communist International*, 3:334.

46. A. Rosenberg, *Der Faschismus als Massenbewegung* (Karlsbad: 1934), reprinted in Wolfgang Abendroth, ed., *Faschismus und Kapitalismus: Theorien über die sozialen Ursprunge und die Funktion des Faschismus* (Frankfurt: Europäische, 1967), pp. 80–90.

47. H. Marcuse, "The Struggle Against Liberalism in the Totalitarian View of the State," originally published in *Zeitschrift für Sozialforschung* (1934), 3, and reprinted in *Negations: Essays in Critical Theory*, Jeremy J. Shapiro, tr. (Boston: Beacon Press, 1968), pp. 14 and 42.

48. Martin Jay, *The Dialectical Imagination: A History of the Frankfurt School and the Institute of Social Research, 1923–1950* (Boston: Little, Brown, 1973), pp. 118 and 141.

49. Reprinted in A. A. Zhdanov et al., *Problems of Soviet Literature: Reports and Speeches at the First Soviet Writers' Congress* (Westport, Conn.: Greenwood Press, 1979), p. 277.

50. Ilya Ehrenburg, *Eve of War, 1933–1941*, vol. 4 of *Men, Years—Life*, Tatiana Shebunina, tr. (London: MacGibbon and Kee, 1963), pp. 43 and 56; Anatol Goldberg, *Ilya Ehrenburg, Revolutionary Novelist, Poet, War Correspondent, Propagandist: The Extraordinary Epic of a Russian Survivor* (New York: Viking, 1984), pp. 151–152.

51. Haslam, "The Comintern," p. 686.

52. Rupnik, *Histoire du Parti Communist Tchécoslovaque*, p. 112.

53. Palmiro Togliatti, *Lectures on Fascism* (New York: International, 1976), pp. 5, 8, and 154.

54. Haslam, "The Comintern," p. 689.

55. Braunthal, *History of the International*, 2:474–476; Droz, *Histoire de l'Antifascisme*, p. 20.

56. International Federation of Trade Unions Archive, file 97: *Report of May 1935*, pp. 1–4, and file 56: *Report of July 1936*, pp. 1–4, International Instituut voor Sociale Geschiedenis, Amsterdam.

57. *International Press Correspondence*, February 9, 1935, p. 162.

58. *Ibid.*, March 16, 1935, pp. 340–341.

59. *Labour Monthly*, June 1935, pp. 385–386.

60. J. Humbert-Droz, *Dix Ans de Lutte Antifasciste, 1931–1941* (Neuchâtel: Editions de la Baconnière, 1972), p. 131.

61. "The Fascist Offensive and the Tasks of the Communist International," reprinted in Georgi Dimitroff, *The United Front: The Struggle Against Fascism and War* (San Francisco: Proletarian, 1975), pp. 10, 19, and 32–39.

62. "Unity of the Working Class Against Fascism," *ibid.*, p. 101.

63. Rupnik, *Histoire du Parti Communiste Tchécoslovaque*, pp. 114–123; Suda, *Zealots and Rebels*, p. 141.

64. Trotsky, "On the Seventh Congress of the Comintern," *The New International*, October 1935, pp. 177–178.

65. Trotsky, "The New Revolutionary Upsurge and the Tasks of the Fourth International," July 1936, in *Documents of the Fourth International: The Formative Years (1933–1940)* (New York: Pathfinder, 1973), p. 89.

66. Jacques Delperrie de Bayac, *Les Brigades Internationales* (Paris: Fayard, 1968), p. 41; Bill Alexander, *British Volunteers for Liberty: Spain, 1936–1939* (London: Lawrence and Wishart, 1982), pp. 51–52.

67. Andreu Castells, *Las Brigadas Internacionales de la Guerra de España* (Barcelona: Editorial Ariel, 1974), pp. 381–383; Academy of Sciences of the USSR/Soviet War Veterans' Committee, *International Solidarity with the Spanish Republic, 1936–1939* (Moscow: Progress, 1975).

68. Stephen Spender, *World Within World* (London: Readers Union, 1953), p. 161.

69. Philip Toynbee, ed., *The Distant Drum: Reflections on the Spanish Civil War* (London: Sidgwick and Jackson, 1976), p. 178.

70. G. Orwell, "Spilling the Spanish Beans," *New English Weekly*, July 29 and September 2, 1937, in *The Collected Essays, Journalism, and Letters of George Orwell*, vol. 1: *An Age Like This, 1920–1940*, Sonia Orwell and Ian Angus, eds. (Harmondsworth: Penguin, 1970), pp. 302 and 303.

71. *Ibid.*, pp. 308–309.

72. Quoted in Paolo Spriano, *Stalin and the European Communists*, John Rothschild, tr. (London: Verso, 1985), p. 26.

73. Parti Socialiste, SFIO, *35è Congrès National, Tenu à Royan, les 4–7 Juin 1938, Rapports*, Paris, 1938, p. 211.

74. "United Front of Struggle for Peace," *The Communist International* (June 1936), 13:721.

75. E. H. Carr, *The Comintern and the Spanish Civil War* (New York: Pantheon paperback, 1984), pp. 89–90.

76. Phyllis Auty, "Yugoslavia," *Journal of Contemporary History* (1970), 5:52.

77. Spriano, *Stalin and the European Communists*, p. 37, n.18.

78. Nigel Hamilton, *The Brothers Mann: The Lives of Heinrich and Thomas Mann, 1871–1950 and 1875–1955* (New Haven: Yale University Press, 1979), p. 277.

79. *Ibid.*, pp. 268, 275, 285, and 292.

80. Arthur Koestler, *Invisible Writing* (London: Collins with Hamilton, 1954), p. 198.

81. Karl Dietrich Bracher, *The German Dictatorship: The Origins, Structure, and Effects of National Socialism*, Jean Steinberg, tr. (New York: Praeger, 1970), p. 375.

82. *Ibid.*

83. Lewis J. Edinger, *German Exile Politics: The Social Democratic Executive Committee in the Nazi Era* (Berkeley and Los Angeles: University of California Press, 1956), pp. 24–38 and 71; Jacques Droz, "Le Socialisme en Allemagne," in *Histoire Générale du Socialisme* (Paris: Presses Universitaires de France, 1977), 3:234–236.

84. Carola Stern, *Ulbricht: A Political Biography*, Abe Farbstein, tr. (New York: Praeger, 1965), pp. 55, 60, and 62; Edinger, *German Exile Politics*, pp. 153–154 and 162–163.

85. "The New Path to the Collective Battle of All Workers for the Destruction of the Hitler Dictatorship," reprinted in Hermann Weber, ed., *Der deutsche Kommunismus: Dokumente* (Cologne: Kiepenheuer und Witsch, 1963), p. 325.

86. Stern, *Ulbricht*, pp. 65–66.

87. Droz, "Le Socialisme en Allemagne," p. 237.

88. Albert C. Grzesinski, *Inside Germany*, Alexander S. Lipschitz, tr. (New York: Dutton, 1939), p. 175.

89. Reprinted in Weber, *Der deutsche Kommunismus*, pp. 382–384.

90. Jorgen Schleimann, "The Life and Work of Willi Münzenberg," *Survey* (April 1965), no. 55, p. 79.

91. David Pike, *German Writers in Exile, 1933–1945* (Chapel Hill: University of North Carolina Press, 1982), pp. 315 and 357.

92. Jiri Hochman, *The Soviet Union and the Failure of Collective Security, 1934–1938* (Ithaca, N.Y.: Cornell University Press, 1984), p. 92.

93. Schleimann, "Willi Münzenberg," pp. 81–82.

94. Fritz Max Cahan, *Men Against Hitler*, Wythe Williams, tr. (Indianapolis: Bobbs-Merrill, 1939), p. 247.

95. Quoted in Pike, *German Writers in Exile*, p. 192.

96. Edinger, *German Exile Politics*, pp. 212–223.

97. Schleimann, "Willi Münzenberg," pp. 83–84; Droz, *Histoire de l'Antifascisme*, 116–117.

98. *Rundschau über Politik, Wirtschaft, und Arbeiterbewegung*, March 23, 1939, pp. 449–450.

99. *International Press Correspondence*, April 3, 1937, p. 355, and April 10, 1937, p. 391; Dimitroff, *The United Front*, p. 232.

100. "ECCI Manifesto on the 21st Anniversary of the Russian Revolution," November 5, 1938, in Degras, *The Communist International*, 3:428–433.

101. Leslie Derfler, *Socialism Since Marx: A Century of the European Left* (New York: St. Martin's Press, 1973), pp. 165–166; Braunthal, *History of the International*, 2:489–490; Bergounioux, "L'Internationale Ouvrière Socialiste," p. 37.

102. Sturmthal, "Austromarxism," p. 182.

103. *World News and Views*, September 2, 1939, pp. 937–938.

104. Humbert-Droz, *Dix Ans*, pp. 386–387.

105. E. Delgado, *J'ai Perdu la foi à Moscou* (Paris: Gallimard, 1950), p. 47

106. Reprinted in Herbert Steiner, "L'Internationale Socialiste à la Veille de la Seconde Guerre Mondiale, Juillet-Août 1939: Documents de Friedrich Adler," *Le Mouvement Social* (January–March 1967), 58:109–111.

107. "ECCI Manifesto on the 22nd Anniversary of the Russian Revolution," November 11, 1939, in Degras, *The Communist International*, 3:447.

108. Braunthal, *History of the International*, 2:491–492.

5. Pragmatic Anti-Fascism in the Soviet Union

1. Hans W. Gatzke, "Russo-German Military Collaboration During the Weimar Republic," in *European Diplomacy Between Two War, 1919–1939* (Chicago: Quadrangle, 1972), p. 43.

2. V. I. Lenin, *Collected Works* (Moscow: Progress, 1970), 45:540.

3. *Ibid.*, 45:592.

4. Jane Degras, ed., *Soviet Documents on Foreign Policy* New York: Oxford University Press, 1953), 1:409.

5. Humbert-Droz, Report to Presidium of Communist International, October 14, 1924, *Archives de Jules Humbert-Droz*, vol. 2: *Les Partis Communistes des Pays Latins et l'Internationale Communiste dans les Années 1923–1927*, Siegfried Bahne, ed. (Dordrecht, Holl.: D. Reidel, 1983), pp. 322–323.

6. Humbert-Droz, Report to Presidium of Communist International, October 20, 1924, *ibid.*, p. 328.

7. J. W. Stalin, *Works* (Moscow: Foreign Languages, 1954), 7:14.

8. Alan Cassels, *Mussolini's Early Diplomacy* (Princeton: Princeton University Press, 1970), pp. 182 and 349–352; Degras, *Soviet Documents*, 2:138.

9. Degras, *Soviet Documents*, 2:354 and 428.

10. Jonathan Haslam, *Soviet Foreign Policy, 1930–1933: The Impact of the Depression* (London: Macmillan, 1983), p. 50.

11. Josef Korbel, *Poland Between East and West: Soviet and German Diplomacy Toward Poland, 1919–1933* (Princeton: Princeton University Press, 1963), pp. 269–271.

12. Degras, *Soviet Documents*, 3:57.

13. *Ibid.*, 3:70.

14. Gustav Hilger and Alfred G. Meyer, *The Incompatible Allies: A Memoir-*

History of German-Soviet Relations, 1918–1941 (New York: Hafner, 1971), pp. 252 and 256.

15. Quoted in Henry L. Roberts, "Maxim Litvinov," in Gordon A. Craig and Felix Gilbert, eds., *The Diplomats, 1919–1939* (Princeton: Princeton University Press, 1953), p. 352.

16. Hilger and Meyer, *The Incompatible Allies*, p. 277.

17. *Ibid.*, p. 271; Litvinov, *Against Aggression: Speeches by Maxim Litvinov* (London: Lawrence and Wishart, 1939), pp. 18–19; *The Communist International*, April 20, 1935, pp. 383 and 386.

18. Jane Degras, ed., *The Communist International, 1919–1943: Documents* (New York: Oxford University Press, 1965), 3:373.

19. Jonathan Haslam, *The Soviet Union and the Struggle for Collective Security in Europe, 1933–1939* (London: Macmillan, 1984), pp. 82, 86, 90, and 103; Jiri Hochman, *The Soviet Union and the Failure of Collective Security, 1934–1938* (Ithaca, N.Y.: Cornell University Press, 1984), pp. 108–120.

20. Haslam, *The Soviet Union and the Struggle for Collective Security in Europe*, pp. 62–63.

21. Degras, *The Communist International*, 3:373.

22. Degras, *Soviet Documents*, 3:150.

23. Lowell R. Tillett, "The Soviet Role in League Sanctions Against Italy, 1935–36," *The American Slavic and Eastern European Review* (February 1956), 15:11–15.

24. Degras, *Soviet Documents*, 3:154.

25. *The Communist International* (April 1936), 13:488.

26. Litvinov, *Against Aggression*, speeches of March 17 and July 1, pp. 23, 38, and 43.

27. *Ibid.*, p. 44.

28. Bohdan B. Budurowycz, *Polish-Soviet Relations, 1932–1939* (New York: Columbia University Press, 1963), pp. 88–89.

29. Degras, *Soviet Documents*, 3:220.

30. I. Maisky, speech of November 12, 1936, *ibid.*, 3:217.

31. Teddy J. Uldricks, *Diplomacy and Ideology: The Origins of Soviet Foreign Relations, 1917–1930* (London: Sage, 1979), p. 173; John Erickson, *The Soviet High Command: A Military-Political History, 1918–1941* (London: St. Martin's Press, 1962), pp. 505–506.

32. E. H. Carr, *The Comintern and the Spanish Civil War* (New York: Pantheon paperback, 1984), p. 24.

33. Hugh Thomas, *The Spanish Civil War* (New York: Harper, 1961), pp. 640–641; Pierre Broué and Emile Témine, *The Revolution and Civil War in Spain*, Tony White, tr. (Cambridge: MIT Press, 1972), pp. 369–371.

34. Haslam, *The Soviet Union and the Struggle for Collective Security in Europe*, p. 146.

35. Degras, *Soviet Documents*, 3:221.

36. G. Ciano, *Ciano's Diplomatic Papers*, Malcolm Muggeridge, ed. (London: Odhams, 1948), p. 86.

37. Edmund Clubb, *China and Russia: The "Great Game"* (New York: Columbia University Press, 1971), p. 309.

38. Jean-Baptiste Duroselle, "La Politique Soviétique à l'Egard de l'Allemagne, du Pacte Anti-Komintern à Mai 1939," in *Les Relations Germano-Soviétique de 1933 à 1939* (Paris: Colin, 1954), pp. 54–55.

39. Haslam, *The Soviet Union and the Struggle for Collective Security in Europe*, p. 160.

40. Litvinov, *Against Aggression*, p. 116.

41. Carl E. Schorske, "Two German Ambassadors: Dirksen and Schulenburg," in Craig and Gilbert, *The Diplomats*, p. 489.

42. Hilger and Meyer, *The Incompatible Allies*, p. 288.

43. Józef Beck, *Final Report* (New York: Speller, 1957), p. 156.

44. Duroselle, "La Politique Soviétique," pp. 66, 68, 72, and 77.

45. John Erickson, "Threat Identification and Strategic Appraisal by the Soviet Union, 1930–1941," in Ernest R. May, ed., *Knowing One's Enemies: Intelligence Assessment Before the World Wars* (Princeton: Princeton University Press, 1984), p. 404.

46. Wacław Jedrzejewicz, ed., *Diplomat in Paris, 1936–1939: Papers and Memoirs of Juliusz Łukasiewicz* (New York: Columbia University Press, 1970), p. 120.

47. Trotsky, "After the Collapse of Czechoslovakia, Stalin Will Seek Accord with Hitler," in *Writings of Leon Trotsky (1938–1939)* (New York: Pathfinder, 1974), p. 30.

48. *History of the Communist Party of the Soviet Union (Bolsheviks), Short Course* (Moscow: Foreign Languages, 1939), pp. 333–335.

49. Jan F. Triska and Robert M. Slusser, *The Theory, Law, and Policy of Soviet Treaties* (Stanford: Stanford University Press, 1962), pp. 374–375.

50. N. Chamberlain, speech to the House of Commons, March 15, 1939, in *The Struggle for Peace* (London: Hutchinson, 1939), p. 410.

51. "Soviet-British-French Talks in Moscow, 1939 (a Documentary Survey)," *International Affairs* (July 1969), 7:81.

52. Keith Feiling, *The Life of Neville Chamberlain* (London: Macmillan, 1970), p. 403.

53. *Rundschau über Politik, Wirtschaft, und Arbeiterbewegung*, March 31, 1939, p. 530.

54. *World News and Views*, March 29, 1939, p. 316.

55. Haslam, *The Soviet Union and the Struggle for Collective Security in Europe*, p. 212.

56. Schorske, "Two German Ambassadors," p. 504.

57. *World News and Views*, June 3, 1939, pp. 646–647.

58. Dated April 18, 1939, in Degras, *Soviet Documents*, 3:329.

59. Schlorske, "Two German Ambassadors," p. 508.

60. *International Affairs*, November 11, 1969, p. 78.

61. Charles E. Bohlen, *Witness to History, 1929–1969* (New York: Norton, 1973), p. 76.

62. Degras, *Soviet Documents*, 3:357.

63. Bohlen, *Witness to History*, p. 82.

64. Degras, *Soviet Documents*, 3:359–361.

65. Conversation of October 1, 1939, in *Les Archives Secrètes du Comte Ciano, 1936–1942*, Maurice Vassard, tr. (Paris: Plon: 1948), p. 319.

66. *The Communist International* (September 1939), 16:952–954 and 957.

6. Popular Front Anti-Fascism in France

1. Stanley Hoffmann, "Paradoxes of the French Political Community," in Stanley Hoffmann, et al., *In Search of France: The Economic, Social, and Political System of the Twentieth Century* (New York: Harper Torchbooks, 1965), p. 17.

2. Stephen A. Schuker, *The End of French Predominance in Europe: The Financial Crisis of 1924 and the Adoption of the Dawes Plan* (Chapel Hill: University of North Carolina Press, 1976), pp. 3, 6, and 384.

3. E. Beau de Loménie, *Les Responsabilités des Dynasties Bourgeoises*, vol. 3: *Sous la Troisième République: La Guerre et l'Immédiat Après-Guerre (1914–1924)* (Paris: Denoël, 1954), pp. 488–490; vol. 4: *Du Cartel à Hitler, 1924–1933* (1963), pp. 55–58 and 190–194.

4. A. Treint, "Thèses sur la Situation Internationale," *Cahiers du Bolchevisme*, November 28, 1924, pp. 90 and 95.

5. Treint, "Le Fascisme en France," *ibid.*, January 30, 1925, pp. 692–693.

6. F. Loriot, "Thèses," *ibid.*, May 1, 1925, pp. 1180–1185.

7. *Cahiers du Bolchevisme*, July 1926, pp. 1503–1504, and April, 1927, p. 373.

8. *Le Populaire*, May 8, 1928, reprinted in Léon Blum *L'Oeuvre de Léon Blum*, Robert Blum, ed., vol. 3, part 2: *1928–1934* (Paris: Michel, 1972), p. 57.

9. David Caute, *Communism and the French Intellectuals, 1914–1960* (New York: Macmillan, 1964), p. 81.

10. *Monde*, June 9, 1928.

11. Michel Ragon, *Histoire de la Littérature Prolétarienne en France* (Paris: Michel, 1974), pp. 181–182.

12. Daniel Guérin, *Front Populaire: Révolution Manqué* (Paris: Julliard, 1963), p. 31.

13. Bruno Jasienski, "Comment 'Monde' Combat le Social-Fascisme," *Cahiers du Bolchevisme*, June 15, 1932, p. 830.

14. *Monde*, July 21, 1928.

15. *La Vérité*, August 1, 1930.

16. Henri Barbé, *Souvenirs de Militant et de Dirigeant Communiste*, typescript, Hoover Institution Archives, Stanford University, n.d., pp. 271–272.

17. A. Gide, entry of July 24, 1931, *Journal, 1889–1939* (Paris: Gallimard, 1948), p. 1066.

18. Peter Campbell, *French Electoral Systems and Elections Since 1789* Hamden, Conn.: Archon, 1965), p. 100.

19. Jacques Duclos, "Temoignages sur les Origines et la Victoire du Front Populaire," *Cahiers de l'Institut Maurice Thorez* (July–September 1966), 2:12; Georges Cogniot, "Le front Unique de la Classe Ouvrière: Fondement du Front Populaire, *ibid.* (October 1966–March 1967), 3 and 4:37.

20. Michel Winock, *Histoire Politique de la Revue 'Esprit,' 1930–1950* (Paris: Seuil, 1975), pp. 24 and 94.

21. Georges Izard, "La Troisième Force: L'Unique Problème: Le Pouvoir, le Programme, et l'Avenir," *Esprit*, March 1933, pp. 1056–1061.

22. "Notes sur la Revue 'Esprit,' " *Commune*, July 1933, p. 77.

23. M. Martinet, "Le Chef Contre l'Homme," *Esprit*, January 1934, pp. 541 and 553.

24. V. Serge, *Memoirs of a Revolutionary, 1901–1941*, Peter Sedgwick, tr. (New York: Oxford University Press paperback, 1967), p. 343.

25. "Contre le Fascisme: Front Commun," *Monde*, April 8, 1933.

26. *Monde*, June 3, 1933.

27. *Ibid.*, June 10, 1933.

28. *Front Mondial*, October 15, 1933.

29. Tobier, "Vers le Front Unique de Lutte," *Cahiers du Bolchevisme*, April 1, 1933, p. 487.

30. Parti Socialiste SFIO, *30è Congrès National, Tenu à Paris, les 14–17 Juillet 1933, Compte Rendu Stenographique*, Paris, 1933, pp. 63, 69–73, and 518.

31. *L'Humanité*, February 6, 1934; Duclos, "Temoignages," pp. 12–13.

32. Lucie Mazauric, *Avec André Chamson, 1934–1939: "Vive le Front Populaire"* (Paris: Plon, 1976), p. 19.

33. Alexander Werth, *France in Ferment* (London: Jarrolds, 1935), pp. 161–162.

34. Jules Moch, *Rencontres avec Léon Blum* (Paris: Plon, 1970), p. 92.

35. André Delmas, *A Gauche de la Barricade: Chronique Syndicale de l'Avant-Guerre* (Paris: Editions de l'Hexagon, 1950), pp. 17–23.

36. Dieter Wolf, *Doriot: du Communisme à la Collaboration*, Georgette Chatenet, tr. (Paris: Fayard, 1969), pp. 98–99; Philippe Robrieux, *Maurice Thorez: Vie Secrète et Vie Publique* (Paris: Fayard, 1975), pp. 179–181.

37. Thorez, "Contre l'Opportunisme," *Cahiers du Bolchevisme*, February 1, 1934, p. 135.

38. Barbé, *Souvenirs*, pp. 333–336; Jean-Paul Joubert, *Révolutionnaire de la S.F.I.O.: Marceau Pivert et le Pivertisme* (Paris: Presses de la Fondation Nationale des Sciences Politiques, 1977), p. 36.

39. Wolf, *Doriot*, pp. 108–112.

40. Mazauric, *Avec André Chamson*, p. 45.

41. A. Prost, "Les Manifestations du 12 Février 1934 en Province," *Le Mouvement Social*, (January-March 1966), 54:15–16.

42. "Au Travailleurs," *Commune*, March–April 1934, p. 859.

43. Simone de Beauvoir, *The Prime of Life*, Peter Green, tr. (Cleveland: World, 1962), p. 132.

44. E. Mounier, "La Révolution Contre les Mythes," *Esprit*, March 1934, pp. 906 and 913.

45. Guérin, *Front Populaire*, p. 57.

46. *Front Mondial*, June 1, 1934, and Supplément Spécial.

47. Parti Socialiste SFIO, *31è Congrès National, Tenu à Toulouse, les 20–23 Mai 1934, Compte Rendu Stenographique*, Paris, 1934, pp. 94–95, 370–371, and 373.

48. Cilly Vassart, *Le Front Populaire en France*, typescript, Paris, 1962, Hoover Institution Archives, Stanford University, pp. 35–36; Daniel R. Brower, *The New Jacobins: The French Communist Party and the Popular Front* (Ithaca, N.Y.: Cornell University Press, 1968), pp. 48–49; Georges Cogniot, *Parti Pris: Cinquante Ans au Service de l'Humanisme Réel*, vol. 1: *D'un Guerre Mondial à l'Autre* (Paris: Editions Sociales, 1976), p. 373.

49. E. H. Carr, *Twilight of the Comintern, 1930–1935* (New York: Pantheon, 1982), p. 194; Vassart, *Le Front Populaire*, p. 36; Thorez, "L'Organisation du Front Unique de Lutte," *Cahiers du Bolchevisme*, July 1, 1934, pp. 772–774.

50. *Le Populaire*, July 7 and 8, 1934, in Blum, *L'Oeuvre*, vol. 4, part 1, pp. 159–160; Pierre Naville in *La Vérité*, July 6, 1934.

51. Delmas, *A Gauche de la Barricade*, pp. 38–39.

52. *Le Populaire*, July 10, 1934, in Blum, *L'Oeuvre*, vol. 4, part 1, p. 171; "L'Intervention de Maurice Thorez: A l'Entrevue des Délégations Socialiste et Communiste du 14 Juillet 1934," *Cahiers de l'Institut Maurice Thorez* (April 1966), 1:39.

53. Reprinted in Blum, *L'Oeuvre*, vol. 4, part 1, pp. 221–223.

54. *La Vérité*, Numéro Spécial, September 1934.

55. Alexander Werth, *Which Way France?* (New York: Harper, 1937), pp. 76–81 and 84.

56. *La Flèche*, November 10, 1934.

57. *Vigilance*, November 20, 1934.

58. Letter from Barbusse to Rolland, November 2, 1934; letter from Guy Jerram to Barbusse, January 4, 1935, both in Romain Rolland Folder, Hoover Institution Archives, Stanford University.

59. Quoted in John T. Marcus, *French Socialism in the Crisis Years, 1933–1936: Fascism and the French Left* (Westport, Conn.: Greenwood Press, 1976), p. 119.

60. *Le Populaire*, May 17, 1935, quoted *ibid.*, pp. 121–122.

61. *La Flèche*, May 25, 1935.

62. *La Vérité*, May 25, 1935.

63. Reprinted in Jean-Pierre Rioux, *Révolutionnaires du Front Populaire: Choix de Documents, 1935–1938* (Paris: Union Générale, 1973), p. 26; Guérin, *Front Populaire*, p. 71.

64. *Vigilance*, June 15, 1935.

65. *Que Faire?* June 1935, p. 1.

66. Peter J. Larmour, *The French Radical Party in the 1930s* (Stanford: Stanford University Press, 1964), p. 173.

67. Parti Socialiste, SFIO, *32è Congrès National, Tenu à Mulhouse, les 9–12 Juin 1935, Compte Rendu Stenographique*, Paris, 1935, pp. 561–562.

68. Victor Basch, "Le Front Populaire," *Les Cahiers des Droits de l'Homme*, November 10, 1935, p. 695.

69. Reprinted in Jules Moch, *Le Front Populaire, Grande Espérance* . . . (Paris: Perrin, 1971), pp. 373–375.

70. Henri Noguères, *La Vie Quotidienne en France au Temps du Front Populaire, 1935–1938* (Paris: Hachette, 1977), pp. 77–79 and 83.

71. David H. Weinberg, *A Community on Trial: The Jews of Paris in the 1930s* (Chicago: University of Chicago Press, 1977), p. 125.

72. Jean Guéhenno, *La Foi Difficile* (Paris: Grasset, 1957), p. 178.

73. *Esprit*, July 1935, p. 633.

74. Jean Daniel, *Le Temps Qui Reste: Essai d'Autobiographie Professionnelle* (Paris: Stock, 1973), p. 19.

75. Claude Estier, *La Gauche Hebdomadaire, 1914–1962* (Paris: Colin, 1962), p. 77.

76. "Vendredi Paraît," *Vendredi*, November 8, 1935.

77. Giulio Ceretti, *A l'Ombre des Deux T: 40 Ans avec Maurice Thorez et Palmiro Togliatti* (Paris: Julliard, 1973), p. 159; Duclos, "Temoignages," p. 17.

78. Reprinted in Blum *L'Oeuvre*, vol. 4, part 1, pp. 225–229.

79. Claude Jamet, *Notre Front Populaire: Journal d'un Militant (1934–1939)* (Paris: Table Ronde, 1977), p. 102.

80. de Beauvoir, *The Prime of Life*, p. 211.

81. *Vendredi*, January 17, 1936; *La Flèche*, February 29, 1936.

82. Werth, *Which Way France?* p. 237.

83. Georges Dupeux, *Le Front Populaire et les Elections de 1936* (Paris: Colin, 1959), pp. 138–139; Joel Colton, *Léon Blum: Humanist in Politics* (New York: Knopf, 1966), pp. 125–126.

84. Mazauric, *Avec André Chamson*, p. 129; Ilya Ehrenburg, *Eve of War, 1933–1941*, vol. 4 of *Men, Years—Life*, Tatiana Shebunina, tr. (London: MacGibbon and Kee, 1963), p. 106; Jean-Louis Barrault, *Memories for Tomorrow*, Jonathan Griffin, tr. (London: Thames and Hudson, 1974), pp. 90 and 94.

85. M. Valière, *L'Ecole Emancipée*, May 17, 1936, reprinted in Rioux, *Révolutionnaires*, p. 136; Guérin, *Front Populaire*, p. 106.

86. Ehrenburg, *Eve of War*, pp. 107–108.

87. Jacques Julliard, "Le Mouvement Syndical," in Alfred Sauvy, ed., *Histoire Economique de la France Entre les Deux Guerres* (Paris: Fayard, 1972), 3:192.

88. Maurice Thorez, *Oeuvres Choisis*, vol. 1: *1924–1937* (Paris: Editions Sociales, 1967), pp. 340–343.

89. M. Gitton, "Tout N'Est Pas Possible," *L'Humanité*, May 29, 1936, in Rioux, *Revolutionnaires*, p. 160.

90. Werth, *Which Way France?* p. 382.

91. Blum, *L'Oeuvre*, vol. 4, part 1, p. 393.

92. Werth, *Which Way France?* p. 388.

93. J. R. Bloch, "Empêchons le Suicide de France!" *Vendredi*, August 14, 1936.

94. *Vendredi*, August 21, 1936; Delmas, *A Gauche de la Barricade*, p. 121.

95. Annie Kriegel, "Les Communistes et le Pouvoir," in Annie Kriegel and Michelle Perrot, *Le Socialisme Français et le Pouvoir* (Paris: EDI, 1966), p. 137.

96. Brower, *The New Jacobins*, p. 142.

97. Thorez, *Oeuvres Choisis*, 1:354.

98. Charles Tillon, *On Chantait Rouge* (Paris: Laffont, 1977), p. 219.

99. Jamet, *Notre Front Populaire*, pp. 151–154 and 157.

100. *Cahiers du Bolchevisme*, November 1, 1936, pp. 1272–1274.

101. *La Gauche Révolutionnaire*, November 20, 1936.

102. Delmas, *A Gauche de la Barricade*, p. 108; Werth, *Which Way France?* p. 403.

103. Serge Berstein, "Le Parti Radical-Socialiste: Arbitre du Jeu Politique Français," in René Rémond and Janine Bourdin, eds., *La France et les Français en 1938–1939* (Paris: Presses de la Fondation Nationale des Sciences Politiques, 1978), p. 278.

104. André Gide, *Littérature Engagée*, Yvonne Davet, ed. (Paris: Gallimard, 1950), p. 18.

105. Gide, letter of August 29, 1936, in *Cahiers André Gide*, vol. 10: *Correspondence André Gide/Dorothy Bussy*, part 2: *Janvier 1925–November 1936* (Paris: Galllimard, 1981), p. 616.

106. Gide, entry of September 5, 1936, *Journal*, pp. 1254–1255.

107. Gide, *Retour de l'USSR* (Paris: Gallimard, 1937), p. 67.

108. *Ibid.*, pp. 13 and 15–17.

109. *L'Humanité*, January 18, 1937, quoted in Frederick John Harris, *André Gide and Romain Rolland: Two Men Divided* (New Brunswick, N.J.: Rutgers University Press, 1973), p. 144.

110. Jonathan Haslam, *The Soviet Union and the Struggle for Collective Security in Europe, 1933–1939* (London: Macmillan, 1984), p. 149.

111. Maria van Rysselberghe, *Les Cahiers de la Petite Dame: Notes pour l'Histoire Authentique d'André Gide* (Cahiers 6–12, 1929–1937), in *Cahiers André Gide* (Paris: Gallimard, 1974), 5:607 and 624–625; André Gide, *Retouches à Mon Retour de l'URSS* (Paris: Gallimard, 1937), p. 109.

112. Gide, letter to Dorothy Bussy, February 8, 1937, in *Cahiers André Gide*, vol. 11: *Correspondence André Gide/Dorothy Bussy*, Part 3: *Janvier 1937–Janvier 1951*, p. 24; letter to Roger Martin du Gard, February 18, 1937, in *André Gide/ Roger Martin du Gard: Correspondence*, vol. 2: *1935–1951* (Paris: Gallimard, 1968), p. 92.

113. André Chamson, *Devenir Ce Qu'On Est* (Paris: Wesmael-Charlier, 1959), p. 62; Madeleine Berry, *André Chamson, ou L'Homme Contre l'Histoire* (Paris: Fischbacher, 1977), p. 106.

114. James Joll, *Intellectuals in Politics: Three Biographical Essays* (London: Weidenfeld and Nicolson, 1960), pp. 41–42.

115. *Les Cahiers des Droits de l'Homme*, April 1, 1937, p. 195.

116. Wacław Jedrzejewicz, ed., *Diplomat in Paris, 1936–1939: Papers and Memoirs of Juliusz Łukasiewicz* (New York: Columbia University Press, 1970), pp. 32–33.

117. Noguères, *La Vie Quotidienne*, p. 148.

118. *L'Humanité*, June 12, 1937, p. 2; *Le Populaire*, June 12, 1937, p. 1; *L'Oeuvre*, June 12, 1937, p. 5; *Nouvel âge*, June 16, 1937, p. 2.

119. Moch, *Rencontres*, p. 235.

120. Joubert, *Révolutionnaire de la S.F.I.O.*, p. 129.

121. Mazauric, *Avec André Chamson*, p. 189.

122. Weinberg, *A Community on Trial*, p. 136.

123. Noguères, *La Vie Quotidienne*, p. 194; Caute, *Communism and the French Intellectuals*, p. 132; *Les Cahiers des Droits de l'Homme*, January 1, 1937, p. 17; April 15, pp. 249–250; November 1, pp. 692–693; Wladimir Drabovich, *Les Intellectuelles Français et le Bolchevisme* (Paris: Libertés Françaises, 1937), pp. 211–212.

124. The letters and articles are collected in Gide, *Littérature Engagée*, pp. 194–210.

125. Elisabeth Young-Bruehl, *Hannah Arendt: For Love of the World* (New Haven: Yale University Press, 1982), pp. 142–143.

126. Antoine Prost, "Le Climat Social," in René Rémond and Janine Bourdin, eds., *Edouard Daladier, Chef du Gouvernement, Avril 1938–Septembre 1939* (Paris: Presses de la Fondation Nationale des Sciences Politiques, 1977), p. 101.

127. *Vendredi*, January 10, 1938.

128. Jean-Jacques Becker, "Le Parti Communiste," in Rémond and Bourdin, *La France et les Français*, pp. 233–239.

129. Maurice Honel (PCF deputy from Clichy) to Maurice Thorez, May 13, 1938, in Rioux, *Révolutionnaires*, p. 361; *La Révolution Prolétarienne*, May 10, 1938, ibid., pp. 347 and 358; *Cahiers du Bolchevisme*, August 1938, p. 486; Kenneth Harris, *Atlee* (New York: Norton, 1982), p. 154.

130. Philip J. Jaffe, *The Rise and Fall of American Communism* (New York: Horizon, 1975), p. 39.

131. "Après Munich," *Les Cahiers des Droits de l'Homme*, October 1–15, 1938, p. 563.

132. Delmas, *A Gauche de la Barricade* p. 152.

133. Albert Bayet, "Paul Langevin et la Défense des Droits de l'Homme," *La Pensée*, May-June 1947, p. 61.

134. Jean Zay, *Souvenirs et Solitudes* (Paris: Julliard, 1945), p. 164.

135. Jean Bruhat, "La CGT," in Rémond and Bourdin, *La France et les Français*, pp. 175–176.

136. *Ibid.*, p. 178.

137. Prost, "Le Climat Social," p. 211; see also Joubert, *Révolutionnaire de la*

S.F.I.O., pp. 178–181; Delmas, *A Gauche de la Barricade*, pp. 179–185; Guy Bourdé, *La Défaite du Front Populaire* (Paris: Maspero, 1977), pp. 128–137.

138. Sean Niall [Sherry Mangan], "Paris Letter," *Partisan Review* (Spring 1939), 6:100.

139. Thorez, *Oeuvres Choisis*, vol. 2: *1938–1950* (1966), p. 100.

140. Becker, "Le Parti Communist," pp. 230–231.

141. *Ibid.*, p. 231.

142. *L'Humanité*, August 25, 1939.

143. *Le Populaire*, August 23 and 25, 1939, in Blum *L'Oeuvre*, vol. 4, part 2, pp. 309 and 313.

144. Maurice Goldsmith, *Frédéric Joliot-Curie: A Biography* (London: Lawrence and Wishart, 1976), p. 105.

145. *Juin 1936*, August 15, 1939

146. de Beauvoir, *The Prime of Life*, pp. 299–300.

147. Quoted in Tillon, *On Chantait Rouge*, pp. 279–280.

148. *Ibid.*, p. 289.

7. The Books and Bricks of British Anti-Fascism

1. Gerald D. Anderson, *Fascists, Communists, and the National Government: Civil Liberties in Great Britain, 1931–1937* (Columbia: University of Missouri Press, 1983), p. 193.

2. Siegfried Sassoon, *The Complete Memoirs of George Sherston* (London: World, 1940), p. 230.

3. Winifred Holtby, *South Riding* (New York: Macmillan 1936), p. 80–81; see also Vera Brittain, *Testament of Experience* (London: Virago, 1979), pp. 76–77.

4. Martin Ceadel, "The 'King and Country' Debate, 1933: Student Politics, Pacifism, and the Dictators," *The History Journal* (1979), 22:418; and Ceadel, *Pacifism in Britain, 1914–1945* (Oxford: Clarendon Press, 1980), p. 131.

5. Lord Vansittart, *The Mist Procession* (London: Hutchinson, 1958), p. 452.

6. Jessica Mitford, *Hons and Rebels* (London: Quartet, 1978), p. 56.

7. E. Romilly and G. Romilly, *Out of Bounds: The Education of Giles Romilly and Esmond Romilly* (London: Hamilton, 1936), pp. 181 and 185.

8. The totals are reprinted in Labour Party, *Reports of Annual Conferences*, 35th, Brighton, October 1, 1935 (London: Transport House, 1935), p. 15.

9. Robert H. Ferrell, *Peace in Their Time: The Origins of the Kellogg-Briand Pact* (New Haven: Yale University Press, 1952), p. 18.

10. Noreen Branson, *Poplarism, 1919–1925: George Lansbury and the Councillors' Revolt* (London: Lawrence and Wishart, 1979), p. 226.

11. Noreen Branson and Margot Heinemann, *Britain in the Nineteen Thirties* (London: Weidenfeld and Nicholson, 1971), pp. 9—17; John Stevenson and Chris Cook, *The Slump: Society and Politics During the Depression* (London: Cape,

1977), pp. 145–165 and 173–176; Wal Hannington, *Unemployed Struggles, 1919–1936: My Life and Struggles Among the Unemployed* (London: Lawrence and Wishart, 1936); Harry MacShane, *No Mean Fighter* (London: Pluto, 1978).

12. [Lord] Walter Citrine, *Men and Work: An Autobiography* (London: Hutchinson, 1964), p. 253.

13. *Ibid.*, pp. 300–301.

14. Colin Cross, *The Fascists in Britain* (London: Barrie and Rockliff, 1961), p. 47.

15. Henry Pelling, *A Short History of the Labour Party*, 3d ed. (New York: St. Martin's Press 1968), p. 76.

16. Brittain, *Testament of Experience*, p. 65.

17. *Action*, October 15, 1931, p. 3.

18. *The Outpost*, May 1932, p. 47.

19. Reg Groves, *The Balham Group: How British Trotskyism Began* (London: Pluto, 1974), pp. 64–69.

20. Jack Gaster, "The Present Position of the ILP," *Labour Monthly*, January 1933, p. 35; R. Palme Dutt, "Notes of the Month," *ibid.*, April 1933, pp. 211–216.

21. *Labour Monthly*, July 1933, pp. 461–463.

22. G. D. H. Cole, *A History of the Labour Party from 1914* (London: Routledge and Kegan Paul, 1948), p. 286; *New Leader*, June 9, 1933, p. 11.

23. Labour Party, *Reports of Annual Conferences*, 33d, Hastings, October 2, 1933 (London: Transport House, 1933), pp. 277–278.

24. *New Leader*, January 6, 1933, p. 5.

25. *Ibid.*, January 13, 1933, p. 2, and March 31, 1933, p. 1.

26. *Ibid.*, February 10, 1933, p. 4, and March 10, 1933, p. 4.

27. Fenner Brockway, *Inside the Left: Thirty Years of Platform, Press, Prison, and Parliament* (London: Allen and Unwin, 1942), p. 252.

28. D.N. Pritt, *The Autobiography of D. N. Pritt*, part one: *From Right to Left* (London: Lawrence and Wishart, 1965), p. 56.

29. *Times*, December 21, 1933, p. 16; *Daily Herald*, December 21, 1933, p. 4.

30. Cross, *The Fascists in Britain*, p. 107; Robert Skidelsky, *Oswald Mosley* (London: Macmillan, 1975), p. 331.

31. *Daily Worker*, May 29 and June 1, 1934; Joe Jacobs, *Out of the Ghetto: My Youth in the East End, Communism and Fascism, 1913–1939* (London: Simon, 1978), pp. 138–139.

32. Brittain, *Testament of Experience*, p. 108.

33. *Daily Herald*, June 8, 1934, p. 2.

34. *Daily Worker*, June 9, 1934, p. 1; *Times*, June 8, 1934, p. 15.

35. Jacobs, *Out of the Ghetto*, p. 144.

36. *Daily Herald*, September 8, 1934, p. 8.

37. Gisela C. Lebzelter, *Political Anti-Semitism in England, 1918–1939* (London: Macmillan, 1978), p. 116.

38. *Times*, September 10, 1934, p. 9.

39. J. Strachey, "The Prospects of the Anti-Fascist Struggle," *Labour Monthly*, October 1934, pp. 608–611.

40. Jacobs, *Out of the Ghetto*, p. 118.

41. Labour Party, *Reports of Annual Conferences*, 34th, Southport, October 1–6, 1934 (London: Transport House, 1934), pp. 10–13.

42. Kenneth Harris, *Atlee* (New York: Norton, 1982), p. 118.

43. Hugh Thomas, *John Strachey* (London: Methuen, 1973), p. 21.

44. *Ibid.*, p. 68.

45. *Ibid.*

46. Mitford, *Hons and Rebels*, p. 60.

47. David Corkill and Stuart J. Rawnsley, eds., *The Road to Spain: Anti-Fascists at War, 1936–1939* (Dunfermline: Borderline, 1981), p. 64.

48. "Stephen Spender," *The God That Failed*, Richard Crossman, ed. (New York: Bantam, 1965), pp. 208 and 210.

49. Spender, "Writers and Manifestoes," *Left Review*, February 1935, pp. 149–150.

50. Spender, *World Within World* (London: Readers Union, 1953), pp. 164 and 174.

51. Jason Gurney, *Crusade in Spain* (London: Faber and Faber, 1974), p. 23.

52. Philip Toynbee, *Friends Apart: A Memoir of Esmond Romilly and Jasper Ridley in the Thirties* (London: MacGibbon and Kee, 1954), p. 146; Stuart Samuels, "English Intellectuals and Politics in the 1930s" in Philip Rieff, ed., *On Intellectuals: Theoretical Studies, Case Studies* (Garden City, N.Y.: Doubleday, 1969), p. 229.

53. Romilly and Romilly, *Out of Bounds*, p. 203.

54. *Ibid.*, p. 228.

55. Toynbee, *Friends Apart*, p. 18.

56. Romilly and Romilly, *Out of Bounds*, p. 239; Kevin Ingram, *Rebel: The Short Life of Esmond Romilly* (London: Weidenfeld and Nicolson, 1985), pp. 61–62.

57. Ingram, *Rebel*, pp. 62–65.

58. *Out of Bounds*, March-April 1934, p. 2.

59. Romilly and Romilly, *Out of Bounds*, pp. 285 and 286.

60. *The Ploughshare*, January 1934, p. 1.

61. *New Verse*, October and December 1934.

62. *Left Review*, October 1934, p. 38.

63. John Lehmann, *In My Own time: Memoirs of a Literary Life* (Boston: Little, Brown, 1969), p. 151.

64. *International Press Correspondence*, October 30, 1935, p. 1406.

65. Dean E. McHenry, *The Labour Party in Transition, 1931–1938* (London: Routledge and Kegan Paul, 1938), pp. 351–352.

66. Hannington, *Unemployed Struggles*, p. 326.

67. Samuels, "English Intellectuals," p. 238.

68. Thomas, *John Strachey*, pp. 148 and 154.

69. *Left Book News*, May 1936, pp. 2–3.

70. John Lewis, *The Left Book Club: An Historical Record* (London: Gollancz, 1970), pp. 26 and 107–108.

71. John Strachey, "Topic of the Month: A People's Front for Britain?" *Left Book News*, August 1936, p. 62; Strachey to Gollancz, July 1936, quoted in Thomas, *John Strachey*, p. 156.

72. Strachey, "Topic of the Month: Peace or War in the New Year?" *Left Book News*, January 1937, p. 199; Gollancz, Editorial, *ibid.*, March 1937, p. 249.

73. Skidelsky, *Oswald Mosley*, p. 393.

74. Jacobs, *Out of the Ghetto*, pp. 104, 118, and 129.

75. Anderson, *Fascists, Communists, and the National Government*, pp. 141–144.

76. Jacobs, *Out of the Ghetto*, pp. 148, 151, and 205; Josh Davidson and Bob Cooney, in Corkill and Rawnsley, *The Road to Spain*, pp. 118 and 161.

77. Jacobs, *Out of the Ghetto*, p. 238.

78. *Daily Worker*, October 1, 1936, p. 1.

79. Jacobs, *Out of the Ghetto*, p. 241.

80. *Daily Worker*, October 2, 1936, p. 1.

81. Phil Piratin, *Our Flag Stays Red*, (London: Lawrence and Wishart, 1978), pp. 19–20.

82. *Daily Herald*, October 5, 1936, p. 1.

83. Branson and Heinemann, *Britain in the Nineteen Thirties*, pp. 293–294.

84. *Times*, October 5, 1936, p. 13.

85. Cross, *The Fascists in Britain*, pp. 166–167 and 177–178.

86. Corkill and Rawnsley, *The Road to Spain*, p. 38.

87. Bill Alexander, *British Volunteers for Liberty: Spain 1936–1939* (London: Lawrence and Wishart, 1982), pp. 54 and 61; Jonathan Guinness with Catherine Guinness, *The House of Mitford* (New York: Viking, 1985), p. 400. Esmond Romilly, *Boadilla* (London: Hamilton, 1937).

88. Hadley Cantril and Mildred Strunk, *Public Opinion, 1935–1946* (Princeton University Press, 1951), pp. 808–809.

89. Cole, *A History of the Labour Party*, p. 330.

90. Toynbee, *Friends Apart*, p. 115.

91. *Tribune*, January 22, 1937, p. 11.

92. Brockway, *Inside the Left*, p. 265.

93. Patrick Seyd, "Factionalism Within the Labour Party: The Socialist League, 1932–1937," in Asa Briggs and John Saville, eds., *Essays in Labour History, 1918–1939* (Hamden, Conn.: Archon, 1977), p. 220.

94. Brockway, *Inside the Left*, p. 269.

95. Patricia Cockburn, *The Years of "The Week"* (London: MacDonald, 1968), p. 207.

96. Laski, "The Labour Party and the Left Book Club," *Left Book News*, August 1937, p. 456.

97. Quoted in Bernard Crick, *George Orwell: A Life* (Boston: Little, Brown,

1980), p. 228; see also Kingsley Martin, *Editor: A Second Volume of Autobiography, 1931–1945* (London: Hutchinson, 1968), p. 216, and C. H. Rolph, *Kingsley: The Life, Letters, and Diaries of Kingsley Martin* (London: Gollancz, 1973), pp. 226–228.

98. *Reynolds News*, March 20, 1938, p. 10, and March 27, 1938, p. 10.

99. "Notes of the Month," *Labour Monthly*, June 1938, p. 331; Cole, *A History of the Labour Party*, p. 353.

100. *Tribune*, April 14, 1938, p. 5, and April 29, 1938, p. 7.

101. *New Leader*, May 6, 1938, p. 4.

102. *Left Review*, May 1938, pp. 959–960.

103. Brittain, *Testament of Experience*, p. 193.

104. Mitford, *Hons and Rebels*, p. 152.

105. Roger Eatwell, "Munich, Public Opinion, and Popular Front," *Journal of Contemporary History* (October 1971), 6: 123.

106. Cantril and Strunk, *Public Opinion*, p.276.

107. Thomas, *John Strachey*, p. 180; *Left Book News*, October 1938, p. 997, and November 1938, p. 1034.

108. *Tribune*, February 10, 1939, p. 13.

109. Mitford, *Hons and Rebels*, p. 174.

110. Thomas, *John Strachey*, p. 184.

111. *Tribune*, August 25, 1939, p. 1.

112. *Daily Herald*, August 22, 1939, p. 8; *New Leader*, August 25, 1939, p. 1; *The New Statesman*, September 23, 1939, p. 420; *Reynolds News*, August 27, 1939, p. 8.

113. "The LBC in War Time," *Left Book News*, September 1939, p. 1381.

114. MacShane, *No Mean Fighter*, p. 231; John Mahon, *Harry Pollitt: A Biography* (London: Lawrence and Wishart, 1976), p. 249.

115. Quoted in Labour Party, *The Communist Party and the War* (London: Transport House, 1943), p. 3.

116. Mahon, *Harry Pollitt*, pp. 250–252; Henry Pelling, *The British Communist Party: A Historical Profile* (London: Black, 1958), p. 110.

117. Claud Cockburn, *Crossing the Line* (London: MacGibbon and Kee, 1958), p. 49.

8. *"Premature" Anti-Fascism in the United States*

1. Larry Ceplair and Steven Englund, *The Inquisition in Hollywood: Politics in the Film Community, 1930–1960* (Garden City, N.Y.: Anchor Press/Doubleday, 1980).

2. Thomas R. Brooks, *Toil and Trouble: A History of American Labor* (New York: Delta, 1964), p. 148; James R. Green, *The World of the Worker: Labor in Twentieth Century America* (New York: Hill and Wang paperback, 1980), p. 133.

3. Philip G. Altbach, *Student Politics in America: A Historical Analysis* (New York: McGraw-Hill, 1974), pp. 44, 45, and 72–73.

4. Eileen Eagan, *Class, Culture, and the Classroom: The Student Peace Movement of the 1930s* (Philadelphia: Temple University Press, 1981), pp. 32–35.

5. *Ibid.*, p. 33; Altbach, *Student Politics*, p. 47.

6. Robert H. Ferrell, "The Peace Movement," in Alexander de Conde, ed., *Isolation and Security* (Durham, N.C.: Duke University Press, 1957), pp. 101 and 103.

7. *Ibid.*, p. 93; Ferrell, *Peace in Their Time: The Origins of the Kellogg-Briand Pact* (New Haven: Yale University Press, 1952), pp. 21–30.

8. John B. Diggins, *Mussolini and Fascism: The View from America* (Princeton: Princeton University Press, 1972), pp. 111–122; David F. Schmitz, " 'A Fine Young Revolution': The United States and the Fascist Revolution in Italy, 1919–1925," *Radical History Review* (1985), 33:118, 121, and 130–131.

9. *Report of Proceedings of the 43d Annual Convention of the American Federation of Labor, Held at Portland, Oregon, October 1–12, Inclusive, 1923* (Washington, D.C.: Law Reporter, 1923), pp. 66 and 272.

10. *Report of Proceedings of the 47th Annual Convention of the American Federation of Labor, Held at Los Angeles, California, October 3–14, Inclusive, 1927* (Washington, D.C.: Law Reporter, 1927), p. 272.

11. *Report of Proceedings of the 48th Annual Convention of the American Federation of Labor, Held at New Orleans, Louisiana, November 19–28, Inclusive, 1928* (Washington, D.C.: Law Reporter, 1928), p. 374.

12. Frank A. Warren, *An Alternative Vision: The Socialist Party in the 1930s* (Bloomington: Indiana University Press, 1974), p. 23; Irving Howe, *Socialism and America* (San Diego: Harcourt Brace Jovanovich, 1985), p. 49.

13. *The Militant*, June 1, 1929, p. 1.

14. Harvey Klehr, *Communist Cadre: The Social Background of the American Communist Party Elite* (Stanford: Hoover Institution Press, 1978), p. 115.

15. Frederick Vanderbilt Field, *From Right to Left: An Autobiography* (Westport, Conn.: Lawrence Hill, 1983), p. 179.

16. Maurice Isserman, *Which Side Were You On? The American Communist Party During the Second World War* (Middletown, Conn.: Wesleyan University Press, 1982), p. 9.

17. Dorothy Healey, *Tradition's Chains Have Bound Us*, UCLA Oral History Program, 1982, 1:154–155.

18. A. J. Muste, in Rita James Simon, ed., *As We Saw the Thirties: Essays on Social and Political Movements of a Decade* (Urbana: University of Illinois Press, 1967), pp. 136–137.

19. Undated memo among the summer 1929 material, Earl Browder Papers, microfilm, reel 3, section 2–13, UCLA Research Library.

20. William Wilson, "The Second Congress of the Anti-Imperialist League," *The Communist*, February 1930, p. 169.

21. Philip J. Jaffe, *The Rise and Fall of American Communism* (New York: Horizon, 1975), p. 32.

22. James Wechsler, *Revolt on the Campus* (New York: Covici Friede, 1935), p. 95.

23. *Ibid.*, pp. 99–100 and 108; Joseph Lash, "Students in Kentucky," *The New Republic*, April 20, 1932, p. 269.

24. Wechsler, *Revolt on the Campus*, p. 139.

25. Matthew Josephson, *Infidel in the Temple: A Memoir of the Nineteen-Thirties* (New York: Knopf, 1967), pp. 160–162.

26. Harvey Klehr, *The Heyday of American Communism: The Depression Decade* (New York: Basic, 1984), pp. 82–83.

27. Sidney Hook, "Breaking with the Communists: A Memoir," *Commentary*, February 1984, p. 53.

28. Alan M. Wald, "The Menorah Group Moves Left," *Jewish Social Studies* (Summer-Fall 1976), 38:305–307; Wald, *James T. Farrell: The Revolutionary Socialist Years* (New York: New York University Press, 1978), p. 6.

29. Alan M. Wald, "Herbert Solow: Portrait of a New York Intellectual," *Prospects: An Annual of American Cultural Studies*, Jack Salzman, ed. (New York: Franklin, 1977), 3:434–435.

30. Hillman W. Bishop, *The American League Against War and Fascism: A Study in Communist Tactics*, typescript, New York, 1937, p. 6, in Benjamin Gitlow Papers, box 7, Hoover Institution Archives, Stanford University.

31. *New York Herald Tribune*, October 1, 1933; *The Communist*, November 1933, pp. 1120–1124; Klehr, *The Heyday*, pp. 110–111; Dorothy Detzer, *Appointment on the Hill* (New York: Hart, 1948), pp. 188–189.

32. Herbert Solow, "Stalin's Great American Hoax: The League for Peace and Democracy," *American Mercury* (December 1939), 48:394; Earl Browder in Simon, *As We Saw the Thirties*, p. 221.

33. Solow, "Stalin's Great American Hoax," p. 400.

34. Altbach, *Student Politics*, pp. 59–60.

35. Eagan, *Class, Culture, and the Classroom*, p. 60.

36. *The Nation*, April 12, 1933, pp. 386–387.

37. *Ibid.*, May 17, 1933, pp. 554–555, and May 24, 1933, p. 571.

38. Altbach, *Student Politics*, p. 89.

39. *Report of Proceedings of the 53d Annual Convention of the American Federation of Labor, Held at Washington, D.C., October 2–13, Inclusive, 1933* (Washington, D.C.: Judd and Detweiler, 1933), pp. 141 and 167.

40. Altbach, *Student Politics*, pp. 67, 89, and 95–6; Eagan, *Class, Culture, and the Classroom*, pp. 116–117; Healey, *Tradition's Chains*, 1:139; Klehr, *The Heyday*, p. 320.

41. *American Socialist Quarterly*, July 1934, special supplement, pp. 6 and 59.

42. Donald R. McCoy, *Angry Voices: Left-of-Center Politics in the New Deal Era* (Lawrence: University of Kansas Press, 1958), p. 72.

43. *New York Times*, February 17, 1934, p. 1; for a different version, see "The Lesson of Madison Square Garden," *New Masses*, February 27, 1934, p. 9.

44. Townsend Ludington, *John Dos Passos: A Twentieth Century Odyssey* (New York: Dutton, 1980), pp. 324–325; Bishop, *The American League*, pp. 8–9; Browder Papers, reel 3, section 2–7, UCLA Research Library.

45. *Modern Monthly*, March 1934, pp. 89–92.

46. Melech Epstein, *The Jew and Communism: The Story of Early Communist Victories and Ultimate Defeats in the Jewish Community, U.S.A., 1919–1941* (New York: Trade Union Sponsoring Committee, 1959), pp. 285, 293, and 300–302; Epstein, *Jewish Labor in U.S.A., 1914–1952: An Industrial Political and Cultural History of the Jewish Labor Movement* (New York: Trade Union Sponsoring Committee, 1953), pp. 258–259. The papers of the Jewish Labor Committee reside in 849 as yet unprocessed boxes at the Robert F. Wagner Labor Archives of the Tamiment Institute Library, New York University. The general inventory indicates that two of the boxes (20–1 and 44–1) contain material pertinent to 1930s' anti-Fascism.

47. Pierre Van Paassen and James Waterman Wise, eds, *Nazism: An Assault on Civilization* (New York: Smith and Haas), 1934.

48. Roger Keeran, *The Communist Party and the Auto Workers Unions* (Bloomington: Indiana University Press, 1980), pp. 107 and 120; see also Wyndham Mortimer, *Organize! My Life as a Union Man* (Boston: Beacon Press, 1971), p. 57.

49. Mark D. Naison, *The Communist Party in Harlem, 1928–1936*, Ph.D thesis, Columbia University, 1975, pp. 232–233.

50. Upton Sinclair, *I, Governor for California—and How I Got Licked* (Los Angeles: End Poverty League, 1935), p. 5.

51. *Ibid.*, pp. 10 and 79.

52. *Reuben W. Borough and California Reform Movements*, UCLA Oral History Program, 1968, pp. 104 and 106–107; Greg Mitchell, "Summer of '34," *Working Papers* (November–December 1982), 9:36.

53. *Reuben W. Borough*, pp. 118–119.

54. Sinclair, *I, Governor*, p. 20.

55. *EPIC News*, March 1934, p. 6.

56. Earl Browder, *Communism in the United States* (New York: International, 1935), p. 270; *New Masses*, September 11, 1934, p. 6.

57. Mitchell, "Summer of '34," part 2, *Working Papers* (January–February 1983), 10:25.

58. Eagan, *Class, Culture, and the Classroom*, p. 120.

59. "On the Main Immediate Tasks of the CPUSA," *The Communist*, February 1935, pp. 122–123.

60. Lowell K. Dyson, *Red Harvest: The Communist Party and American Farmers* (Lincoln: University of Nebraska Press, 1982), pp. 97–98 and 129–130.

61. Browder, *Communism in the United States*, p. 313.

62. *EPIC News*, March 4, 1935, pp. 1 and 11.

63. *Ibid.*, May 27, 1935, p. 7.

64. Arne Swabeck, "The Real Meaning of the United Front," *The New International*, October 1935, p. 182.

65. Eric Leif Davin and Staughton Lynd, "Picket Line and Ballot Box: The Forgotten Legacy of the Local Labor Movement," *Radical History Review* (Winter

1979–1980), 22:54; see also Staughton Lynd, "A Chapter from History: The United Labor Party, 1946–1952," *Liberation*, December 1973, p. 38.

66. Eagan, *Class, Culture, and the Classroom*, p. 134; Hal Draper, in Simon, *As We Saw the Thirties*, pp. 176 and 178–180; Patti McGill Peterson, "Student Organizations and the Anti-War Movement in America, 1900–1960," in Charles Chatfield, ed., *Peace Movements in America* (New York: Schocken, 1973), p. 124.

67. Harold Draper, "The American Student Union Faces the Student Anti-War Strike," *American Socialist Monthly*, April 1936, pp. 7–8; the ASU's national executive secretary, Joseph Lash, refuted those charges in the May issue, "Another View of the American Student Union," pp. 28–30.

68. William Z. Foster, "Fascist Tendencies in the United States," *The Communist*, October 1935, p. 898; Heywood Broun, "We Want a United Front," *The Nation*, December 11, 1935, p. 673.

69. Healey, *Tradition's Chains*, 1:221.

70. Melvin Dubofsky and Warren Van Tine, *John L. Lewis: A Biography* (New York: Quadrangle, 1977), p. 249; McCoy, *Angry Voices*, p. 107; William H. Riker, *The CIO in Politics, 1936–1946*, Ph.D. thesis, Harvard University, 1948, p. 149.

71. *The Communist*, April 1936, p. 394; "Report of the Central Committee to the Ninth National Convention," June 24, 1936, in Earl Browder, *The People's Front in the United States* (London: Lawrence and Wishart, 1937), p. 36; Browder, in Simon, *As We Saw the Thirties*, 234; Steven Nelson, James R. Barrett, and Rob Buck, *Steve Nelson, American Radical* (Pittsburgh: University of Pittsburgh Press, 1981), p. 173.

72. Healey, *Tradition's Chains*, 1:218.

73. Morris Schonback, *Native Fascism During the 1930's and 1940's: A Study of Its Roots, Its Growth, and Its Decline*, Ph.D. thesis, UCLA 1958, pp. 236, 326, and 346.

74. David H. Bennett, *Demagogues in the Depression: American Radicals and the Union Party, 1932–1936* (New Brunswick, N.J.: Rutgers University Press, 1969), p. 268; Alan Brinkley, *Voices of Protest: Huey Long, Father Coughlin, and the Great Depression* (New York: Knopf, 1982).

75. See John Gerassi, *The Premature Antifascists: North American Volunteers in the Spanish Civil War* (New York: Praeger paperback, 1986).

76. *Report of Proceedings of the 56th Annual Convention of the American Federation of Labor, Held at Tampa, Florida, November 16–27, Inclusive, 1936* (Washington, D.C.: Judd and Detweiler, 1936), p. 578; Riker, *The CIO in Politics*, p. 90.

77. F. Jay Taylor, *The United States and the Spanish Civil War* (New York: Bookman, 1956), pp. 129 and 237–242.

78. *The Student Advocate*, February 1937, p. 13, and April 1937, pp. 3–4.

79. *Ibid.*, May 1937, p. 4.

80. Klehr, *The Heyday*, p. 318.

81. John W. Masland, "The 'Peace' Groups Join Battle," *Public Opinion Quarterly* (December 1940), 4:669–670.

82. Louis Adamic, *My America: 1928–1938* (New York: Harper, 1938), p. 83; Sidney Hook, "Memories of the Moscow Trial," *Commentary*, March 1984, pp. 57–63; Alan Wald, "Memories of the John Dewey Commission: Forty Years Later," *Antioch Review* (Fall 1977), 35:438–451; Wald, *James T. Farrell*, pp. 63 and 66.

83. *The New Republic*, March 17, 1937, pp. 169–170.

84. *New Masses*, May 3, 1938, p. 19.

85. *The New Republic*, February 2, 1938, p. 354; "Draft Resolution for the Tenth Party Convention," March 18, 1938, in Browder Papers, reel 3, section 2–45, UCLA Research Library.

86. Hathaway, "Building the Democratic Front," *The Communist*, May 1938, pp. 404 and 405; Dennis, "Some Questions Concerning the Democratic Front," *ibid.*, June 1938, p. 535.

87. Eagan, *Class, Culture, and the Classroom*, p. 198; Peterson, "Student Organizations," p. 125.

88. Young Communist League Papers, box 2, Hoover Institution Archives, Stanford University.

89. *The New Republic*, October 19, 1938, p. 311.

90. Isserman, *Which Side Were You On?* pp. 26–27.

91. Haskell Lookstein, *Were We Our Brothers' Keepers? The Public Response of American Jews to the Holocaust, 1938–1944,* (New York: Hartmore House, 1985), p. 59.

92. Riker, *The CIO in Politics*, p. 242.

93. *The Nation*, May 27, 1939, pp. 626 and 605, and June 17, 1939, p. 710.

94. *The New Republic*, June 14, 1939, p. 162.

95. *Ibid.*, June 28, 1939, p. 202; *The Nation*, June 17, 1939, p. 711.

96. *Partisan Review*, Fall 1939, p. 125; *The New Republic*, July 26, 1939, p. 336.

97. *The Communist*, October 1939, p. 899.

98. Earl Browder, *Unity for Peace and Democracy* (New York: Workers Library, September 1939); Nelson, Barrett, and Buck, *Steve Nelson*, p. 248.

99. Lillian Symes, "The War and the Communists," *Socialist Review*, September–October 1939, pp. 4–5.

100. John P. Diggins, *Up from Communism: Conservative Odysseys in American Intellectual History* (New York: Harper Torchbooks, 1977), p. 185.

101. Josephson, *Infidel in the Temple*, p. 480; Richard Rovere, *Final Reports: Personal Reflections on Politics and History in Our Time* (Garden City, N.Y.: Doubleday, 1984), p. 67.

Epilogue

1. S. Spender, *World Within World* (London: Readers Union, 1953), p. 266.

2. C. D. Lewis, *Collected Poems of C. Day Lewis* (London: Cape, 1954), p. 228.

3. J. P. Sartre, *The War Diaries of Jean-Paul Sartre, November 1939/March 1940*, Quintin Hoare, tr. (New York: Pantheon, 1984), p. 310.

4. German Foreign Office memo reprinted in Raymond J. Sontag and James S. Beddie, eds., *Nazi-Soviet Relations, 1939–1941: Documents from the Archives of the German Foreign Office* (Washington, D.C.: Department of State, 1948), p. 319.

5. Ivan Maisky, *Memoirs of a Soviet Ambassador: The War, 1939–1943*, Andrew Rothstein, tr. (New York: Scribner's 1968), p. 40.

6. W. Gallacher, *The Last Memoirs of William Gallacher* (London: Lawrence and Wishart, 1966), p. 272.

7. Muriel Gardiner, *Code Name "Mary": Memoirs of an American Woman in the Austrian Underground* (New Haven: Yale University Press, 1983), p. 155.

8. Jorgen Schleimann, "The Life and Work of Willi Münzenberg," *Survey* (April 1965), no. 55, pp. 86–90.

9. Joel Colton, *Léon Blum: Humanist in Politics* (New York: Knopf, 1966), p. 385.

10. G. Orwell, "London Letter," *Partisan Review*, November–December 1941, and "War Time Diary," both in *The Collected Essays, Journalism, and Letters of George Orwell*, vol. 2: *My Country Right or Left, 1940–1943*, Sonia Orwell and Ian Angus, eds. (New York: Harcourt Brace Jovanovich, 1968), pp. 154 and 407.

11. See David Wyman, *Paper Walls: America and the Refugee Crisis, 1938–1941* (Amherst: University of Massachusetts Press, 1968), and *The Abandonment of the Jews: America and the Holocaust, 1941–1945* (New York: Pantheon, 1984).

12. Michael R. Marrus, *The Unwanted: European Refugees in the Twentieth Century* (New York: Oxford University Press, 1985), pp. 170–171.

13. Deborah E. Lipstadt, *Beyond Belief: The American Press and the Coming of the Holocaust, 1933–1945* (New York: Free Press, 1986), pp. 15 and 97.

14. G. Clare, *The Last Waltz in Vienna: The Rise and Destruction of a Family, 1842–1942* (New York: Holt, Rinehart and Winston, 1980), pp. 122–123.

15. Shimon Redlich, "The Jewish Antifascist Committee in the Soviet Union," *Jewish Social Studies* (January 1969), 31:25–36.

Index

Ford, James, 191
For Intellectual Liberty (England), 171
Fortune (journal), 206
Foster William Z., 185, 195
Four Power Pact, 72–73, 110
France, 6, 7, 9, 14, 101; anti-Communism, 204, 205; center-left government in, 77; economic-social divisions in, 123–24; fall of, 180; Fascism in, 67; foreign policy, 117, 125; invasion/occupation of the Ruhr, 47, 48, 59; Popular Front anti-Fascism in, 77, 90, 95, 123–53; relations with Soviet Union, 102, 109, 110, 111, 113, 116, 118, 119–20, 121; Right-wing leagues in, 12, 87; and Spanish Civil War, 115, 142–43; strikes, 33; Third Republic, 123–24; Vichy, 205
France Today (Thorez), 171
Françistes, 72
Franco, Francisco, 74
Franco-Russian Alliance, 136
Franco-Russian treaty, 111
Freeman, Joseph, 186
Freikorps, 12, 13, 16–17, 36, 58
French Front (proposed), 143–44
French Peasant and Worker Group, 153
Friends of Europe, 171
Friends of the Soviet Union (England), 167
Front Commun (France), 129, 136
Front Mondial (journal), 138
Front of National Rebirth (Romania), 71
Front Social (France), 136, 143

Gallacher, William, 171, 204–5
Gamelin, General Maurice, 205
Gandhi, Mohandas, 127
Gardes mobiles (France), 148, 149
Gascoyne, David, 169
Gauchistes (revolutionary Left group), 128, 136, 139, 140–41, 142, 143, 149
General Confederation of Labor (CGL) (Italy), 21, 26, 28, 45; Congress, 23–24
General Federation of German Trade Unions (ADGB), 58, 61, 63, 64
General Jewish Council (U.S.), 200
General strikes, *see* Strikes
Georgian Republic, 41
Georgians, 41
German-American Bund, 196

German Communist Workers Party (KAPD), 37, 39
German Freedom Library (Paris), 97
German Nationals (party, Austria), 67–68
German-Polish Nonaggression Treaty, 110
German-Russian Nonaggression Pact, 5
German-Russian Nonaggression Treaty. see Nonaggression Treaty (USSR/Germany)
German Social Democratic Party Executive (Sopade), 98–99, 100
Germany, 3, 6, 12, 74, 110, 114, 155, 200; Anti-Comintern Pact, 116; anti-Fascist movement, 96; as danger to USSR, 113; defeat, World War II, 203; elections, 61–62, 63, 64–65, 128; expansionism, 74–75; failure of revolution in, 19, 47, 48–49; Fascism, 1, 10, 11: French policy toward, 125; invasion of Poland, 120; invasion of Russia, 205–06; *Lands*, 48–49, 61, 63, 64–65; Law for the Protection of the Republic, 59; military buildup, 150; moral boycott of, 129; nonaggression pact with Soviet Union, 102–3, 105, 179, 180; rearming, 73–74, 111; relations with Italy, 74–75; relations with Soviet Union, 4, 41, 60–61, 102, 106–7, 109, 111–12, 116–17, 118–19, 120–21, 179, 180; revolution in, 15–17, 19, 33, 36, 47, 48–49; Third Reich, 99, 109, 111, 190; *see also* Communist Party (Germany) (KPD); Nazism
Gide, André, 81, 84, 128, 138n, 148; broke with Communists, 144–46; *Retouches à Mon Retour de l'URSS*, 145; *Retour de l'URSS*, 145
Giolitti, Giovanni, 24
Gitton, Marcel, 142
Gollancz, Victor, 94, 165, 171–72, 178, 179
Gömbös, Gyula, 70
Gomes de Costa, Manuel, 12
Gorki, Maxim, 80
Gottwald, Klement, 83, 92, 138
Graham, Frank, 175
Gramsci, Antonio, 24–25, 26, 31, 43, 44–45, 107; sentenced to jail, 45, 46
Grand Rassemblement (National Anti-Fascist Assembly) (France), 133–34
Great Britain, 7, 66, 110, 112, 113, 142; anti-Communism, 204–5; conservative